R i c e

D0987732

PRAISE FOR *SALES AN* *THE SIX SIGM.*

"Sales and marketing are new frontiers for Six Sigma and Michael's book provides practical insights for any organization that is considering how to connect their continuous improvement efforts with top line growth and customer satisfaction."

JOHN BIEDRY, SENIOR VICE PRESIDENT CONTINUOUS IMPROVEMENT
SERVICEMASTER

"The name of the game is not to design the sales process around ourselves, but to create customer value. Sales and Marketing the Six Sigma Way is relevant to all executives who are looking to deliver maximum results internally and externally."

GREGORY T. DEININGER, V.P. NATIONAL ACCOUNTS
MARRIOTT

"It isn't often that I can recommend a Six Sigma book because reducing defects tends to be product-focused and internally-oriented. This book is not only different but better than any other Six Sigma book I've ever seen because it actually shows how to use it to increase the value of your relationships and experiences with your customers. This is the way Six Sigma should be done."

PAUL GREENBERG, AUTHOR
CRM AT THE SPEED OF LIGHT

"Applying Six Sigma to Sales and Marketing? Initially I was skeptical, but after reading this book, I'm a believer. Applying these principles correctly will help sales managers solve many of the challenges they face every day in their quest to improve sales performance."

JACK SNADER, PRESIDENT
SYSTEMA CORPORATION

"If more books on the subject were as concise and fun to read as Sales and Marketing the Six Sigma Way, the business world would be a better place. The book will provide sales and marketing executives with money-making tools they can use daily."

KAMAL HASSAN, GLOBAL VP OF BUSINESS DEVELOPMENT
BMG

"If you don't know what you have done to succeed or what has caused you to fail, you are leaving your destiny to chance. In our experience, when you understand and remove obstacles to your customers achieving their objectives, you create customer value by helping them succeed. In addition, putting your own processes under the microscope can reveal what's inhibiting you from achieving your sales goals. Michael Webb's straightforward approach to sales and marketing using the popular Six Sigma method is presented with a sense of humor and lots of examples. Well worth your time!"

SHEILA MELLO, AUTHOR
CUSTOMER-CENTRIC PRODUCT DEFINITION

"Michael Webb brings true understanding to sales and marketing through process thinking. If you want a harmonious relationship between sales, marketing, and customer service that will drive customer value, you need to read this book!"

WILLIS TURNER, CAE, CSE
PRESIDENT/CEO, SALES AND MARKETING EXECUTIVES INTERNATIONAL (SMEI)

"Webb's breakthrough ideas show how marketing, selling, and servicing functions can be approached as a process—with input and outputs and causes and effects. I highly recommend this book to all senior executives—whether they are aiming for better forecasting, better market share, higher margins, or reduced cost of sales. It will completely change the way you view sales and marketing and help you get a handle on sales process improvement."

FRANK WILEY, PRESIDENT
MAGNITUDE MARKETING, LLC

"Hats off to Mike Webb for tackling this challenging subject. Improving sales and marketing is like training your cat to come when you call it. It's an interesting thing to think about but full of pitfalls to the uninitiated. Mike, however, is very initiated and this book does a good job of showing you how quantitative methods can apply to a traditionally hard to manage business. It's not that sales forces don't have metrics. You could argue that they have the ultimate metric: Did we make the sale? Like your cat, these groups seem to have a mind of their own and the cause and effect of the activities that go into making the sale aren't usually methodically examined and improved. Mike shows you how to do that with style."

BILL BENTLEY, PRESIDENT
VALUE-TRAIN

"Michael Webb has a very incisive, clear-headed approach to untangling complex sales problems. Sales and Marketing the Six Sigma Way breaks the sales funnel into its component parts and systematically identifies bottlenecks and disconnects that waste your time and resources. Selling might have been done by the seat-of-the-pants in the 20th century, but that isn't going to work now. Those who miss this shift will find themselves further and further behind quotas and locked in a corporate pressure cooker. But those who recognize and act will discover that the current business climate can be enormously rewarding and profitable. This book is not a sales rah rah session. It takes enormously successful methods from manufacturing and applies them to the toughest job in your company – getting orders from customers. I wholeheartedly recommend Michael and his innovative methods."

PERRY MARSHALL, PRINCIPAL
PERRY MARSHALL AND ASSOCIATES

"Think about it ... marketing and sales can easily represent nearly half of your company's annual expenses. This expense is far from being optimized when 9 out of 10 leads are typically discarded early in the sales cycle. Companies that do not apply a systematic and truly accountable approach to blending marketing and sales will undoubtedly struggle to survive in this increasingly competitive business climate. This book concisely applies practical Six Sigma methods to help companies boost customer value and realize greater ROI out of their marketing and sales investment. If you know there's room for improvement between your marketing and sales teams, I highly recommend you leverage this book as a key competitive advantage."

JEFF KOSTERMANS, PRESIDENT & CEO
LEADGENESYS

"Michael Webb has once again demonstrated his clear and systematic thinking about delivering value to customers in this must read book, Sales and Marketing the Six Sigma Way. In this book, Mike provides tools to help measure your sales processes in terms important to your customers. Then, you can continuously improve your processes of Finding, Winning, and Keeping Customers."

RAY MCKINNEY, DIRECTOR OF DEVELOPMENT
MATRIX TECHNOLOGIES

.

MICHAEL J. WEBB
WITH TOM GORMAN

SALES AND MARKETING THE
SIX
SIGMA
WAY

SALES PERFORMANCE
CONSULTANTS, INC.
Make Your Sales Funnel Flow Faster

This publication is designed to provide accurate and authoritative information in regard to the subject matter covered. It is sold with the understanding that the publisher is not engaged in rendering legal, accounting, or other professional services. If legal advice or other expert assistance is required, the services of a competent professional should be sought.

Published by Sales Performance Consultants, Inc.

Printed in the United States of America

ISBN-13: 978-0615751887
ISBN-10: 0615751881

Library of Congress Cataloging-in-Publication Data

Webb, Michael J.
  Sales and Marketing the Six Sigma Way / Michael J. Webb; with Tom Gorman.
    p. cm.
  Includes index.
  ISBN-13: 978-1-4195-2150-8
  ISBN-10: 1-4195-2150-0
  1. Marketing—Management. 2. Marketing—Quality control. 3. Six sigma (Quality control standard) I. Gorman, Tom. II. Title.
  HF5415.13W356 2006
  658.8'02—dc22

                                 2006008093

C o n t e n t s

A *c k n o w l e d g m e n t s*

The ideas behind this book have resulted from thousands of hours of conversations with dozens of people over the years. The list includes friends like Ray McKinney, Tom Ribar, Jeff Prince, and Dave Lynn; employers like Dan Kosch and Mark Shonka; and many, many others. While I can't possibly make a list that would do justice to everyone, the value I have received from our conversations has been enormous. Thank you all for sharing with me your questions and your insights into the root causes of sales and marketing problems.

When the time came to begin organizing and writing the book, several people stepped up to the challenge. I want specifically to recognize their contributions: Senior Master Black Belt Rob Tripp generously gave me his time and support as I groped my way through Six Sigma training material, and he has been a valuable sounding board as I worked through logical connections to sales and marketing problems. Likewise, I'd like to thank Michael Cyger of iSixSigma for being so open to considering my articles on the subject and for giving me opportunities to learn and to Ralph Jeswald for his insights to activity based cost accounting. In addition, many patient and intrepid people worked their way through the early versions of this manuscript and provided unvarnished (and invaluable) feedback on some or all of it: Rob Tripp, Frank Wiley, Jack Snader, David Maister, Ann Trampas, Bill Bentley, David Mansfield, Jay Bronec, and Robert Schmonsees.

I am also indebted to many of the previous authors who have taken on some aspect of measurement and process improvement in sales and marketing: James Cortada, Paul Selden, George Smith, Daniel Stowall, Edward Abramowich, and Neil Rackham. A special thanks to Hugh McfarlaneMc-farlane for the concept of the buyer's journey and for the idea of using it to align marketing and selling activities, and for parts of the diagrams used in Chapter 6. Hugh is the author of *The Leaky Funnel* and founder of MathMarketing, based in Australia. As far as writers go, I am very fortunate to have become acquainted with my coauthor, Tom Gorman, whose steady, resilient, and often brilliant contributions and workmanship have made this book as good as it could be.

My thanks also go to the superb team at Kaplan Publishing and particularly to acquisitions editor Karen Murphy, development editor Trey Thoelcke, and production editor Karen Goodfriend for their excellent work on, and support for, this book.

Of course, my family has paid a huge price in putting up with my absence as I have launched the business and finished this book. Thank you Leslie, Frank, and Kira for sticking with me. I'd also like to thank Betty Jo Yoder for her encouragement and support over the years.

And, finally, there are the people and companies who agreed to let me tell their stories. I have gone out of my way to credit them (or protect their identity, as appropriate). Taken individually, I cannot thank them enough for their willingness to work with me. Taken as a whole, their stories offer an expansive illustration of what is right—and wrong—with the management of sales and marketing today.

This book is about making sales easier and more productive in your business.

There it is, as clearly as I can say it.

Yet life is hard for plenty of other business functions as well. What's so special about sales? Aren't we all responsible for our own productivity?

That's the prevailing belief in many companies, but think about this: Is any job in business more difficult than selling? At the same time, is any job more important to a company?

Selling—actual selling, not filling orders for Rolling Stones tickets or refilling Coke machines—exists because someone must persuade someone else to (1) listen carefully, (2) speak frankly, (3) make a decision, and typically (4) part with his or her money. None of these four activities comes naturally to most members of the human race. That's why we need salespeople and why their job is so difficult.

As to importance, if no one buys what a company sells, then the projected life-span of that company roughly equals that of a goldfish in a plastic bag of water in the hands of a five-year-old at a county fair in Kansas on a hot August afternoon.

Moreover, it's actually the job of many people, most obviously (or perhaps not so obviously) marketing people, to make selling easier and more productive. Indeed, if a company's marketing function isn't making selling easier, it is probably making it harder. In addition, sales managers; sales support people; service people; and providers of advertising, sales training, and customer relationship management (CRM) software all make selling easier and more productive or harder and less productive.

So this book is about making the job of selling easier and more productive.

Now, how are we going to do that?

A SYSTEMATIC APPROACH

Several months ago, a friend of mine named Steve visited Las Vegas for the first time. He planned to play roulette, mainly because it looks cool and allows straight-up bets on black or red, which even mathematically challenged Steve can mentally track. Steve also looked into roulette betting systems. Some of these systems are sold at Web sites, which are, of course, operated by people who became fabulously wealthy by playing roulette and who now want to share their good fortune with others.

Steve visited several of these sites and found some of the systems appealing. One was based on the fact that, in any set of 36 spins of the roulette wheel, only 15 to 20 different numbers will come up. The payout on a specific number is 36 to 1. So the system was to watch the wheel for a while, pick a number that comes up, and then bet on it until it comes up again, you reach 36 spins, or your budgeted money runs out. Another system was to choose red or black and progressively double your bet on that color until either you win (and then go back to your original bet) or you lose your budgeted money.

Thanks to the wide-open nature of the Web, some sites explain roulette betting systems for free, so Steve didn't lose any money there. These free sites also point out that the systems cannot and do not help you win at roulette because the house, being a business, skews the odds in its favor in various ways.

But these free sites also mentioned something that Steve and I found interesting. Although a roulette system will not necessarily help you win, it will help you play a far more disciplined game than if you just laid down bets willy-nilly or bet on your birthday, as most gamblers do. Most of the roulette "systems" are actually methods of managing your money at the table. They guide the size of your bets and—key benefit—tell you when to stop. On these grounds, even the antisystem folks believe that using a system beats not using one! (As luck would have it, Steve played blackjack and basically following the same system as the dealer—request a card at 16 or below, don't at 17 and above—won $40.)

Now, aside from the fact that Las Vegas holds more interest for most of us than Six Sigma, why am I telling you this?

Because in marketing and sales at most companies, a systematic approach is as rare as it is at the MGM Grand—among the players. But that is changing, because a number of companies are proving that truly systematic management approaches make both marketing and selling easier and more productive.

When I say systematic approaches, I'm using shorthand. In fact, when I say *Six Sigma*, I'm using shorthand. If you're not familiar with the term Six Sigma, don't worry. I'll explain it and other process improvement approaches in Chapter 2. Even if you are deeply familiar with Six Sigma and other process improvement methods, you'll find that applying them in marketing and sales differs from applying them in any other area of business. I'll be showing how to apply them in marketing and sales in every chapter of this book.

Some readers may believe that most companies now manage marketing and sales in a systematic way. At the risk of seeing hordes of marketing and sales managers wielding torches and pitchforks on my front lawn some night, I vigorously disagree.

The current "system" usually starts with arbitrary sales growth targets and moves on to staggeringly wasteful lead generation, then to highly subjective lead qualification. Then salespeople do their best to present to prospects the product or service and its features and benefits and to move the sale toward the close. I would describe all of this, charitably, as hit or miss. The proof that it is hit or miss, aside from my own experience and that of hundreds of other salespeople I've known, rests in the widespread belief that "Sales is a numbers game."

The numbers game works for Mother Nature. A salmon can lay millions of eggs to produce a few fish. An oak tree can produce thousands of acorns to sprout one new tree. And enough baby ducks, turtles, and jungle cats figure out how to live long enough so that duck hunters, pet shops, and circuses don't run out. But while Mother Nature has the unlimited time and resources that the numbers game demands, companies do not. The numbers game translates to massive inefficiency in most business endeavors. That is why most business functions, particularly manufacturing, have developed far more systematic management methods than marketing and sales.

Now, however, companies are bringing those methods into marketing and sales, thereby achieving previously unattainable results.

WHY PROCESS IMPROVEMENT, AND WHY NOW?

Many of the methods you'll learn in this book, which I've bundled into the term *sales process improvement*, grew out of the quality movement that has transformed manufacturing over the past 30 years. You've probably heard of Total Quality Management (TQM), benchmarking, balanced scorecards, quality circles, Lean, or Six Sigma. These approaches all have two things in common: They focus attention on the way people work and the results they produce, and they employ systematic ways of improving the way people work and the results they produce. These specific quality improvement or process improvement approaches vary. But all of them, in one way or another, rely on gathering and analyzing data on how people work, the materials they work on, the results they produce, and—on the basis of that analysis—developing ways to improve the work, materials, and results.

You may be aware that quality and process improvement approaches have driven down costs, improved product quality, and increased productivity in factories around the world. Companies that have embraced these methods include Allied Signal, Bank of America, Dell, General Electric, Honeywell, Johnson & Johnson, Motorola, Sun Microsystems, 3M, and many more.

However—and this is why I've written this book at this time—companies now are applying these approaches in marketing and sales as well with remarkable success. For example:

- ServiceMaster, a company of meat-and-potatoes businesses such as TruGreen ChemLawn, and American Residential Services (heating, cooling, and plumbing repair), realized a $23 million return on one pricing initiative alone. That initiative used Six Sigma to identify and drive the improvements.
- Hong Kong Shanghai Bank Corporation overcame traditional biases in its sales and marketing departments to increase revenues by $10 million in one European brokerage business alone, while achieving profitability in that area for the first time in more than five years. Again, management credits Six Sigma with driving the improvement.
- Standard Register, an established business forms manufacturer,

has used Six Sigma in marketing and sales and to generate process improvements in *its customers'* businesses. Management had to find a method for developing ways to remain relevant as business forms went electronic. It found that method in Six Sigma. Standard Register's Six Sigma initiatives, and migration from regional to national accounts, have generated tens of millions of dollars in new revenue.

WHAT, EXACTLY, IS SIX SIGMA?

In writing this book, I've found many answers to that question among quality improvement experts, marketing and sales professionals, and executives and consultants. Indeed, *Six Sigma* has several meanings. I've found that people in each of these groups, and even people hosting Six Sigma conferences, often use the term Six Sigma to indicate process improvement in general. Some use Six Sigma to indicate almost any process improvement or fact-based management approach. Yet others avoid saying Six Sigma, even when using it in its most strictly defined sense (and there is a very strict definition) to avoid the inevitable quip, "It's Greek to me."

Indeed, *sigma* (σ) is the 18th letter in the Greek alphabet. Six Sigma is a statistical measure. It's also a five-step approach to problem solving. The term is often used to designate an organizational initiative to improve a company's business processes, as in, "We're a Six Sigma company now." In some circles, Six Sigma has become a catchall term for management and problem-solving approaches that employ certain tools to improve business processes and results.

At its best, Six Sigma improves the way managers manage by establishing the context in which, and the means by which, they can decide what is important and what isn't, what requires attention and resources and what doesn't. Six Sigma is the systematic alternative to managing by the seat of the pants, by the way it's always been done, or by assumption, opinion, table pounding, or wishful thinking. In marketing and sales, it is also the alternative to the numbers game. Process improvement doesn't do away with management principles such as responsibility, authority, chain of command, and span of control. Nor does it ignore management practices such as goal setting, planning, delegating, and controlling to plan. Instead, it enables managers at all levels to adhere to those principles and employ those practices. It does this by keeping them focused on the customer, on the organization's purpose, and on the facts of a business situation.

Six Sigma and most process improvement methods depart from the management practices found in most marketing and sales functions. The title of this book, *Sales and Marketing the Six Sigma Way*, sums up my view that decisions affecting these functions must be based on objective measurement and analysis of specific sales and marketing activities and their results. This book explains that view and how to manage based on that view. Process improvement methods aim to portray the objective reality of a business situation: inputs and outputs, workflows and behaviors, causes and effects, problems and solutions. They therefore have the power to end marketing and sales managers' overreliance on gut instinct and standard practices and to introduce "scientific" management to an area that benefits tremendously from it.

Some marketing and salespeople worry that the scientific management of process improvement does away with the fun and creativity of marketing and selling. Others, quite frankly, worry about the exposure such management can generate. Process improvement doesn't do away with fun and creativity or with the need for gut instinct and standard practices. Marketing and sales will always call for creativity, personal expression, and relationship building as well as a "good nose" and diligent execution of the basics. Process improvement merely points to where and how these capabilities can be put to best use.

THE PURPOSE OF THIS BOOK

This book shows how to use process improvement to boost the performance of marketing and sales. Therefore, this book is written for anyone with a stake in an organization's marketing and sales results, including:

- Sales and marketing managers in companies of all sizes and in most industries, and in nonprofits with fundraising operations
- Quality management and process improvement professionals who want to apply the tools of their trade to their organization's sales and marketing functions

- Senior executives with responsibility for their company's financial performance
- Sales and marketing consultants, sales trainers, and sales software providers who want to understand, and perhaps improve, their clients' marketing and sales processes, which in turn will improve the effectiveness of their offerings

I especially want to help bridge the language and knowledge gaps between marketing and sales professionals on the one hand and quality improvement professionals on the other. In practice, I have found that although the gap between these two groups can be wide, reliable ways of closing it exist. For instance, marketing and sales professionals and quality professionals both focus on value for the customer. Quality professionals help their company do more of what adds value for customers (and less of everything else). Marketing and sales professionals make customers aware of that value, guide them to purchase it, and then deliver as much of that value as possible to as many customers as possible. Once the two sides understand their mutual role, they usually lay down their rubber bands and paper clips.

This book can benefit sales and marketing managers in search of new ways to improve their business. Six Sigma practitioners who want to help their sales and marketing departments to understand the power of their methods should pass this book along to forward-thinking managers in those functions. Again, this book is meant to bridge gaps.

This book will have achieved its purpose if marketing and sales managers realize that to manage sales, they must look beyond sales figures and measure and manage the activities and interim results that produce those figures. This book will have achieved its purpose if quality improvement professionals grasp the unique challenges that marketing and sales departments face in trying to influence customers' thinking and behavior. It will have achieved its purpose if senior executives see that process improvement is not a business fad having to do with cutting costs, justifying decisions, or raising a company's profile but rather a method of making decisions in the best way yet developed.

THE STRUCTURE OF THIS BOOK

This book is composed of eight chapters serving the following functions:

- *Chapter 1: The Crisis in Marketing and Selling—and What to Do about It* examines the mounting challenges that companies face in their efforts to find, win, and keep customers, and explains how sales process improvement can help deal with these challenges.
- *Chapter 2: What Is Six Sigma, and Why Should You Care?* explains, for readers unfamiliar with these methods, how process improvement applies to sales and marketing, provides some background on the quality movement, and briefly describes some of the terminology of Lean and Six Sigma.
- *Chapter 3: The New Sales and Marketing Management Strategy* shows how to implement process improvement to change the basic ways in which marketing and sales are managed. This represents a radical—but extremely rational—departure from current practices.
- *Chapter 4: An End-toEnd Six Sigma Sales Project That Increased Revenue by 94 Percent* is based on a project conducted to improve sales at a revenue-generating Web site. This chapter shows how a Six Sigma project works in a live but relatively controllable sales environment.
- *Chapter 5: Tools for Aligning Marketing and Sales Functions* describes marketing and selling as an integrated endeavor and illustrates important tools managers can use to capture the voice of the customer, map what customers value, and translate that data into practical tools that help marketers market and salespeople sell *together.*
- *Chapter 6: Designing a Sales Process That Works* shows how to establish a measurable production system for marketing and selling. This involves understanding the buyer's journey and designing the right sales and marketing tactics for helping buyers move through that journey in ways you can measure.
- *Chapter 7: Making Marketing and Sales Decisions That Get Results* describes how sales training, CRM, promotional campaigns, and other efforts produce more powerful results when applied in a process improvement context. Some are formal Six Sigma projects,

whereas others are less formally defined but no less important.

- *Chapter 8: Moving to High-Performance Marketing and Sales Management* illustrates how process improvement and Six Sigma deployments should be implemented in marketing and sales, how to avoid pitfalls, and how to maximize your gains from these powerful techniques.

ARE YOU SKEPTICAL?

If so, that's good. That's good for two reasons. First, this book is not one that you read to have your preconceived ideas confirmed. It's a book that you read to learn new methods for solving long-standing, seemingly intractable marketing and sales problems. Given the nature of these problems, you naturally would tend to question the claim that you'll find solutions in the pages that follow. Second, a skeptical mind—make that a skeptical but open mind—is the main resource you will need to put these approaches to use in marketing and sales. People with skeptical but open minds quickly learn how to use these approaches and find that they actually do work.

However, you will not find the solutions to your marketing and sales problems in this book. You will find the path to those solutions. You will find new ways of developing those solutions for the marketing and sales functions in your unique organization.

So please turn the page and turn your skeptical, open mind to the marketing and sales problems that most organizations now face.

1

THE CRISIS IN MARKETING AND SELLING—AND WHAT TO DO ABOUT IT

Astute marketing and sales professionals may recognize the formula at work in the title of this chapter: Pose a problem and then offer the solution, which is what you are selling. Some of these professionals might be thinking, "Crisis in marketing and selling? There's no crisis—we're doing fine." The majority, however, will likely have an awareness of the situation I'm about to describe. Even those not in crisis will recognize that the challenges of marketing and selling have intensified.

Consider these two findings from CSO Insights, a firm that regularly surveys the marketing and sales industry:

1. In 2004, for the first time since organized records were kept, more than 50 percent of salespeople in the United States were under quota. (CSO Insights 2004 State of the Marketplace).
2. In 2005, while the number of sales reps who made their targets increased, most of those reps worked more hours on more opportunities, made more sales calls, and submitted more proposals than in the previous year. (CSO Insights 2005 State of the Marketplace).

Are marketing and sales actually becoming tougher? And if so, why?

POWER HAS SHIFTED TOWARD CUSTOMERS

Two basic forces drive free markets: supply and demand. In any given market, the stronger of those two forces will shift economic power toward either the buyer or the seller. When the *supply* of a product is high or increasing (relative to demand), the advantage shifts to the buyer. When *demand* for a product is high or increasing (relative to supply), the advantage shifts to the seller. As those of us who stayed awake through Economics 101 know, in a free market the interaction of supply and demand sets the price of a product. When supply is high, prices fall because there's more product than people want, so buyers cut the price to get customers to buy it. When demand is high, there's not enough product to go around, so customers bid up the price, and sellers are happy to go along with that.

But supply and demand affect more than prices. When a product or service is "in demand," sellers don't have to sell very hard. Buyers will go out of their way for a good deal or even an okay deal. They'll put up with long lines and waiting lists, even tolerating slipshod service. This is why in most of the United States, so many of us pump our own gasoline. When demand is high, selling is easy.

That's a major reason that selling has become more difficult. In the developed world, the supply of most products and services is high relative to demand. That's true of food and beverages, clothing and furniture, air travel and fast food, Internet access and brokerage services, and scores of other categories. From farms to factories and from New York to Seattle and beyond, modern technology and production methods have made developing, producing, and delivering products easier and cheaper. The reasons? More efficient production methods, updated plant and equipment, and the ever-increasing benefits of high technology.

As always, exceptions exist, such as health care and higher education, where demand outstrips supply. Hospitals and universities don't typically employ salespeople, although they use marketing to compete for the best customers. But many, if not most, U.S. industries now resemble the auto industry. Where the United States once had three domestic car manufacturers, who divvied up 90 percent of the market, today foreign car companies compete far more effectively on both quality and price than they did the first three-quarters of the last century. Foreign manufacturers now have plants in North America and close to 60 percent of the U.S. market. (We'll touch on some reasons for the Japanese auto industry's success in Chapter 2.)

When power shifts toward customers, companies compete on low price and high quality—in other words, value—which includes selection, service, and other parts of the customer's experience. So it's no accident that over the past 20 years, companies have developed an intense interest in The Customer. Bankers who once scowled at borrowers now compete for loans. Grocers who basically stocked shelves and gave out coupons now offer fresh sushi, gourmet cheeses, and organic broccoli. Parallels in the business-to-business world include solution selling, consultative selling, customer councils, and customer relationship management (CRM) systems. Many of us might like to think that this focus on The Customer sprang from human kindness, but no: it's economics, plain and simple. When supply outstrips demand and most companies can deliver high quality at a fair price and run a loyalty program, salespeople must work harder to win customers.

Sometimes demand does exceed supply. The phenomenon was vividly portrayed by Geoffrey Moore in his book *Inside the Tornado,* which explains how markets for successful new high-tech products can ramp up rapidly. Moore describes a "stampede" in which "demand dramatically outstrips supply, and a huge backlog of customers appears." He says that the lucky company's strategy at this point must be "just ship!" He adds, "Don't focus on the customer; in other words, just focus on yourself." That's because a company in a market tornado doesn't need to worry about the customer. The key success factor is getting the product out the door.

But *Inside the Tornado* was published in 1995. While the 1990s were a time of tornados for high-tech industries, many businesses now appear to be in a decade of doldrums.

WHY THE CORPORATE PRESSURE COOKER IS EVEN HOTTER

Other forces have made life tougher for those toiling in the marketing and sales fields:

- *The growth imperative never ceases.* The relentless pressure on publicly held companies to increase their profitability shows no signs of abating. Yet they must do this in the high-supply environment described above. Marketing and sales must deliver increasing sales amid high competition at lower costs or, at best, with the same resources.

- *Few untapped production cost savings remain.* Thanks to technology-driven gains in productivity (and thanks to quality improvement), huge cost savings have been achieved in production and throughout the supply chain. With precious few dollars, Euros, or yen left to squeeze out there, companies must look to other areas, such as sales and marketing, for lower costs and higher return on investment (ROI).

- *Change can kill companies.* As Jeff Watts, vice president of account services for Creata Promotion, points out, an inability to detect and respond to market changes can be fatal. Victims include DEC, Howard Johnson, Burroughs, Polaroid, and scores of others. Companies need a distant early warning device to help them anticipate change and respond accordingly.

- *Going global means a world of trouble.* In multinational organizations, global marketing and sales operations magnify and compound the usual challenges.

- *We're still figuring out the Internet.* The World Wide Web is a great leveler and arguably the greatest direct marketing medium ever invented. But we're in the early innings. Many companies, including a good number in health care, financial services, travel, and retailing, have sophisticated Web-based sales strategies—but many more, even in those sectors, do not. In fact, the opportunity that the Web presents to create and monitor metrics on customer behavior has barely been recognized, let alone developed.

These forces are battering companies already beset by long-standing marketing and sales problems, long-standing because their root causes are rarely identified and removed.

Classic Marketing and Sales Problems

Consider these typical marketing and sales problems:

- *Poor lead generation.* Actually this problem goes deeper to poor lead *definition.* Every company needs higher-quality leads, yet rarely do marketing and sales sit down and clearly define the characteristics of high-quality and low-quality leads. How can people pursue high-quality leads if they don't know what one looks like? Leads are now evaluated mainly by salespeople using their experience and intuition. Or they are "evaluated" after the fact—a good lead is one we could close, and a poor lead is one we couldn't close—and stops right there.
- *Black holes.* An HVAC (heating, ventilation, and air conditioning) company spent tens of thousands of dollars to generate poorly defined leads. Then they sent those leads to their distributors without requesting or receiving any feedback on action taken or the outcome.
- *Marketing and sales silos.* Even when marketing and sales report to the same senior executive, they typically are managed separately. Service is also off in a separate world. The result? Poor communication, incomplete handoffs, turf wars, competition for resources, and confused or stranded customers. Marketing is rarely held accountable for producing revenue, while sales is held accountable for little else (often not even for bringing in profitable business at a reasonable cost).
- *Lack of true sales support.* Most salespeople are left to work independently, like basket weavers. In more than one company, I and other salespeople wrote our own sales presentations and even brochures, mailers, and ads, because the marketing materials were useless. As you sit in comfort reading this, salespeople everywhere are fighting tooth and claw to make things happen for customers despite vigorous, wrong-headed internal efforts seemingly

aimed at scuttling sales. Okay, maybe I'm exaggerating, but let's be honest: For all the talk of "alignment" over the past several years, very few of the lines seem directed toward salespeople.

- *NEC (not elsewhere classified):* Here we can bundle other forms of waste and inefficiency, usually expressed (or at least thought of) in terms of long sales cycles, low close ratios, and too many sales going down to no decision. And let's not forget finger-in-the-wind sales "forecasts" and lack of predictable, or even measurable, results from sales training, advertising, CRM, and product development.

These problems are so widespread that most marketing and sales professionals barely see them as problems but rather as "part of the job" or "the way things are." Their resignation may be the biggest problem of all, because these are indeed problems and, as such, can be solved but only with dedicated effort and the right approaches.

When these problems are persistent and damaging, they are usually rooted in the sales process—that is, in one or more specific marketing, sales, or service activities—or in the information available (or not available) on those activities. Thus, these problems often point to problems in the sales process and to a lack of information on what is and isn't working. The fundamental problem is therefore twofold: inefficiency or ineffectiveness somewhere in the sales process, and a lack of information on the activities within that process. As Bob Dylan put it: "Something is happening here, but you don't know what it is."

BLUNDERS MANAGERS MAKE DESPITE GOOD INTENTIONS

Every area of business has its problems. That's not the problem. The problem is the way people deal with marketing and sales problems. Here are few examples from my files:

- Every year, a company that provided uniform rental and laundry services stopped accepting new business after November 1. Bringing on new customers committed the company to purchase the uniforms, and the CFO liked to push those expenses into the next year to improve the bottom line. This went on for years, frustrating sales' efforts to land new business for about two months out of every year.

- A technology services company spent over a million dollars on a CRM system to improve sales forecast accuracy. They succeeded, only to learn that the forecast amounted to less than half of the planned level. This was good information, but it revealed that management's revenue targets had far exceeded the marketing and sales organization's capacity to produce customers. Rather than increase that capacity—tough to do after that million-dollar outlay—management pushed the salespeople harder to make plan. It didn't work.

- A software firm enjoyed real success in its early years, when a salesperson could make 100 prospecting calls and land appointments with about 10 qualified prospects. But over time that ratio rose to 500 to 10 and even higher. The sales managers couldn't understand the new salespeople's lack of prospecting skill. (Most of the original salespeople had moved on.) "I found business when I was starting out," managers would say, "Why can't they?" Only as the company went bust did management realize that the market had moved on. Any systematic yield analysis of prospecting activity would have revealed that fact two to three years earlier.

Marketing and sales managers have been conditioned, encouraged, and trained to focus mainly on sales figures. Meanwhile, management of the activities that generate the leads, opportunities, and sales tends to be haphazard. Most sales managers rely far too heavily on what I call the usual fixes:

- Demand more marketing and selling activity—more leads, more sales calls, more proposals, more distribution channels
- Train salespeople in a new "selling system" or new selling skills
- Tweak the compensation or incentive system or hold a sales contest
- Reassign salespeople to different territories or accounts
- Replace the sales manager or salespeople, or both
- Hire a new ad agency or marketing communications firm
- Try a new CRM system or other sales support software

Don't get me wrong. These initiatives are not bad. At certain times in certain situations any one or more of them might be the solution to a company's sales problem. Yet decisions to employ these solutions are usually made on the basis of very little, if any, actual analysis. Without an analysis of the problem, how can any of these represent a solution? Only with luck.

Managers decide which of these fixes to use based on gut instinct, their experience with what worked for them in the past, or their preference for a particular vendor. They employ such decision making because they see marketing and sales as subject to the vagaries of human nature and therefore as mysterious and uncontrollable. They see marketing and sales as art rather than science, as emotional and competitive rather than rational and cooperative.

These beliefs generate management by slogans like "Go for Growth!" or "I'm for the Customer!" complete with banners and buttons but little real backing. Managers foster sales contests and competitive ranking of salespeople, which actually discourages them from sharing successful sales tactics. (In some shops, it encourages them to undermine one another.) They can lead to the Superman Theory of Sales in which management looks to a few "born salespeople" to carry the load. If all else fails, some companies try to use distributors or independent reps as their sales force rather than a channel, which rarely works. These beliefs also coincide with the view that sales is a numbers game.

Seeing marketing and sales as mysterious and uncontrollable, management focuses on results—How are this month's sales? Is that better or worse than last year? Are we making plan or not?—rather than on the process that produces the results. In a sense, management tries to change the room temperature by talking to the thermometer. The metrics, such as they are, focus on the company's goals, such as revenue, revenue growth, sales trends, and revenue per head count. However, that focus tends to leave out the customers or reduce them to a necessary evil that exists to help us make our numbers. That just might undermine an outfit's ability to find, win, and keep customers. A focus on revenue results also undermines genuine efforts to change marketing and sales methods, because change involves knowing what needs to be changed. That, as we will see, requires analysis that goes far beyond the usual fixes outlined above.

THE SUCCESSFUL ALTERNATIVE: PROCESS THINKING

Given this litany of changes, challenges, problems, false fixes, skewed beliefs, and gut-level decisions, what, exactly, can managers do differently? What is the alternative to the current state of affairs in most organizations?

The alternative is to address the fundamental questions that marketing and sales executives in every company must face when trying to solve a sales problem:

- Where is the problem? In the product? In the organization? Out there, in the marketplace? And where in the product, the organization, or the marketplace?
- What, exactly, is causing the problem? What is causing low sales, slow product adoption, withering markets, or low responses to direct marketing efforts?

Answering these questions calls for an understanding of marketing and sales as a process. A process—any process—is a series of activities designed to produce certain results. Process thinking enables you to measure activities and results and to analyze them for causes and effects. Process thinking is the foundation for the quality movement and for Six Sigma. A business process is simply the way work is organized, a series of activities designed to generate certain results. A process takes inputs—such as raw materials, components, numbers, or ideas—and transforms them into outputs—such as products, services, ledgers, reports, books, or films. A production process generates finished goods. An accounting process generates orderly records of transactions. And a sales process generates customers.

I define the sales process to include everything that a company does to find, win, and keep customers. Broadly, marketing finds customers, sales wins customers, and service keeps customers. Each of these three subprocesses consists of activities. Each activity produces a result that advances the process of finding, winning, and keeping customers.

It is up to management to design, build, maintain, and execute a process for finding, winning, and keeping customers. The process will be unique to the company, and it cannot be purchased in a software system, nor should it be mistaken for the sales funnel. With the right sales process in place, marketing, sales, and service people will be positioned to work more efficiently and effectively. In fact, working within a first-rate sales process, ordinary people can produce extraordinary results.

CAUSE AND EFFECT IN MARKETING AND SALES

The principle of cause and effect underpins much of process thinking and most quality improvement methods. Quite simply, the principle states that every problem has a cause and that cause must be located and removed to produce an improved effect. The cause can be reliably located and removed only by means of a systematic, objective approach to the situation.

Consider these situations:

- To bring in more business, the private banking division of a major financial institution decided to hire more salespeople. But first, it asked an internal quality improvement expert to examine its sales process. This person found that the division's procedure for opening accounts—and the information it required—caused customers to drop out at that point. By changing its account-opening procedure, the division increased its revenue by 18 percent in one year with no increase in staff.

- A telecom carrier hired a sales training firm to improve the sales skills of its account executives. Early on, the sales trainer asked the salespeople, "What's the biggest barrier to a sale that you face?" "That's easy," they said, "getting the prospect's old phone bills." Their practice was to ask prospects for copies of their phone bills so they could gauge the call volume and propose a competitive price. But prospects often couldn't find those bills or couldn't get them from accounting. Sometimes they used the request as an excuse to stall. Meanwhile, the company actually competed more on service than on price. By changing the sales presentation to focus on service rather than on costs, the company helped salespeople eliminate a major sales barrier and start addressing customers' telecommunications problems.

- To increase its flow of leads, a software firm launched and promoted a Web site. The firm soon found that it had more leads than it could handle. However, Mickey Mouse was a frequent visitor. In fact, to avoid sales calls, 28 percent of visitors supplied false contact data. The site's data collection capability was so rudimentary that the company couldn't tell who had visited a specific page or why. As it turned out, the site had been designed around the company's products rather than visitors' needs. By redesigning the site to offer useful information and diagnostic tools, and to request contact data in return, the company dramatically increased the quality of leads generated by the site.

Each of these companies initially took a standard approach to solving a sales problem. The first wanted to add salespeople. The second wanted to train salespeople. The third wanted more leads. On the surface these solutions made sense. In effect, the bank said, "We need more sales, so let's hire more salespeople." The telecom company said, "Let's learn the prospect's call volume, then beat the competition's price." The software firm said, "Everyone who visits our site is a potential customer."

Each company based its initial thinking on an erroneous assumption about its sales process: sales volume depends on the size of the sales force; to make a good proposal, salespeople must know the prospect's current costs; or people who visit a company's Web site are leads. As baseball great Saitchel Paige said, "It's not what you don't know that will hurt you. It's what you know that isn't so that will do you in."

The actual solutions to these companies' sales problems differed sharply from those they initially contemplated. They were able to formulate these solutions only when they examined their sales processes for value to the customer on the one hand and for bottlenecks and waste on the other.

- The bank examined its sales process and discovered a bottleneck at the account-opening stage. So it measured and analyzed the way it opened accounts—the procedure, the number of employees involved, the number of touches a customer required, and the actual and elapsed time involved. It also examined the results—customer satisfaction, customer complaints, instances of troubleshooting by salespeople, and deals lost at this stage. This analysis led the company to fix the bottleneck and thus the problem in the sales process.

- In its analysis, the telecom company examined the way salespeople interacted with customers—the focus on price, requests for bills, elapsed time to get the bills, number of proposals actually based on lower prices. It also looked at results—lag in sales time, prospects' frustration and stalling, and deals lost at this stage. The company saw that the biggest barrier to the sale was one they could eliminate simply by changing the focus of the sales presentation.

- The software company examined the design of its Web site—page content, information given for free, method of requesting contact data, links within the site—and the results—the number of visitors giving bogus contact information, the percentage and type of leads that qualified as prospects, and the purchase volume for various types of leads. This examination led to the conclusion that the site had not been designed around customers' needs. The redesigned site centered on serving those needs, identifying problems, and providing useful information in exchange for contact data.

In these cases, educated, experienced, well-intentioned executives were about to make expensive mistakes because what they thought they knew wasn't so. There was more to the picture, and there was a way to see those things. A more effective, more certain approach was within their grasp. As these cases demonstrate, to identify and fix a sales problem, you must understand the activities in the sales process and their results.

Therein lies another problem: Lack of measures on marketing and sales activities and results that can be agreed upon, communicated, monitored, evaluated, and affected by management decisions. The lack of such measures on lead generation, prospecting, qualifying, sales calls and presentations, proposal writing, and interactions leading to the close—and on their outcomes—means that management cannot truly manage many aspects of the sales process. Gross measures such as close ratios and revenue booked tell us almost nothing. For example, if Mary closes 25 percent of her sales opportunities and Bob closes 15 percent of his, what does that tell us? Does it say that Mary is a more effective salesperson? Or does it mean that Mary has a richer territory or better opportunities? Should Mary be given Bob's territory and Bob Mary's? Or should Bob should go on a few calls with Mary to see how she operates?

Does Bob need additional training? Without more facts, we can't answer any of these questions.

In marketing, the old gag goes, "Half of our advertising dollars are wasted. Trouble is, we don't know which half." Actually, it might be more than half. Moreover, that lack of knowledge extends to elements of marketing like collateral material, Web sites, trade shows, public relations, and even product development.

I believe that the fundamental questions about the location, causes, costs, and solutions to marketing and sales problems can be answered only when managers view sales as a process. It's a beautiful view once you get used to it. At first, however, it can be dizzying or even off-putting. So stay with me. In a short time, you'll see that the clarity that comes with seeing sales as a process makes up for any initial disorientation.

MARKETING AND SALES IS A VALUE-ADDING PROCESS

As you know, customers are not found under cabbage leaves, nor does the stork deliver them. Very rarely do they just show up on the doorstep. Customers come from the marketing and sales process. Therefore, marketing and sales constitute a production process. This process takes the "raw materials" of people in the marketplace who have the kinds of problems your company solves and adds value to them until they are transformed into customers. Those who do not become customers either opt out or are moved out of the sales process, temporarily or permanently.

How do marketing and sales add value? By using communications, media, knowledge, and marketing and sales tools to help prospects solve the problems that the company can solve. In every customer organization, people hold an ongoing conversation about goals, challenges, resources, problems, and priorities. The job of marketing and sales is to engage in that conversation as it relates to their company's products and services. The marketing and sales professionals who best comprehend and contribute to that conversation will find, win, and keep the most customers.

Thus the sales process—marketing, sales, and service—must add value for customers by understanding, engaging, and educating them and helping them make the purchase decision, when it would benefit both buyer and seller. Every step of the sales process must add value for customers in this way and do so efficiently and effectively.

The purpose of the sales process is *not* to vacuum money out of customers' wallets. Rather, it is to add value for customers and for the company by solving problems for customers. This approach is not a good idea for altruistic reasons but for selfish reasons: Adding value for customers is the only way to gain value for your company. This, of course, is the core principle of Adam Smith's analysis of the free market system, in which we all provide value in exchange for value and the markets, guided by Smith's "invisible hand," determine the distribution of goods and services.

In performing their value-adding roles, marketing and sales amount to services in and of themselves—information services and problem-solving services. (If this sounds like "consultative selling" or "solution selling," it actually goes well beyond those approaches, and neither of those techniques will solve sales process problems.) Particularly in sales of complex products and services in a business-to-business environment, buyers need huge amounts of information to make a purchase decision. Price often represents a relatively small part of the decision, with the major issues being uses and applications, compatibility with current systems, upstream and downstream effects, and support and maintenance. If such issues cannot be resolved, low price becomes meaningless. This information component and the need to resolve issues are why we need salespeople.

Some truly creative ways are available to add value for customers through information and issue resolution. For instance, Bellevue, Washington, homebuilder Quadrant Homes takes a creative approach to selling homes. Customers come to Quadrant through multipronged marketing efforts. "We have decided to treat marketing as an investment with an associated ROI," says William Boucher, vice president of communications at Quadrant Homes. "Unlike most builders, who see it as too expensive, we are willing to build the necessary traffic and sales velocity our business model requires by doing some things most builders would never do: television and radio, aggressive public relations and outreach to real estate agents via formal integrated programs, and a Web site." Quadrant's value proposition is "More House, Less Money." It advertises a unique home-buying process "designed to be a hassle-free, even fun, experience" while providing you with more choices than any other homebuilder.

When constructing houses to order, many builders send customers around to various stores and suppliers to select from a limited set of color schemes, flooring materials, lighting fixtures, appliances, and so on after the contract is signed. This generates delays, difficulty, and frustration for all parties while adding no value for customers. In contrast, Quadrant prospects prequalify for a mortgage and then visit the company's state-of-the-art showroom. This is not the usual office setup in the garage of a model home. Instead, the company maintains a 10,000-square-foot facility showcasing the design options available to buyers. After the customer visits one of Quadrant's new-home communities and selects a lot, the salesperson accesses detailed information about the lot location and floor plan online. Then the salesperson helps the customer select from more than 5,000 interior and exterior finishing and fixture options and choices of millwork and appliances.

We'll revisit Quadrant in Chapter 6 because it used process improvement principles to link its production and its marketing and selling into one well-managed process. In this process, customers enjoy greater choice and convenience and a predictable building schedule instead of the limited choices, unlimited hassles, and stop-and-start construction usually associated with new-home construction. This process design makes sales far easier for Quadrant's salespeople as well as for its customers.

The business results? Quadrant has become the number one home builder in Washington and was voted "Best Company to Work For" by *Washington CEO* magazine in June 2004. The company's president, Peter Orser, says, "Ninety-three percent of our customers are willing to refer a friend to Quadrant Homes, and 37 percent actually do, which is four times the national average among homebuilders."

I believe that the marketing and sales process itself must add value for customers. This may seem odd or maybe even idealistic given that most people associate marketing and sales with moving money from buyer to seller and thus as adding value mainly for the seller. But given the reality described by Adam Smith, every company must create a sales process that creates value for customers. When it does, both the customers and—key point—salespeople will follow that process. We'll return to this theme in Chapters 3 and 6, but as you read along, start thinking about ways in which your company's sales process could add more value for customers (and about ways in which it might now be subtracting it).

Marketing and Sales Is a Production Process

Quality and process improvement methods have roots in manufacturing, where they add value in very obvious and tangible ways. In contrast, sales adds value by providing information and resolving issues, both of which are intangible. Given process improvement's roots in manufacturing, it's worth considering a few analogies between sales and manufacturing:

- *Leads are analogous to raw materials in manufacturing.* Advertising and promotion produce leads, people who may need the company's products and services or who actively seek information about them.
- *Sales opportunities are analogous to work-in-process in manufacturing.* Salespeople qualify sales opportunities, people who are considering a purchase and who fit the company's qualification criteria.
- *Customers are analogous to finished goods.* Salespeople close deals with people who buy their products and services and thus become customers.

Other parallels exist between sales and manufacturing, which we will explore as they arise. For now, the main point is that sales is indeed a process that produces customers, which every company needs to survive. It produces customers by adding value for people in the marketplace who have the kinds of problems that the company solves. The value that the sales process adds is not tangible as it is in manufacturing, but it is no less real.

If it's not tangible, how do we know when the sales process is creating value? How do we know whether the process or any of its parts, such as an advertisement, a mailing, a Web page, or a sales call, are producing the intended result?

We know whether value has been added by the actions taken or not taken by the customer. In the sales process, value is most clearly and measurably defined as *that which the customer will take action to obtain or keep.* We know that the process has created value when the prospect reads and responds to the advertising copy, requests the offer presented by the mailing, opts in to the electronic newsletter, accepts our phone calls, or openly shares vital information with the salesperson. Prospects and cus-

FIGURE 1-1

Sales and Marketing Is a Production Process

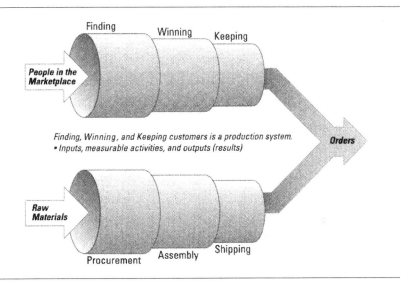

Finding, Winning, and Keeping customers is a production system.
• Inputs, measurable activities, and outputs (results)

tomers take these actions to obtain value, and these actions can be measured. The most obvious measures are sales figures, which every company, manager, and salesperson already tracks. However, to truly improve a sales process, we need to go beyond sales figures and measure activities and results at various stages of the process.

Figure 1-1 illustrates the idea. Your purchasing and production departments are busy sourcing the right materials and adding value to them until they are ready to ship. Your marketing and selling departments are trying to attract people with problems you can solve and adding value to them until they are ready to buy.

Of course viewing sales as a production process raises some questions too complex to address right now. How do we measure actions and analyze the results? How do we know how much value is being created? Don't some marketing and sales efforts generate value but not action on the part of the customer? I'll answer these kinds of questions, but for now the point is that sales produces customers by adding value, and we can measure that value by means other than sales figures. *And* we can apply process improvement approaches to marketing and sales.

Effective analysis calls for learning what prospects and customers are doing at each stage of the marketing and sales process and what results are occurring at these stages and why. This entails gathering data on what marketing and sales people are doing and on the results they're producing. We must discern cause and effect, then decide what needs to be changed and how to change it to improve the result.

As noted, in the sales process, each activity that adds value to customers and prompts an action is also a point where a prospect can drop out or be qualified out. That's why we must identify every phase of the process and measure each phase's results. Examining the process in this way produces yields. These yields can point to the location of the problem. That, in turn, can point toward the kind of solution that's required. For instance, the international bank mentioned earlier discovered that customers were dropping out at the account-opening procedure. The telecom company found that it lost prospects at the point where it requested copies of past phone bills. The software company learned that it lost potential prospects at the point where it asked for contact data without providing anything of value in return.

PROOF THAT INVESTING IN QUALITY IS GOOD BUSINESS

Do quality and process improvement approaches really generate higher revenues and profits? Aside from anecdotal evidence from executives and managers, and stories of companies such as GE under Jack Welch, is there evidence that these approaches deliver increased financial performance?

Minnesota-based Kopp Investments has been investing in companies managed with quality improvement approaches for the past seven years. Kopp chooses stocks to invest in by applying two types of criteria to companies in the S&P 500. According to Craig Robinson, the cofounder of the firm's total quality management (TQM) strategy, the firm bases 50 percent of its decision on standard measures of financial performance, such as market capitalization and return on investment. It bases the other 50 percent of its investment decision on a measure of management's commitment to quality and ability to manage for quality.

The latter measure has three components. The first uses the six-part Baldridge criteria (leadership, strategic planning, customer and market focus, measurement and analysis, human resources, process management and business results). The second component is a survey of quality experts that Kopp has created. "We survey quality experts to learn which companies among the S&P 500 they believe are managed by quality principles," Craig explains. Each company gets a score from 1 to 5, with 5 the highest. "It can be a Six Sigma company or a Lean company. Whatever the semantics, the main thing is that it manages for quality." The third component is an aggregate of all the international, national, and state quality awards, such as the Baldridge Award, the Deming Prize, and similar honors.

The result is a composite score for each company in the S&P 500. The 100 companies that score the highest relative to their peers become part of Kopp's Q100. "If I am buying stocks," Craig said, "I want to buy the stocks of companies that I believe are run better than their competitors. In the long run, being good at quality is the only way you can compete."

Has this investment approach worked?

Craig points out, "We have outperformed the S&P 500 for six of the last seven years—and dramatically outperformed it. The one year we didn't, the S&P 500 was up 21.05 percent and we were up 20.87 percent. For the past three years, our annualized return is 13.8 percent versus 8.3 percent for the S&P 500. For the past five years, the portfolio is up 7.4 percent and the S&P 500 is down 2.4 percent.

Special **R**esource

Identifying companies that are serious about quality management is good business. You, too, can select companies to invest in based on their management's quality strategy. Craig Robinson of Kopp Investments and Michael Webb have prepared a white paper describing this approach: "How to Select Winning Companies for Your Investment Portfolio." You can download this white paper for free by visiting *www.qualitymanagementinvestor.com*.

"We may not be able to say, 'Six Sigma will produce X percent of incremental performance,'" Craig says. "That isn't how it works. But because Six Sigma is so tied to business results, it correlates with our financial measures. It also shows up in areas such as the Baldridge criteria for measurement and analysis and process management."

It's significant that Kopp Investments followed a philosophy of value investing and long-term stability well before creating the Q100. Focusing on companies managed according to quality improvement principles simply helps Kopp make investments according to that philosophy.

DON'T LOOK FOR MAGIC WANDS OR SILVER BULLETS

While our goal is to make selling easier and more productive, managing with quality improvement methods sometimes requires more work than standard practices. The result, as in most endeavors in which people work more effectively, is higher performance. However, while you may achieve higher performance quickly, the real benefits are long term. A manager, department, or organization must recognize that these methods are like diet and exercise: It is in their interest to adopt them for life. If you ever hear anyone say, "We tried process improvement for a year, and we found it just didn't work," they are not talking about process improvement. A commitment to quality must, by definition, be a long-term commitment to manage with a certain philosophy and certain methods.

Another caveat: By no means does Six Sigma—or any management method—do away with problems and challenges. It simply provides the best method yet devised for identifying, analyzing, and dealing with them. That's no small contribution. Earlier I noted that managers often cannot locate a marketing or sales problem or its cause. That's why they often choose one of the usual fixes. Process improvement unearths causes by clearly defining activities and results in the sales process and thus the location of problems.

You may be familiar with the serenity prayer: "Lord, grant me the courage to change the things that I can change, the patience to accept the things that I cannot change, and the wisdom to know the difference between the two." In marketing and sales, and in business in general, process improvement approaches enable us to do a better job of knowing the difference between the two. Come to think of it, they often also help managers develop the courage and patience to deal with what they can and cannot change.

KEY POINTS

- A host of forces are shifting the dynamics of market power in favor of customers.
- Traditional approaches to managing marketing and sales make it difficult for managers to know with any certainty what changes they should make. As a result, managers often rely on gut instinct and experience instead of systematic thinking and hard data. When the inevitable mistakes happen, they are extremely costly.
- While marketing and sales have been thought of as art rather than science, companies are beginning to make great progress in applying a process approach to them. This means being more precise with words and measurements so that work can be understood in terms of cause and effect.
- Customers have free will and will act only when they see value to themselves. Key to a process approach in marketing and sales is realizing that, just as in manufacturing, everything you do must create value for customers.
- The product of marketing and sales activities is a series of customer actions, ultimately resulting in orders. These actions can and should be measured as carefully as raw material, work-in-process, and finished goods inventories are measured in manufacturing.
- Over the long term, the investment values of companies where management is committed to a quality philosophy have consistently outperformed the S&P 500 for Kopp Investments.

2

WHAT IS SIX SIGMA, AND WHY SHOULD YOU CARE?

To readers unfamiliar with process improvement, the whole thing can seem like a cult. The term *Six Sigma* sounds mysterious, even a bit sinister. Practitioners sometimes pore over odd-looking charts and arcane statistics or talk in the alphabet soup beloved by administrators. And although most of them have learned to stop saying, "We're from quality improvement, and we're here to help!" some practitioners like to appear as if they have all the answers.

Yet process improvement professionals have helped scores of major companies and hundreds of midsized companies boost their bottom lines. Now those companies are turning to process improvement to increase their revenues. Sooner or later, there's a good chance that your company will consider adopting Six Sigma if only for competitive reasons. So every businessperson should know about Six Sigma, at least in broad outlines.

In this chapter, I explain Six Sigma from the marketing and sales perspective. If you are unfamiliar with process improvement, you'll learn the basics here. If you are a process improvement professional, you'll learn a bit about how Six Sigma applies to marketing and sales. You'll also see process improvement at work in marketing and sales. This will position you to start thinking about your marketing and sales function in new ways. It will also underscore what every solid process improvement professional knows: You always have to use Six Sigma in service of your business goals, never for the sake of Six Sigma.

Here's an example that illustrates that concept. American Home Shield (AHS), a company of ServiceMaster, provides repair warranties on residential plumbing, heating and cooling systems, and home appliances. Vice President Steve Burnett explains:

> In our business, as in any annual contract business, some customers are going to cancel. At one point, we found that requests to cancel were queuing up and taking too long. So we designed a Six Sigma project to reduce the time it took to cancel customers.
>
> And it worked. We improved our process and were able to cancel contracts faster and cheaper. That seemed to make sense. But to me, from a business standpoint, it didn't get to the root cause of the problem, as in, "Gee, why are customers canceling?" Because it's nice that we can cancel contracts quickly, but our real goal is to keep customers, right?
>
> Now we had been tracking customer satisfaction, and we knew we were doing well. But we weren't getting at why people left us. So we started monthly surveys of lost customers—good, statistical samples of customers who canceled or didn't renew. That uncovered some root causes of lost customers, which we learned were often service issues. If you look at it from the customer's viewpoint, service issues have to do with 'not fixing my problem,' 'not communicating with me,' 'not getting back to me'—very basic things. Using Six Sigma, we found that we just weren't aware of many unresolved service issues. Our normal business processes didn't close the loops and tie things off.
>
> So we established a service call follow-up process. Two days after placing a work order with us, the customer gets an automated call. We ask if the technician fixed the heating system or the appliance, showed up on time, etcetera. The customer presses "1" if everything was fine and "2" if not, in which case we get back to him or her to find out what's unresolved.
>
> As a result, we've seen much higher customer satisfaction scores, particularly in problem resolution. We had been doing such a good job with most customers that we weren't great at exception management, and this process really fixed that.

But that's not all. Getting back to the cancellations, we also designed a process to funnel those requests to a Save Desk. This is a group of highly trained service technicians with accounting training and excellent soft skills. When someone calls saying, "I want out of this contract," they now hear us say, "What's the problem? I'm sorry this happened. Let me help you." Most often, we uncover errors in our previous processing or handling of the customer, and we spend very few incremental dollars to fix these issues.

With the Save Desk, 69 percent of those customers decide not to cancel. We've even surveyed them on buyer's remorse, and we found only 4 percent degradation there. So we now save 65 percent of those people who call to cancel. We also did a small test on this without the Six Sigma methodology and found that 40 to 45 percent of the saved customers renewed again.

Here's the thing: We went from looking at Six Sigma very operationally—how we could cancel contracts faster—to looking at the customer's real need and how to fill that need. We measured the heck out of everything, found the problems, and put processes in place to fix them. To me, that's the real issue—meeting the customers' needs. We think bigger about Six Sigma than we did before. We're not interested in saving two people off a headcount if we can reduce our cancellations by two-thirds and have 40 percent of them renew.

This case charts the course that many companies are now traveling. They are moving from an operational focus on cutting costs to a marketing and sales focus on generating and protecting revenue. But what does Steve mean by Six Sigma? What does "measure the heck out of everything" mean? Why hadn't someone at American Home Shield just said, "Hey, let's try a Save Desk"? This chapter answers those questions while providing an overview of process improvement and Six Sigma. However, this is not a technical primer. (You'll find some very good ones listed in the Appendix.) Instead, this chapter conveys the basic principles and practices of process improvement while showing how they apply in marketing and sales.

FIVE THREADS OF SALES PROCESS IMPROVEMENT

All process improvement methods share the following five principles to at least some degree.

Creating Value for Customers

A company exists because it creates value for customers. Quality professionals want to learn how customers define value and help the company deliver it. Do customers want 14 colors? Or was that our idea? What does it cost us—and customers—to offer 14 colors? Would customers pay for that choice? If not, why are we providing it?

Which created more value for ServiceMaster customers? Canceling them faster or fixing their problems and maintaining their warranties? In some cases, perhaps the former. But in most cases, fixing their problems created more value for customers and thus for the company. In addition, many regular customers who didn't call to cancel were helped by the new problem resolution process. That's still more value added.

Managing on Data and Facts

Sales figures measure the end result, not the activities and results within the sales process. Without data and facts on those activities and results, managers must rely on gut instinct, standard practices, and the usual fixes. A better approach is to see sales as a process and to understand the inputs, the outputs, and the many steps that turn inputs into outputs. With that viewpoint plus data and facts, you can manage the sales process.

Managing on the basis of data and facts implies a commitment to measurement. Six Sigma underscores the need to measure what people are doing and producing at discrete levels. This, in turn, usually reveals a lack of good data, which is why data collection is often a big part of a Six Sigma project.

ServiceMaster "measured the heck out of everything," not to do Six Sigma but to understand what was going on in its processes. Without data, facts, and measures regarding contract cancellations, nobody could say, "Hey, let's try a Save Desk!"

Analyzing Cause and Effect

Data and facts enable us to analyze cause and effect. We can see what is happening and discover why it's happening, then do something about it. In formal Six Sigma terms, we say that Y is a function of X. Technically:

$$Y = f(X)$$

That is Y, which is the result or effect (the dependent variable), depends on or is caused by certain activities, conditions, or situations, which are the Xs (independent variables).

AHS found that unresolved service problems caused many cancellations. The Y of cancellations was caused by the Xs of unresolved service problems. So they established post-service call follow-up and problem resolution processes and experimented with the Save Desk, which proved successful.

Of course, you can't solve every problem. For instance, the company's research surely showed that some cancellations were due to customers relocating overseas. That's useful information, because there's nothing a Save Desk can do about it. Remember the Serenity Prayer? This is how Six Sigma gives you the wisdom to know what you can and can't change. It identifies the Xs, so you can decide which ones you can and can't affect.

Minimizing Waste, Errors, and Defects

In most companies, sales and marketing is a sort of black box. No one really knows what goes on inside. Figure 2-1 reflects this state of affairs. Leads go in, customers come out. Some leads and customers are better than others, and no one really knows why.

Most approaches to improving sales attempt to pack more into the process. More leads. More salespeople. More products. As shown in Figure 2-2, you might get more out of the system by putting more in, but output becomes a case of diminishing returns.

FIGURE 2-1

Current State of Most Businesses: No Process, No Control

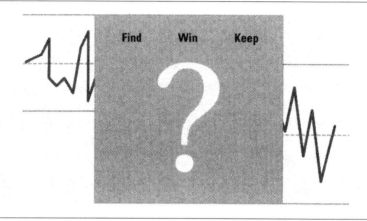

FIGURE 2-2

Traditional Approach—Work Harder!

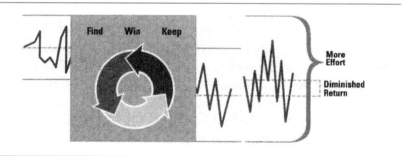

In process improvement, waste is any activity or result that doesn't add value for the customer. Errors and defects are unwanted results. The causes of waste, errors, and defects lie in the way people work or the materials they work on, and those causes can be discovered and removed. But when sales managers hear about eliminating waste and errors, they often object. For instance, in "qualityspeak" a useless sales lead is an "error" or "defect." Yet all salespeople know that companies generate far more leads than sales opportunities. How can a lead that doesn't qualify as a sales opportunity be an error or defect? Aren't such leads just part of the process?

FIGURE 2-3

Sales Process Improvement—Reduce Defects

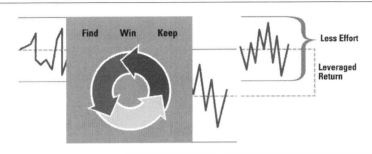

Well, yes, but in process improvement terms, because we can't add value to them, they're scrap. Unfortunately, if you're like most business professionals, you might just accept that. After all, sales is a numbers game, right? Isn't every no just another step on the way to a yes? Given this, if you're a quality professional, you might just call them bad leads or leads that don't qualify. But no matter what you call them, leads that don't become customers represent an opportunity to improve. (See Figure 2-3.) The business goal is to avoid a wasteful, error-prone numbers game by actively managing waste, errors, and defects. Notice I said managing, not eliminating.

Consider the approval processes that companies use to decide whether to sell to a customer on credit. A bad debt is clearly an error or defect. Yet if you shoot for zero bad-debt expense, you will turn away many qualified customers. You don't want that strict of a credit policy. However, if you allow a bad-debt expense of 5 or 10 percent of sales, you'll kill your profits. So you target a level of bad debt that balances the need to sell against the need to collect your receivables, say 2 percent of sales.

What bothers me is that we all see the sense of this in the credit area but not in lead generation. Remember the outfit where salespeople went from 100 calls to 500 calls to find 10 prospects? If that company's bad-debt expense had jumped fivefold, management would have overhauled the credit approval process the next day. But they tolerated a similar situation in prospecting for years, then went out of business. Talk about waste.

We are not salmon or oak trees, which can make do with Mother Nature's yield ratios. We are men and women who know that the war against waste is worthwhile even in marketing and sales.

Setting the Context for Collaboration

Collaboration. Teamwork. Pulling together toward the same goal. Who can argue against these notions? No one! Who can work against them? Everyone! Professionals across all functional areas are united by a single idea: Their colleagues in other functions are preventing them from doing their job.

Six Sigma and other process improvement methods recognize the interconnectedness of every element in a business, every activity and result, every input and output, every function and person. Some people believe that a butterfly in Beijing can cause a hurricane in Honolulu. Yet many people fail to see the effect of poor product literature on a potential customer. Process improvement makes these connections explicit by making the activities in the process, and their results, explicit.

Imagine a company culture characterized by these five principles: delivering value to customers, managing on data and facts, analyzing cause and effect, minimizing waste and defects, and working in true collaboration. Or just look at the experience of Toyota, GE, or Kopp Investments. In companies that embrace process improvement, these principles organize and align everyone's beliefs, thoughts, and actions. In this way, the five threads of sales process improvement set the context in which management makes decisions and people carry them out. I develop this thought a bit more in Chapter 3, but here's what it amounts to: Senior executives often make major decisions without thinking through the hundreds of small decisions and actions that people must execute to implement those major decisions. Without thinking them through—and measuring the activities and results—how will executives know whether all those decisions and actions are occurring?

True, they broadly define objectives such as deadlines, headcounts, budgets, and sales goals. But how will middle managers, employees, and the executives themselves know if people are doing what they must do every day to reach those objectives? Quarterly and annual metrics on deadlines, headcounts, expenses, and sales provide scores at the end of each inning (month) and game (year). But we must keep track of the strikes, balls, hits, runs, and—yes—errors whenever there's action on the field. At the highest level, that is why—and that is how—process improvement works: It sets the context in which everyone knows what to do and how well all of them are doing it.

WHAT IT REALLY TAKES TO IMPROVE RESULTS...PERMANENTLY

It has often been said that the definition of insanity is doing the same thing over and over while expecting a different result. Yet without understanding the system of causes and effects they are dealing with, managers cannot know what changes they should make to produce the results they desire.

What marketing and selling needs is a more scientific approach; an approach that allows managers to understand and analyze information about the performance of their organization and to reliably connect inputs/causes with outputs/results.

To permanently improve the results that a process produces, you have to improve the process itself. You have to improve the methods by which the work gets done. The lack of such an approach is why many people shy away from accountability in marketing and sales and why many others are held accountable—and even penalized—for things they can not control. They are basically told to improve their performance within the same process. That leaves an awful lot outside their control, including the materials they are working on and the ways in which they are supposed to work on them, while usually leaving the activities upstream and downstream from them unchanged.

These are exactly the sorts of things that the quality movement addressed in manufacturing organizations, where many factors were beyond the control of the people doing the work, including the quality of raw materials, the uneven performance of equipment, and the demands of the ordering and expediting functions. The quality movement (TQM) and now Lean and Six Sigma have provided repeatable, structured, proven approaches for distinguishing what can be controlled from what can't in manufacturing organizations. These techniques showed managers the specific changes they needed to make to their business to produce the results they desired. Those who made the changes got the results.

This book is based on the idea that the principles of the quality movement, up to and including Six Sigma, apply to sales and marketing when applied correctly. Given this book's premise and the impact of the quality movement on modern industry, let's survey a bit of background on the quality movement.

A NANO HISTORY OF QUALITY IMPROVEMENT

Scientific management began with Frederick Taylor's efforts in the early 1900s to make factories more efficient. Taylor is most famous for time-and-motion studies on assembly line workers and for designing work processes that increased worker productivity, particularly at Ford and other auto manufacturers. His methods were revolutionary at a time when the carrot and the stick were the main managerial tools.

The actual quality movement traces its roots to the work of Walter Shewhart of Bell Labs in the 1920s. Shewhart pioneered the use of statistics to analyze product and process performance. Starting in the 1940s, two students of Shewhart, W. Edwards Deming and Joseph M. Juran, established the principles of Total Quality Management (TQM). Deming worked with Japanese engineers in the 1950s as their nation rebuilt after World War II. The Japanese enthusiastically adopted his management principles and statistical methods for controlling processes and quality. When Japanese manufacturers captured a large share of the U.S. auto market in the 1970s (and in other industries, such as cameras and consumer electronics), U.S. companies got serious about improving quality. Foreign competition ignited the quality movement in the United States. That movement promulgated structured methods of improving the quality of a product by improving the process that produces it.

In 1951, Dr. Joseph M. Juran published the *Quality Control Handbook*, one of the first books on the subject. Then in 1964 came his book *Managerial Breakthrough*, which described a step-by-step sequence for achieving quality improvement. This eventually evolved into Six Sigma. In 1986, Six Sigma emerged as an improvement model at Motorola, and in 1988, Motorola won the Malcolm Baldridge National Quality Award. Within a few years, Six Sigma had been adopted by IBM, Texas Instruments, Xerox, Allied Signal, GE, and many others and became popularized as a management method. Its impact has been felt not just in manufacturing but also in services, health care, hospitality, banking, and education.

Total Quality Management

In the 1980s and 1990s, the work of Deming, Juran, and Philip Crosby found expression in Total Quality Management (TQM), one of the best-known approaches. TQM assumes that quality depends upon every activity and person in the company (hence, the term *total*). It also assumes that improvement never ends. TQM was responsible for major improvements in quality and business results in such companies as Ford, Motorola, and Toyota.

Unfortunately, in U.S. companies TQM implementers tended to have a rather unfocused approach of "quality for quality's sake." Techniques such as Quality Circles, which regularly brought employees together to collaborate on ways to improve quality, fell into disrepute as companies failed to gain measurable and timely results. Many of the methods had value, but something was missing. That something was the customer's needs, which Lean brought into focus. For that reason—and for its usefulness in marketing and sales—let's take a look at Lean.

Lean Has Worked Wonders for Businesses Worldwide

Lean, also known as Lean Thinking, grew out of lean manufacturing as developed by Toyota and documented in the 1990 book *The Machine That Changed the World: The Story of Lean Production,* by James P. Womack and Daniel T. Jones. The basic Lean principles are value, value stream, flow, pull, and perfection. In applying these principles, you identify *value;* analyze the *value stream;* eliminate waste and make the value stream, that is, the value-creating process, *flow* more quickly; let customers *pull* the product as they need it; and constantly strive toward *perfection.*

Lean aims to add value for the customer, who may be internal or external, by identifying waste, which is anything that does not add value for the customer. Lean begins with 5S, which roughly translated from the Japanese stands for sort, straighten, sweep, schedule, and sustain. These represent basic housekeeping techniques designed to enable consistency, eliminate wasted time and energy, and prevent mistakes by being organized.

Then Lean examines each work activity from the *customer's* point of view. You ask, "What value does this activity add for the customer?" Then you classify each activity in the process as a value-adding or non-value-adding activity. You "lean" a process—make it lean—by retaining and strengthening the value-adding steps while eliminating, or at least minimizing, the non-value-adding steps. (Lean does recognize "enabling activities," which the company needs even if the customer doesn't, such as accounting and the cafeteria.) Waste includes waste of materials, motion, effort, energy, talent, and time—including waiting time, elapsed time, and cycle time. Waste also includes overproduction, underproduction, and fixing errors (rework). The more waste you remove from a process, the leaner it becomes. The leaner it becomes, the more efficient it becomes.

Lean provides a tremendously useful way of looking at marketing and sales. Many a hungry salesperson has said, when asked to attend a meeting about nothing, "If there's not a dollar on it, I don't do it." Lean turns that mindset to the customer's advantage by saying, in effect, "If there's no value in it for the customer, we as a company don't do it." This way of thinking controls the urge to do things that have (usually short-term) value to the company but not to the customer. For instance, slash-and-burn salespeople, out to enrich themselves at the customer's expense, can say, "If there's not a dollar on it, I don't do it," and leave a trail of dissatisfied customers in their wake. Lean, however, presupposes that you make money by creating value for customers. That's the premise of Lean in manufacturing, in marketing, and in selling. It's also the reason I say that the sales process itself must create value for customers.

Lean can help you readily identify marketing and sales activities that create no value for either the company or its customers. Activities crying out for scrutiny include attending trade shows just to show the flag, low-yield cold calling, many forms of advertising, and most promotional items of the coffee mug and embossed pen variety. Ultimately, however, judgments about the value of a marketing or sales activity to the customer and the company must be based on *measured* results and costs versus benefits. We'll examine ways to develop a sales process that adds value for customers—and ways of measuring that value—in Chapters 5 and 6.

BETTER TOGETHER: LEAN AND SIX SIGMA

Sometimes you'll hear the term *Lean Six Sigma* or hear the two methods discussed together. That's because some companies have implemented both Lean and Six Sigma, either separately or in an integrated way. This joint implementation makes a lot of sense. Lean provides ways of making processes flow faster, smoother, more efficiently, and more consistently. It is used mainly when the problems and the solutions are known. Six Sigma provides ways of defining measurements so you can identify variations ("errors" and "defects"), identify their causes, and eliminate them to improve performance. Six Sigma is used mainly when the problems are known but the solutions are not.

Many companies have succeeded in first implementing Lean and then Six Sigma. This works by first eliminating the obvious (and not so obvious) non-value-adding activities in the process along with wasted time, motion, materials, and money. Then, with a basically efficient process in place, people turn to improving the effectiveness of the process, that is, the predictability and quality of the results.

SIX SIGMA, SEVEN WAYS

Although you can use process improvement techniques without implementing a full Six Sigma approach, Six Sigma represents the most rigorous and sophisticated approach available (as of this writing). It's also the approach widely credited with the success of such companies as GE under Jack Welch, Allied Signal, Motorola, and many others. But Six Sigma means different things in different contexts to different people. So to help you get your arms around these meanings, here are the most widely accepted definitions of Six Sigma, some of which I have alluded to earlier.

Definition #1: Six Sigma = Management Philosophy

Six Sigma is a management philosophy and approach based on the five principles discussed earlier in this chapter. The key one is value for customers, which Six Sigma aims to deliver in the most effective and efficient possible ways. This differs sharply from hanging posters saying "The Customer Is King" in the cafeteria. Instead, senior executives must consistently manage on the basis of all five principles and have people "measure the heck out of everything."

Definition #2: Six Sigma = Scientific Method

Six Sigma is a business application of the scientific method. The scientific method demands that you observe, measure, analyze, hypothesize, experiment, and replicate the results of the experiment. This method moves management from the realm of opinion, standard procedures, and the usual fixes to the realm of facts, data, and measurable realities.

The scientific method provides much of the rigor for which Six Sigma is famous, but Six Sigma is not rigorous for the sake of being rigorous. It is rigorous for the same reason that boot camp is rigorous. You need incredible discipline and skill to survive in the real world of business with its sketchy data, hidden processes, changing variables, human foibles, and rabid competitiveness.

Definition #3: Six Sigma = Formal Initiative

The term Six Sigma often means an organization-wide, formal effort to improve quality and processes. You'll hear people say, "We're doing Six Sigma now" and "We're a Six Sigma company." A key element in such efforts is a quality department or project office that oversees implementation of Six Sigma projects. Whether this is a quality czar, a manager with only two professionals, or a larger department, this function is accountable for quality and process improvement and is essential to a formal Six Sigma initiative.

Definition #4: Six Sigma = Applied Statistics

I'm not going to geek out on you, but Six Sigma's statistics supply much of its objectivity and precision. The rocket science in the approach rests on the scientific nature and reliable behavior of numbers. Thus, when you try to learn how a process works, basic questions arise. What do you need data on? What kind of data do you need? How much do you need? What is the data telling you? How certain can you be about what it's telling you? You need statistics to answer these questions. If you're not a geek, don't be intimidated by the statistics in Six Sigma. They can almost always be translated into business terms, and the statistics themselves are calculated by standard software packages or by technically inclined folks who actually like the stuff.

Some Six Sigma practitioners do focus on statistics instead of the underlying business process and goals. That not only turns off businesspeople but can lead the project team down the wrong path or even kill the initiative. Statistics are simply some tools of Six Sigma, not the solution to everything.

Definition #5: Six Sigma = Specific Tools

You'll often hear about the tools of Six Sigma or the Six Sigma toolbox. The term *Six Sigma* is often used to designate the use of certain methods of gathering, organizing, and analyzing ideas, data, facts, statistics, and parts of processes. For instance, Voice of the Customer uses surveys, focus groups, interviews, and other methods to define customers' needs and requirements for a product, service, or process. A SIPOC diagram depicts the suppliers, inputs, process, outputs, and customers of a process, which helps people clearly identify and discuss its elements.

Certain tools are used in specific steps of a Six Sigma project. There are so many tools, however, that I can't cover them all in depth in this book. You'll find books that do that in the Appendix. However, I will show you some of the most important tools in Chapter 4.

Definition #6: Six Sigma = Quality Measure

In statistics, sigma (σ) is a measure of variation, similar to the more familiar standard deviation from the mean. The higher the sigma value, the less variation in whatever is being measured.

The concept of variation is key. When they think about minimizing waste, errors, and defects, Six Sigma practitioners typically think in terms of minimizing variation. This grows out of the method's manufacturing roots. In a production process, if we can measure the characteristics of inputs and outputs, we can control their quality. How? By using statistical analysis to identify the variations in those characteristics, then asking ourselves, "Why are these variations occurring?" The answers point to the causes of the variations, some of which we can eliminate or

FIGURE 2-4
Why Six Sigma Is a Worthwhile Goal

99% Good (3.8 Sigma)		99.99966% Good (6 Sigma)
20,000 lost articles of mail per hour	→	Seven articles lost per hour
Unsafe drinking water for almost 15 minutes each day	→	One unsafe minute every seven months
5,000 incorrect surgical operations per week	→	1.7 incorrect surgical operations per week
Two short or long landings at most major airports each day	→	One short or long landing every five years
200,000 wrong drug prescriptions per year	→	68 wrong prescriptions per year
No electricity for almost seven hours each month	→	One hour without electricity every 34 years

Courtesy of Breakthrough Managment Group

change. Things that can and need to be controlled, but aren't, are often called defects.

In business, Six Sigma is a measure of quality equal to 3.4 defects per million opportunities for a defect. That's close to perfection. That means that in a million boxes of Kellogg's Raisin Bran, about three will contain burned flakes, foreign matter, short weight, no raisins, or another defect. It means that when Heineken ships a million bottles of beer, only three will be flat, off-tasting, or less than full. In foods, beverages, and consumer packaged goods, major companies can actually perform at that level or close to it.

In our modern world, higher and higher levels of quality are becoming increasingly important. The examples of defect rates in Figure 2-4 show why Six Sigma is a worthwhile goal.

Achieving high levels of quality is critical to profitability, because as products and services grow more complex, the impact of defects doesn't just accumulate, it multiplies. Consider that a modern jet aircraft has more than a million parts. Small variations in the sizes of those parts accumulate to cause supposedly identical planes to vary in length by as much as a few feet. Now, consider the number of steps involved in your company's typical marketing and selling process from product development to promotion, lead generation, channel management, qualification, proposal, negotiation, close, delivery, and through to servicing. If the wrong market is targeted, or the right market targeted incorrectly, an entire product launch can fail. Small errors in the early stages can cause debilitating amounts of waste and inefficiency downstream.

Six Sigma cannot make every process operate perfectly. Instead, it enables people to track down the causes of variation so that processes can be made to operate as effectively—and as inexpensively—as possible.

For the record, here are the standard Sigma quality measures:

Quality Level	Defects per Million	Defect Free Percentage
Six Sigma	3.4	99.99
Five Sigma	233	99.98
Four Sigma	6,210	99.40
Three Sigma	158,655	93.30
Two Sigma	308,538	69.10
One Sigma	691,462	30.90
Zero Sigma	933,193	6.70

Six Sigma performance is usually attained only in narrowly defined processes. As the layers of processes, people, and functions increase, the potential for defects increases geometrically. Vacuum cleaners, automobiles, and anything else with moving parts are tougher to get right than consumer packaged goods such as toothpaste. And in many services, such as restaurants, a Six Sigma level of quality for the entire organization will forever remain a distant dream.

That also holds true in marketing and sales. A company where all except 3.4 of one million leads generates a sale is unimaginable. So what good is Six Sigma as a quality measure in marketing and sales? To be honest, as a practical measure not much. But as a way of thinking, it offers a lot: The pursuit of perfection. It also means knowing how to measure improvement, wherever it occurs on the scale.

Most marketing and sales processes function at One or Two Sigma or less. For instance, a close ratio of 30 percent—that is, salespeople collectively closing 30 percent of their sales opportunities—would translate to One Sigma. A close ratio of 69 percent would equal Two Sigma. (I'm expressing this loosely. As I'll explain in Chapter 3, both "close" and "sales opportunity" would have to be precisely defined for the ratio and the Sigma value to be meaningful.) A close ratio of 69 percent may seem ridiculously high. But depending where in your process you begin the measurement, it might not be ridiculous at all. You can always calculate a Sigma value for a process, but if a process is functioning at One Sigma, you can often dispense with some of the formalities of a Six Sigma project and sometimes even some steps.

Oh, about those steps . . .

Definition #7: Six Sigma = Five Steps

As a formal process improvement method, Six Sigma is composed of five steps: define, measure, analyze, improve, and control. Called DMAIC (*de may' ik*) for short, these steps follow the scientific method. I'll show you the steps in an actual project in Chapter 4 and just briefly explain each one here.

1. *Define* the problem (or error or defect) and the process precisely, whether you are examining the entire process or only one part of it. Here you identify the process that contains the problem, the activities in the process, and the results of those activities—as well as the error or defect.
2. *Measure* the activities and the results while clarifying exactly what you are measuring. Here, having defined the activities and results, you measure them to understand the process. This often involves a significant data collection effort, but without data you don't know what's really happening. In this step, you also generate baseline measures of the process's performance.
3. *Analyze* the data (from the measurement step) for variations in the results and in the activities that produced them and search for cause-and-effect relationships. You often must move back and forth between the measure and analyze steps to clarify how the process really works. The result of this analysis becomes your hypothesis—your theory of cause and effect regarding the problem.
4. *Improve* the process by constructing an experiment or pilot project to test your hypothesis. The change aims to measurably affect one (or more) of the Xs, the causes. If your hypothesis is correct, there will be a measurable (positive) change in the Y, the effect,

and you will have reduced the instances of defects and thus improved the process.

5. *Control* the process to make the change permanent, lock in the gains, and achieve future gains. If your theory proves correct, you institutionalize the change so the problem doesn't recur. This might involve new management reports or financial incentives, as well as a control plan to ensure that the inputs and outputs remain within the targeted ranges.

When necessary, Six Sigma can be applied with a rigorous level of precision, using applied statistics that would impress a seasoned engineer. Fortunately, it can also be applied at a commonsense level, which can be quite effective in the marketing and sales areas, especially at first. As one Master Black Belt put it, "When you've got a process operating at One Sigma, you don't have to worry about design of experiments." In design of experiments, you use statistical techniques to set up an experimental project to identify the interactions between multiple variables. However, Six Sigma's glowing reputation has been built on the rigor of these five steps and statistical methods. These steps and methods enable managers to see things they wouldn't normally see and to make improvements that wouldn't normally occur to them.

Implementing these steps correctly takes knowledge and experience. To be sure, implementing them on a commonsense level can (and should) be done in any company. You'll definitely be able to improve your sales and marketing results using your own common sense just by following some of the examples and techniques you'll learn about later in this book.

Yet a point may come where common sense begins to fail—when reality doesn't behave as you expected it to. In those circumstances, you may need the "rocket science" underlying Six Sigma. That's why Six Sigma people focus so much on education and scientific rigor. To become experts, people must do one or more Six Sigma projects to earn their credentials. Companies engaged in serious deployments of Six Sigma ensure that they reward education and analytical accomplishments. That's because skill with the Six Sigma method takes effort and makes managers better at thinking and decision making.

Our description of Six Sigma would not be complete without describing the ways companies recognize and reward individuals who demonstrate various levels of proficiency and who play certain roles on a typical Six Sigma project team.

YOU MIGHT NEED A FEW BELTS

While some people make fun of them, companies take "Belt" certifications seriously because they serve an important purpose in Six Sigma deployments. They denote levels of achievement in solving difficult problems and, therefore, in helping companies make more money.

Six Sigma practitioners are known as Black Belts, Green Belts, and Master Black Belts. Black Belts have completed Six Sigma Black Belt training and at least one formal Six Sigma project, and they can lead project teams. Green Belts have some Six Sigma training—often as much as Black Belts—but hold positions in operating or support departments; they bring Six Sigma practices into their areas. Master Black Belts oversee Black Belts and have more training and experience in managing Six Sigma projects. Candidates for Belts are assigned projects to work on during formal training. They attend classroom training for a week, work on their projects for three weeks, return to class for another week, and so on, until they have acquired the skills for their role.

The definition of other roles can be squishier but typically are as follows:

- *Sponsor.* A senior executive who sponsors the company's overall Six Sigma initiative
- *Leader.* Senior-level executive responsible for implementing Six Sigma within the business
- *Champion.* Middle- or senior-level executive who sponsors a specific Six Sigma project, ensuring that resources are available and crossfunctional issues are resolved. Leaders and champions usually receive high-level training on the technical aspects of Six Sigma and on leading an initiative.
- *Team Member.* Professional with general awareness of Six Sigma (through no formal training) who brings relevant experience or expertise to a particular project
- *Process Owner.* Professional responsible for the business process that is the target of a Six Sigma project

Please don't think that Six Sigma training alone can make someone a talented Belt. When you've seen a few of them in action, you'll notice that the best Belts can constantly shift between the facts, data, and statistics on the one hand and the problem, process, and goals on the other. They digest data, generate questions, and test ideas, then return to the business issues. They have the knowledge, skills, and experience and the intelligence, insight, and humility to work toward the best solution for the real-world problem. Those things aren't taught in courses, yet they are requirements for excellence in most endeavors, including process improvement.

That's how Steve Burnett was able to realize that American Home Shield's first Six Sigma project may have improved the cancellation process but didn't really achieve the business goal. Indeed, many companies find that the most effective Black Belts and Master Black Belts come from the operating areas of the business. People who understand the business *and* Six Sigma are the greatest resources in these initiatives.

MISCONCEPTIONS AND PITFALLS TO AVOID

Six Sigma, as a management philosophy, scientific approach, or five-step process, is itself a tool. You don't use Six Sigma for its own sake; you use it to accomplish specific tasks. But like any tool, Six Sigma can be used in the wrong ways, for the wrong purposes, and even in a dangerous manner just like a jackhammer, chainsaw, or performance appraisal. Although many companies have been incredibly successful with Six Sigma, it is a challenging initiative and potentially problematic. According to Bruce Hayes, chief operating officer of consulting firm Six Sigma Advantage, the three most often cited problems in implementing Six Sigma are:

1. Lack of senior management engagement
2. Selection of the available people, rather than the best people, to become Black or Green Belts
3. Poor Six Sigma project selection (more on this in Chapter 8)

In addition, I've repeatedly heard Six Sigma practitioners and operating executives cite the following problems and misconceptions:

- *Six Sigma is about cost cutting.* Yes, Six Sigma and Lean increase effectiveness and efficiency and have produced hundreds of millions of dollars in savings. However, many companies, fixated on cost cutting, abandon their programs after achieving savings and soon backslide. They also fail to apply Six Sigma to new problems—and to generating revenue. A true commitment to Six Sigma becomes an ongoing way of managing.

- *Six Sigma is the flavor of the month.* Some management teams—often those that used Six Sigma for cost cutting—view it as a fad and communicate that to their people in various ways. While adopting Six Sigma on a limited basis or holding a few trial projects can make sense, it delivers the greatest benefit when viewed as a long-term commitment. Otherwise, many people will believe they can keep their heads down and wait until it blows over. Moreover, some people, for reasons as depressing as they are obvious, fear precise measurement of their activities and results and may try to portray Six Sigma as temporary, even when it is not.

- *Six Sigma statistics and jargon are overwhelming.* It's a sad fact that some Belts are unrepentant geeks. They miss the point of statistics or lack the knowledge or social skills needed to deal with businesspeople. They don't talk to managers in the manager's own language, and they don't interpret statistics in ways that businesspeople can grasp. Unfortunately, most Six Sigma courses do not help them learn these skills. Six Sigma practitioners *must* relate the data and analysis to business strategies and goals. It's often best to avoid showing tables of data and charts, and to instead persuade managers to follow certain recommendations.

- *Six Sigma uses a sledgehammer to crack walnuts.* Rigid application of Six Sigma can lead to overkill. If the define and measure steps reveal an obvious solution, by all means implement it and move on to the next problem. Rigid application can also lead a company to, as the saying goes, redouble its efforts after losing sight of the objective. In one case, IBM used process improvement to make a superior 5.5-inch disc drive—in the 1990s. Again, the left foot of

Six Sigma must follow the right foot of sound business strategy (and avoid slipping on walnuts).

- *Small companies can find Six Sigma hard to implement.* Six Sigma may be perceived as inefficient for small companies, which lack the scale that generates big payoffs. Small companies may also lack the funding or human resources for full-time Black Belts and find that part-timers are less effective. However, although a major Six Sigma effort may be inappropriate or too costly for a small company, the approach and tools will work even for a Web site.

- *Six Sigma is all about the training.* Some consulting firms and executive programs foster the impression that Six Sigma training will produce Black and Green Belts with extraodinary problem-solving powers. Even though training in Six Sigma can be invaluable, it only imparts knowledge of Six Sigma, which, as valuable as it is, must still be skillfully applied.

- *The gains from Six Sigma slip away.* Some companies have found it difficult to replicate the success of a project across the broader organization. Also, Six Sigma can be harder to employ in a transaction- or people-driven process than in a manufacturing process. By some estimates, as much as 40 percent of the gains of a Six Sigma project are lost because of a poorly implemented control phase, especially in transactional environments. That implies that Six Sigma may be harder to implement in marketing and sales environments, which is indeed often the case.

Any of the foregoing impediments and misconceptions can occur when applying Six Sigma in marketing and sales—in addition to more specific issues. These challenges, however, are caused not by Six Sigma itself but by the people attempting to implement it. Sometimes management rushes into the jargon and rigor of Six Sigma before employees are ready for it. Other times, management makes one or more of the foregoing mistakes. In Chapter 8, I'll address these challenges and illustrate why the reward is worth the effort.

PUTTING PEOPLE— AND DISCIPLINES—TOGETHER

Six Sigma, and indeed any process improvement effort, puts together people who are experts in methods created to boost the performance of business processes with the people who manage and work in those processes. Six Sigma provides a process for improving business processes. That's what has been missing in most organizations.

Six Sigma engages people in a new conversation, quite different from the standard fare in most organizations. It's not an exercise in finger pointing, avoiding reality, covering up mistakes, or placating the customer or management or someone in the next department. It's a conversation about what is happening in a process and why it's happening, and about what's causing whatever you don't want to happen and fixing it.

But these conversations take place only when management creates an environment that encourages people to connect in these ways. That's the subject of the next chapter.

KEY POINTS

- Companies are beginning to recognize that process improvement can be used to increase revenue. This focus on sales process improvement has five underlying premises or principles:
  1. Creating value for customers
  2. Managing on the basis data and facts
  3. Analyzing cause and effect
  4. Minimizing waste, errors, and defects
  5. Setting the context for collaboration

- Even though process improvement can be implemented with simple common sense, it also has deeply scientific underpinnings. Mastering this knowledge requires education and experience. Companies that are serious about Six Sigma recognize and respect those accomplishments through certifications known by colored Belts, modeled after the martial arts.
- The quality movement has a 60-year track record of analyzing work and improving results.
- The Lean manufacturing movement also has a remarkable track record for improving business results via methods similar and complementary to Six Sigma.
- The term *Six Sigma* is actually used to mean seven different things:
  1. Six Sigma = Management Philosophy
  2. Six Sigma = Scientific Method
  3. Six Sigma = Formal Initiative
  4. Six Sigma = Applied Statistics
  5. Six Sigma = Specific Tools
  6. Six Sigma = Quality Measure
  7. Six Sigma = Five Steps (define, measure, analyze, improve, control)
- Applied incorrectly, any management approach can fail. However, learning to applying the right approach for your organization will definitely produce rewarding results.

3

THE NEW SALES AND MARKETING MANAGEMENT STRATEGY

In Chapter 2, I mentioned the five threads of the Six Sigma management philosophy—creating value for customers; managing on the basis of data and facts; analyzing cause and effect; minimizing waste, errors, and defects; and setting the context for collaboration. This chapter weaves these threads into a pattern that provides ways of understanding sales and marketing as a true production process, which means one that can be measured and improved.

If you are from the world of marketing or sales, or general management, you may still be wondering why all this process improvement stuff is necessary. And I know that you're still not completely clear about what constitutes Six Sigma. So here's another example that shows it in action in a sales environment—one in which a number of managers and virtually all of the salespeople harbored suspicions of Six Sigma.

HOW SIX SIGMA OPENED SALES MANAGERS' EYES

Jon Theuerkauf, managing director, head of Six Sigma HSBC USA(Hong Kong Shanghai Bank Corporation USA), explained how HSBC addressed long-standing problems in its futures trading area.

In futures trading, we had been paying our salespeople commissions based on revenue growth, which led them to see all business as good business. But we hadn't calculated our trading costs or the cost of services like custom research. For example, the unit came up with more or less arbitrary prices per trade, and when it came to service gave customers pretty much whatever they wanted. That happens a lot in financial services, where you do whatever you can to get the volume. The unit managers thought high volume would keep costs low, but they didn't really know if this was the case. Anyway, that strategy hadn't been generating acceptable profits. The unit was in trouble, and they knew it.

So we educated the managers and salespeople about the need to really understand customer profitability. We created a menu of services in an Excel model and asked the salespeople to go through their portfolios and check off the services provided to each customer. We had costed out the services and, by adding in the cost of trades, had come up with a profitability hurdle. Bottom line: Less than 30 percent of our customers met that hurdle. This was a real shocker to the managers and the salespeople.

Yet they said, "Wait, you have to look at the whole relationship!" In fact, we had considered things like the business we did with the customer elsewhere in the bank and projected trading volume. We realized that, if we did a lot of business with the customer elsewhere, it might be okay to carry them on the futures trading at a reduced margin; the overall relationship needed to be managed profitably. But everybody can't—and didn't—fit that model. So the costing model told us whether this was a good customer and, if not, how to get the minimal acceptable profit, either by increasing the price per trade, increasing the volume, reducing services, or some of each.

We heard many sad or optimistic stories about how good the customer was or would become. But when we asked for supporting data, we didn't get it. So we developed "expectation pacts" with the salespeople. If a salesperson said that a 1,000 contracts-per-month customer would go to 5,000 per month next year, we'd say that in 30 days, we expected 2,000 contracts, then 3,000 in 6 months. Then we'd wait 12 months to see if the customer went to 5,000.

As a flexible model with strict standards, this also became a tool in bringing customers on board. For example, "Yes, Mr. Customer, you can have this service, but it costs X Euros or we have to see X volume of trades at this price within one quarter." Every prospect was run through the model, which classified them as green, yellow, or red. Green means bring them on. Yellow means the business head has to sign off on it. Red means don't bring them on without a very, very good reason. We would show customers our model and tell them they weren't profitable. We said, "We'll give you options because we'd love you to stay with us, but this has to be a partnership. We need bigger tickets at a different price or lower service requirements or both. Or you can trade with us online." The customers self-selected. Within the first 13 months of the project's findings, we had culled out 50 percent of our existing customer base.

The unit managers had to change their philosophy, to think about profits rather than just volume and to start really dealing with customers. They had to understand costs, calculate profitability, get paid properly, and not treat everybody the same. They came to see that if you keep giving away business, you're just generating more cost.

That stopped the flow of bad business, which resulted in about 35 percent excess capacity. And guess what? We went from filling up the capacity and making $6 million to making over $10 million. The most that business had ever made was under $5 million, but in the year after this project they made $6.7 million, after culling out 50 percent of the customer base. Their target this year is $11 million.

Try telling your sales force they're going to lose 50 percent of their customers and make more money than ever. To them, it was like being in an earthquake that wouldn't stop. But we made sure that every single person in the business was on a Six Sigma project so they could learn firsthand the process we were going through. We overcommunicated and held all-hands meetings every month. Plus, the viability of the business depended upon all of us as a team turning it around. We—and they—knew we weren't going to get there by "trying harder." That just wasn't going to work.

A lot of the success of this effort hinged on the financial analysis. We did activity-based costing [explained later in this chapter], which we had to sell to our finance guys. We also have a long-standing policy that finance must sign off on all projects and analytics involving the financials. Our financial policies for Six Sigma projects document how finance will measure revenue increases and so on. We're very specific about what counts and doesn't count towards crediting Six Sigma with the impact. That's a big part of why we're successful with the methodology.

This case not only shows Six Sigma at work in a sales environment (from a wide-angle view—we'll narrow the focus in Chapter 4). It also shows the five principles in action. Let's look more closely to see how.

THE FIVE PRINCIPLES AT WORK AT HSBC

Here's how marketing and sales and Six Sigma professionals can mesh their efforts when lashed together by those principles.

Give and Receive Value

Recall that in Chapter 2, I said that quality professionals will ask whether the customer wants *and would pay for* a choice of, say, 14 colors. A company must create value for customers and be paid for that value. HSBC provided custom research and other services but was not receiving commensurate value. Many sales organizations make the mistake of focusing on revenue rather than on value provided to, and received from, the customer.

Focusing on revenue rather than on value is not the Six Sigma way. Profitably adding value will build a business, even if total revenue is smaller. Giving value to the customer at the company's expense won't work any more than will getting value at the customer's expense. Marketing and sales must add value, not just revenue, to the business.

Insist on Data and Facts

It's easy in some businesses to assume that rising revenue will cover all costs. But that assumes that either the business model takes care of itself or that someone else worries about profitability. We've established that marketing and sales must be responsible for profitability, but what about that business model belief? Could a business be based on an unprofitable model? Happens all the time. Just think back to the Internet bubble, when companies actually bragged about their "burn rate"—the pace at which they were spending money to build revenue. Even within an essentially sound business model, assumptions about costs, like most assumptions, are often unconsciously formed and passed on to every new manager and employee.

Yogi Berra was right: You *can* learn an awful lot by watching. But to learn anything in business, you have to be watching data and facts. At HSBC, Jon Theuerkauf's team measured the costs of trades and services and learned that 70 percent of customers were not profitable. Even if management could be happy with that number, say, because of profitable business elsewhere in the bank, management must know that number and know where the alleged profits were coming from. In the case of ServiceMaster, Steve Burnett's team found the reasons for contract cancellations, learning that many of them might be addressed by a Save Desk. Until then, the company canceled contracts without knowing why customers were leaving.

If you're a seasoned Black Belt, you've probably had the pleasure of seeing managers' minds blown by data when it's placed in the context of company goals and strategies. If you're a marketing or sales manager, please be open to having your mind blown.

Understand Cause and Effect

Analyzing cause and effect differs from assuming cause and effect. It's easy to assume that certain practices must be having certain effects. HSBC's trading unit believed that low prices and free services generated high volume and that high volume would more than cover its costs. The first belief held some truth, but even without artificially low prices and free service, the unit has been growing and will (as of this writing) soon surpass its preproject volume.

What caused the lack of profits? Unit managers would say, "Our volume's still not high enough," or "Futures trading is a loss leader." But the cause (the X) of the lack of profits (the Y) turned out to be pricing that did not cover the costs of trades and services. As Jon Theuerkauf said, "If you keep giving away business, you're just generating more cost."

Analyzing cause and effect makes these connections clear. It gets behind the general ledger revenue and expense figures that management usually relies on, enabling you to unearth the causes and effects behind those numbers.

Erase Waste

Again, waste is anything that doesn't add value. If you are doing things that don't add value for the customer or your company, you must stop doing them. If you're doing things that customers say they value but won't pay for with their attention, time, or money, then you have to measure the ancillary costs and benefits to see if what you're doing is profitable.

Those costs might include opportunity costs. For instance, Jon Theuerkauf said, "Customers were sucking up a sales guy's resources when he should be looking for new customers or cross-selling business. If he's doing custom research for a marginal customer, that's lunacy. You're not growing the business, and you're consuming resources for a customer that doesn't make you any money."

To minimize waste and defects in the sales process, management must question, or at least tolerate people who question, accepted practices.

Foster Collaboration

As always, management has to lead the charge and make sure that everyone is behind it. Jon points out that he came from GE Capital, which is where, in 1996, Six Sigma was first applied to financial services. "I was brought up in a world where mandates are the way to make things go faster. When you work for somebody like Jack Welch or Larry Bossidy, when they made the decision that the organization was going north, you either got moving in a northerly direction or you got run over."

Is that setting the context for collaboration?

Yes! First, relatively few people get run over because most do head north. Second, Six Sigma closely examines what people do, and that examination involves them in the project. The people doing the work tell you what they are doing and why (if they can) and what they are producing (if they know), which lets them know they are part of things. Third, because all activities in a process are related, so are all the people in it. Six Sigma recognizes the needs of internal as well as external customers. It improves the process by improving the ways in which people work together and by ensuring that changes do not undermine other people in the process. I've found that insights from Six Sigma help people in a process see how interconnected they are, appreciate what the other person does, and work together more smoothly.

On that latter subject, HSBC and ServiceMaster replicated projects in highly individual ways for units and branches across the company. They recognized that people needed to buy in and that minds can't be forced to change. They respected local requirements and frames of reference. They provided data that was specific and relevant to the particular business as well as enough time and resources for people to work through the new approaches.

MAKING CHANGE WORK FOR YOUR SALES AND MARKETING ORGANIZATION

Once the principles are established in an organization, applying Six Sigma becomes fairly straightforward. But if they are not established in the minds of every manager and employee, and integrated into the ways in which performance is managed, measured, and compensated, then you will encounter resistance, reluctance, and evasiveness. People must accept the "rule of data." A popular TQM poster used to say, "In God we trust. Everyone else must bring data."

Sometimes Six Sigma projects prove things that people just don't believe or can't face. Yet even proof can be ignored unless these principles are in place. People who are not used to managing or working this way need senior executives to explain, support, promote, and reward the use of Six Sigma. This means that, given the pressure for short-term results, Six Sigma can be an expensive high road. It pays off in the end, but it takes vision, integrity, determination, and a commitment to building long-term value for your customers and company.

How to Know What's Going On in Marketing and Sales

In Chapter 2, I said that a process approach provides the context in which people can get information, make decisions, and take the actions that implement decisions (especially senior executives' decisions). A process approach will also provide feedback to tell management whether those decisions and actions have occurred and with what results. What emerges is something akin to a corporate nervous system, a feedback loop on the condition, performance, and results of the organization's processes. Note that this kind of feedback loop can be set up for a specific activity, such as generating leads or qualifying prospects, as well as for an entire sales process. A feedback loop is as important in marketing and sales as it is in production, finance, and other functions that traditionally have established them.

Essentially, this nervous system operates according to the following four steps:

1. Define the parts of the sales process and how they fit together
2. Measure the sales process as a production process
3. Distinguish the important from the unimportant
4. Improve the demand plan, sales forecasting, and operations planning

Defining the Parts of the Sales Process and How They Fit Together

Process improvement depends on understanding the parts of the process and how they interact. So you have to define the parts of the sales process or at least the part of it that you want to improve. Figure 3-1 depicts a generic sales process for an outfit with a direct sales force. (Actually, this is one kind of sales process map, which I'll discuss in more detail in Chapter 6.) By "parts of the sales process," I mean the activities that people perform and the decisions they make and the actions that customers take or decline to take.

Most companies structure and think of marketing, sales, and service as departments, reinforcing the idea of separateness. When we "depart," we separate. As a result, managers often don't see how these functions fit together, nor do they see them in terms of the value created for the customer. For example, consider how people treat the sales funnel, which in Figure 3.1 would be considered the "Winning" column. They usually assume that managing the sales funnel is the sales department's problem and no one else's. Process thinking corrects the usual limited view of the sales funnel, a point I'll discuss in more detail later in this chapter. The three columns in Figure 3-1 show how the processes of

FIGURE 3-1

Sample Sales Process Map for a Company with a Sales Force

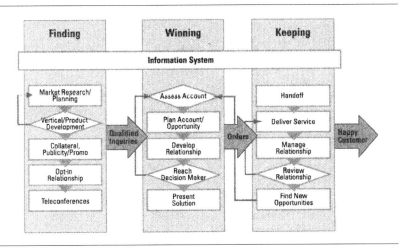

FIGURE 3-2

Process Map Showing Value to the Customer

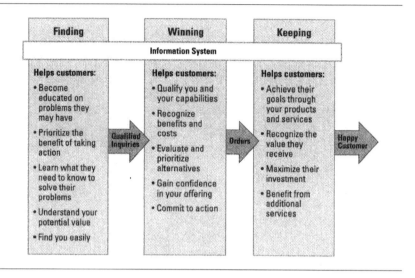

finding, winning, and keeping customers—marketing, sales, and service—relate to one another. The rectangles within each column represent activities; the diamonds represent decisions; the horizontal arrows contain the outputs of finding (qualified inquiries), winning (orders), and keeping (happy customers).

Meanwhile, Figure 3-2 illustrates the value that each of these functions creates for the customer at this sample company. There are, of course, many other forms of value that marketing, sales, and service create for customers.

With the view of the sales process depicted in Figure 3-1 and the kind of information depicted in Figure 3-2, you can ask, "What value does the prospect or customer need us to deliver at this point in the sales process—and are we delivering it?" If you answer that question to your customers' satisfaction, they will get what they need from your sales process, and they are more likely to give you what you want: their attention and interest (qualified inquiries), their business (orders), and their loyalty (happy customers).

Measuring the Sales Process as a Production Process

In Chapter 1, I pointed out the parallels between raw materials, work-in-process, and finished goods in a manufacturing operation on the one hand and leads, opportunities, and deals in a sales operation on the other. Over the past 25 years, manufacturing operations have improved their results by doing a better job of measuring and managing the quantity and quality of their inventories. Marketing and sales have similar opportunities, yet most companies do not really measure their sales process. Instead, they focus on the end result: orders booked. To measure and manage the sales process, you have to measure the activities and the results that lead up to the orders being booked.

Figure 3-3 shows the sales process map from Figure 3-1, modified to include the actions taken by the customer in response to the company's marketing and sales activities. This figure also shows the count of prospects and customers as the process progresses, and I'll explain those counts in a moment.

First, in the columns labeled "Finding" and "Winning," let's look at the marketing and sales activities (in rectangles) and the actions (in the diamonds) and how they relate to the actions taken by the customer, which are in the fourth column. Those customer actions are what we want to measure. Why? Because they indicate that we are creating value for the customer. How so? Because, you'll recall, value is that which the customer will take action to obtain. Therefore, if customers recognize the problem, acknowledge their pain, request assistance, work with the salesperson to define their needs and so on, then we have created value for them.

Now let's follow the counts of prospects as they move through the process, bearing in mind that these counts are the "inventory" produced by marketing and sales, as well as the yields of the various activities. The company distributes 10,238 pieces of collateral material, causing 617 prospects to visit the Web site and sign up in for the newsletter. Of those 617 prospects, 119 take part in a complimentary teleconference run by the company. Of those, 37 request assistance, thus becoming leads, and after the company assesses them, 25 become qualified leads. Of those 25 qualified leads, 19 become actual sales opportunities. From that point on, a salesperson works with each of those sales opportunities, ultimately converting 6 of them into customers. If you haven't examined Figure 3-3,

FIGURE 3-3

Sales Process Map (with Customer Actions and Counts)

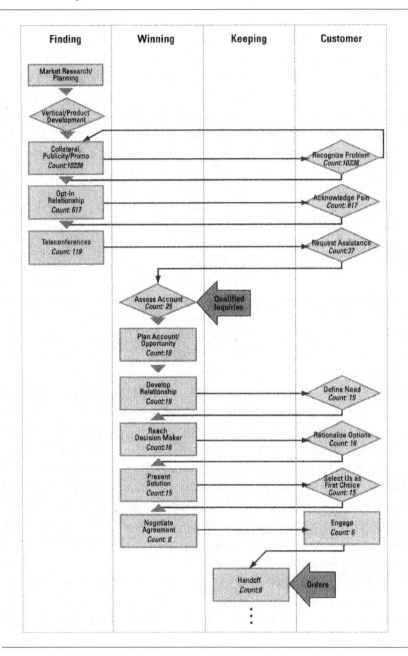

please do so now, because it very logically illustrates the concept of "measuring things" in the sales process.

The concept of measuring activities and results (customer actions that indicate that value has been created) raises several additional points:

- Prospects do not, of course, march in lockstep through the sales process. This means that the count of leads, qualified leads, and sales opportunities at various points in the process is a snapshot of what is actually a flow of prospects through the sales process. The actual number of prospects at any stage will change, perhaps within hours. Prospects can even change their minds and go backwards in some cases. The same thing occurs with inventory counts in manufacturing, which is continually producing finished goods.
- Very few companies measure their leads, qualified leads, and sales opportunities in anything like this manner. As a result, managers have little choice but to focus on the outcome of the process (orders and revenue figures) rather than on what's going on within the process. Yet, as the saying goes, you can manage only what you can measure, which is why I say that most companies don't really manage their sales processes.
- As noted in Chapter 1, rarely do people in marketing and sales sit down and define the characteristics of a lead. In fact, typically no shared understanding exists, even among salespeople, regarding what exactly constitutes a lead, a qualified lead, or a sales opportunity. To develop these measurements, you must first define what you are counting. That's where operational definitions, which I explain below, come into play.
- Finally, it's essential to measure the *quality* as well as the quantity of leads, qualified leads, and sales opportunities. It's important because measuring quality enables you to see where your best prospects, sales opportunities, and customers come from. It also reveals which marketing and sales activities (and salespeople) do the best job of improving the quality of a lead or opportunity. We'll examine this further in Chapter 5.

Operational Definitions

Now about those operational definitions. Yes, if you're not a process improvement professional, that's another pesky bit of nomenclature. But it's a useful one, because an operational definition describes, clearly and in detail, a concept, term, metric, or procedure in a process. For instance, an operational definition of a qualified lead would provide specific, detailed characteristics that a lead would have to possess to be considered qualified. In other words, what actions would a customer have to take to be classified as a lead? Similarly, an operational definition of the sales cycle would precisely define when the sales cycle for a prospect begins and ends in terms of the actions we take and that the customer takes.

When operational definitions are in place, everyone knows how things are defined and measured. Everyone literally knows what they're talking about when they discuss leads, qualified leads, sales opportunities, the sales cycle, a sales call, a proposal, and a closed deal. Without those definitions, all those terms are nebulous, subject to interpretation, and not measurable in any standard way—and measurements must, of course, be standard.

One more point on this topic: If a manufacturing manager were to throw a pile of parts on the factory floor and say, "Okay people, I don't care how you do it, but I want you to take these parts and build a tractor!" people would say he was nuts. Manufacturers have taken great pains to define materials and procedures that guide the production process. They know the precise output of each step. Moreover, they recognize that people must work as a choreographed team. That's where marketing and sales processes need to go. The specifics will be different. You'll be dealing with ways of developing relationships with prospects instead of ways of assembling widgets. You'll have to consider the interests of those prospects, because unlike widgets, they have free will, can move around, and even opt out of the process. You'll also have to track the quality of your work, just as you do in manufacturing.

To manage marketing and sales effectively, you must measure the inventory as you would in a production environment. The existence and outcome of leads and opportunities determine whether we've been productive. When you understand your sales process, how it creates value, and how the prospect or customer acts in response to that value; and when you've clearly defined your terms, then—and only then—can you determine your cost of producing a lead or a customer, the length of your sales cycle, your close ratio, and so on. Only then can you manage these key aspects of your sales process.

Distinguishing the Important from the Unimportant

Six Sigma's focus on identifying and minimizing variation helps managers distinguish the important from the unimportant. Can't marketing and sales managers already do that? Well, they do their best with the limited data they have. But imagine how well they would do with solid data on their sales processes and the right analytical tools. After all, that's what their counterparts in manufacturing are doing.

For example, manufacturing seeks to minimize variations in materials and work methods that undermine the product's quality or performance. So if a component is supposed to be 72 millimeters wide, it must be that width, maybe within some tolerable range such as plus or minus 50 microns. In marketing and sales, the quality of leads, opportunities, and customers also varies, and you need valid measures to gauge those variations. Then you can measure the effectiveness (the yield) of your marketing and sales activities.

At this point, we're not even considering the reasons for variation. Those reasons are important but only when the variation itself is important. Allow to me explain.

Exhibit 3-4 shows a process behavior chart. This type of chart is widely used in process improvement because it provides such useful information. The data points on the chart might be measurements of activities or results (such as prospecting sales calls, qualified leads, or sales per month) or it could be a ratio (such as a close ratio). Variation will occur in any business process, even a manufacturing process, as a result of machine wear if nothing else. The issue isn't eliminating all variation. The issue is understanding variation.

The process behavior chart plots a jagged line by connecting the data points, say, in time series data (data collected over time, such as weekly sales or monthly close ratios). Then it plots a line that describes the average of the values, that is, the average around which the data varies, and upper and lower control limits, which are the horizontal lines above and below the average. Those upper and lower limits (UCL and

FIGURE 3-4
Process Behavior Chart

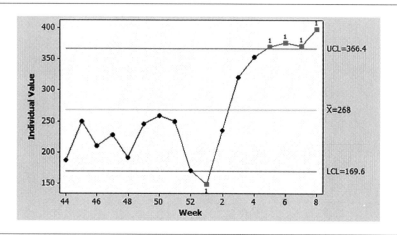

LCL) are plotted on the basis of calculations performed by software and based on the data, just like the line for the average. The control limits depict the "normal" range of variation for the data being considered. (Technically, Figure 3-4 is an ImR or Individual Moving Range chart, the type most appropriate for the kinds of variables typically measured in sales and marketing, where you are not dealing with subgroups. The method of preparing an ImR chart is beyond the scope of this book and is available from other sources, such as those found in the Resources section of this book.)

In statistical terms, we say that normal variation is caused by "noise." Management typically doesn't have to worry about noise. Noise is the result of "common causes" in the environment of the process and is present in virtually all kinds of process measurements.

What management should be concerned about instead are "signals," behaviors of the data points, such as those that lie above or below the control limits or those that show a pattern indicating that future data points will exceed those limits. That kind of variation is the result of "special causes." That is, it is not part of the normal behavior of the process, and whether it's considered good or bad, its causes should be investigated. If the variation is good, perhaps the process could be designed to produce that result more consistently. If the variation is bad, we want to eliminate whatever is causing it.

Let's say that the data points in Exhibit 3-4 depict the weekly ratios of qualified leads to cold calls. What happened in the week that the ratio fell below the lower control limit? It could be any number of things, but do *not* jump to conclusions. It might not be because Charlie was out ill or the economic news turned negative that week. Similarly, you'd want to investigate what happened in the month when the ratio exceeded the upper control limit. The key point is that something outside the normal functioning of the process generated that result.

This type of chart is just one tool that helps managers to know what's going on in their processes and decide what does and doesn't require their attention.

Simply creating such charts from your company's monthly revenue numbers can provide valuable insights. Just bear in mind that the value of these charts hinges on the questions and conclusions you draw from them. How do you locate the real causes of the signals? How certain can you be about your cause-and-effect conclusions? Don't be intimidated by statistics or charts. You can readily hire statistical expertise, and charts are easy to read once they're explained. The hard part is exercising the discipline and judgment required to understand the problem in process terms, which we'll spend time doing later in this book.

Note that to raise the overall performance of a process above the "normal" range you must make systemic improvements to the process. You have to change the process so that it will consistently perform at a higher level and deliver those "outlier" results. You have to shift the entire average and the whole normal range upward. This doesn't happen by exhorting people to try harder or even by offering greater incentives. A business process has a certain capacity and capability, and only changes to the process itself will permanently increase that capacity or capability. Many, many managers don't realize this. For example, it's *extremely* common for management to set revenue targets that are beyond the capability of the sales process, and it rarely works out well.

Improving the Demand Plan, Sales Forecasting, and Operations Planning

Manufacturing managers regularly develop production plans to manage their business more efficiently. These include capacity plans, purchasing plans, and a master schedule that enables them to think through the resources that will be required to achieve their business goals. Likewise, companies need to develop a demand plan that includes promotions, prices, sales forecasts, and details of the resources required and the expected returns.

Various forecasts abound in most companies. Purchasing departments project their requirements, as do production and accounting departments. Marketing produces long-range projections based on such input as market research, market share, and consumer behavior. Sales produces a forecast of what it expects to sell in the next 30 to 90 days, a report that is notoriously inaccurate in most businesses.

Left to their own devices, as is often the case, these departments have little alternative but to create their own forecasts based on the information available to them independently. A sales forecast produced from a statistical projection of past order volumes is invalid the moment a new product line is rolled out or a competitor signs on a new distributor. A sales forecast rolled up from salespeople's wild guesses with fudge factors added by middle managers will be equally unreliable. With each department marching to its own version of the music, it's no wonder conflicts and missed opportunities arise.

Balancing the opposing forces of the demand plan and the production plan is key to managing profitability. The most widely accepted method for doing this, Sales and Operations Planning (S&OP), is composed of a series of meetings that require information from the key departments, including the sales department's short-term forecast. Rather than trying to force the sales department to make a long-term forecast at the level of, say, individual part numbers or stock-keeping units (SKUs), which is impossible, S&OP separates long-term forecasts (aggregates with no SKU-level details) and short-term sales forecasts (with at least some SKU information based on the flow of opportunities). Properly practiced, S&OP improves decisions about materials, labor, equipment, and logistics, because it drives managers to work with a common forecast.

Measuring the number and quality of your leads, prospects, and sales opportunities at various stages of the sales process means that sales managers gain visibility into the flows of their business and see the bottlenecks and what might be done about them. This not only improves the short-term forecast but also renders managers more accountable, because they have the information needed to improve their processes.

FIGURE 3-5

Sales Process Activities and Results (with Counts/Yields)

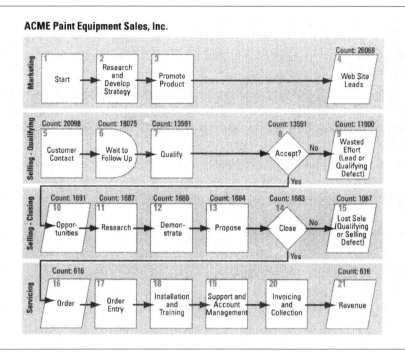

Figure 3-5 shows a flowchart of a sales process for a sample company. The information is similar to that provided in Figure 3-3, but it is for a different sample company and presented in a different format. This chart breaks the sales process into four parts—marketing, qualifying, closing, and servicing—and shows the activities (in rectangles), results (parallelograms), and decision points (diamonds) within those parts. I won't explain this chart in much depth, given that it includes fairly generic activities, results, and decisions, all numbered from 1 to 21. Instead, I want to point out that the counts show the results and yields of these activities and decisions as prospects work their way through the sales process. The count begins with 26,068 Web site leads (box #4), which convert to 1,691 opportunities (box #10), which convert to 616 revenue-generating orders (box #16). These numbers represent a snapshot of the transactions as each potential sale moves through the system, and they reveal the work-in-process as well as the throughput (number of leads converted to revenue) at a given point in time.

Companies that do not track sales process yields in this way (most companies) are ignoring a mother lode of useful information. Tracking these yields and using process behavior charts as shown in Figure 3-4 can help you improve the sales process itself, as well as the sales forecast, because they can show the actual effect of changes such as promoting the product, changing your prices, or hiring more salespeople.

If you're familiar with S&OP, think of what this analysis would mean to those planning efforts. If you're not, just consider how better sales forecasts could help your production and financial people plan more effectively. In fact, good sales forecasts are essential to operations planning. S&OP tears down the typical company's Tower of Babel by creating one integrated operating forecast and updating it monthly as sales orders come in, shipments consume finished inventory, and production replenishes it.

In their book *Sales Forecasting—A New Approach,* Thomas Wallace and Robert Stahl make the point that "better production, purchasing, and scheduling processes yield better forecasts." Likewise, better sales processes contribute to improved sales forecasts. Although sales forecasts will remain estimates, when the sales process is properly designed, sales forecasting no longer amounts to guessing what will close in the next period. Instead, it becomes a supportable estimate based on the organization's ability to perform a certain set of activities with a known set of prospects, arriving at reasonably predictable results.

GETTING THE INFORMATION YOU NEED IS EASIER THAN YOU THINK

You may be wondering, how can we possibly get this information? Although assembling this information represents a significant shift in the way most sales organizations operate, it is easier than it may appear. Figure 3-6 shows the track record of an engineering company that had clear operating definitions of qualified opportunities and deals and tracked the close ratio. This was a hard number, representing the proposals that were won divided by all those that were proposed in a given month (including those that were canceled or went down to no decision). This data showed that the firm's sales process was fairly stable around a 43 percent close ratio. Other information calculated from the same set of data allowed them to understand how many deals a given sales engineer could

FIGURE 3-6
Close Ratio Process Behavior Chart

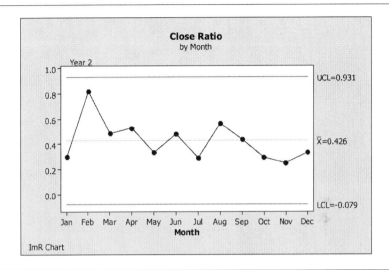

typically handle in a month. Combining the close ratios and the data on the deals that an engineer could handle gave the firm realistic information on its capacity to produce—and a way to predict—revenue. This accomplishment required little more than good operating definitions and a commitment to compiling a decent monthly sales activity report.

Spending the 15 minutes per month required to update their information proved fairly easy for salespeople, once they realized the information would not be used to pressure or criticize them unfairly. The key was providing useful operational data in a consistent manner to everyone who needed it. With this foundation in place, the firm could begin working on the quality of the opportunities, thus finding ways to increase the close ratio even more.

THE DIFFERENCE BETWEEN THE SALES PROCESS AND THE SALES FUNNEL

Many managers talk in terms of managing the sales funnel rather than the sales process. Let me distinguish between the two, because whereas both are descriptive, only the sales process can actually be managed.

The metaphorical sales funnel depicts a world of potential buyers floating above the larger opening. Many salespeople call these folks "suspects" to distinguish them from prospects, who are considered potential buyers. Prospects move through the ever-narrowing funnel until they come out the smaller end as customers. Salespeople qualify prospects, usually with the help of questions of the Can-they-buy? and Will-they-buy? type. If a prospect qualifies, a salesperson tries to move that prospect through the funnel by securing an appointment, asking questions to learn about the prospect's problems, proposing a solution, and trying to close the sale. A prospect occupies a position within the funnel, at least in the mind of the salesperson, depending on the real or perceived stage of the sale.

Although used widely, the sales funnel metaphor has three huge shortcomings:

1. It does not describe a value-adding process.
2. It ignores the buyer's journey.
3. It makes unwarranted assumptions about the volume of work in each phase.

The funnel analogy becomes more useful if it is broadened to take these points into account. I'll take these one at a time.

First, rather than specify a value-adding process, the sales funnel focuses on things that the company does to promote and sell its product—the marketing mix of newsletters, direct mail, advertisements, Web sites, e-mail, product literature, sales techniques, and so on. The company promotes itself, touts its products, offers specials, sends "closers" into the field, and by and large tries various means of pushing people through the funnel.

Second, the buyer's journey, as described in Hugh Macfarlane's book *The Leaky Funnel,* is the process the customer goes through in making a purchase. (I'll discuss Hugh's ideas in more depth in Chapter 6.) This isn't the "purchasing procedure," although that's part of it. It's actually the sequence of actions by which customers become aware of a problem, acknowledge the problem, define their needs, investigate solutions, and choose and implement a solution.

See the difference? The sales funnel focuses inward and prompts us to ask, "What can we do to the customer given the customer's position in the funnel?" The other focuses outward and prompts us to ask, "How can we help the customer get what he or she wants at this point in the buying process (while getting what we want at the same time)?" or, in true process terms, "How can we add value to the customer at this point?" This is no small distinction; rather, it enables a company to design a sales process that adds value for prospects and customers in measurable ways. Adding measurable value is the key to making the process more effective.

Finally, the shape of the funnel often causes managers to make unwarranted assumptions. For example, when sales is not closing enough business, management may jump to the conclusion that its salespeople do not know how to close. But this assumes there are plenty of qualified opportunities in the earlier stages of the funnel. Without careful measurement of the actual quantity and quality of lead opportunities and deals in the funnel, this assumption is dubious at best. In fact, the inability to generate qualified opportunities is one of the most common problems companies have.

DEVELOPING THE RIGHT SALES PROCESS

The right sales process is the one that adds the most value for both the customer and the company. The sales process that will achieve this depends on the industry, company, and customer base, and it will change as markets, products, and business conditions develop. Most companies do not currently have the right sales processes in place, because so few have taken a process approach. Sales processes are generally where manufacturing processes were before the quality revolution that began in the late 1970s. Therefore, to develop the right sales process, most companies would have to change, and change is never easy. Indeed, marketing and sales tend to be particularly resistant to change. Also, these functions attempt to influence human behavior, a considerably more challenging task than influencing the width of a component. But even though human behavior is not as controllable as the width of a component, it can be fairly predictable once you have measured and analyzed it in a given situation. With that information in hand, you can design a new sales process or modify an existing one.

To change your sales process, you must make the new process the path of least resistance, particularly for your salespeople. For instance, salespeople must qualify prospects, so you can give them clear qualification criteria and require them to use and record the criteria before they start selling to a prospect. You make doing this the path of least resistance by integrating the criteria into your systems and management expectations and by updating and sharpening the criteria as you gain experience with them. As salespeople see that the criteria actually help them sell, they use them even more willingly. This goes for distributors as well, although it's a bit harder there.

The right sales process also becomes the path of least resistance for prospects and customers. (Notice I'm saying least resistance, not no resistance!) If the sales process adds value for the customers at each step of the buyer's journey, then customers on that journey will listen to those salespeople and frankly discuss their needs with them. They will be honest and helpful instead of reluctant or evasive. Of course, the salesperson must be willing to let go of prospects who aren't ready to buy, and the sales process must direct those prospects to a "back burner" activity, such as a newsletter or a "wave marketing" (or "drip marketing") campaign, to maintain contact and provide updates. As we'll see in Chapter 6, you can design a sales process to work this way.

HOW YOUR VP OF FINANCE CAN HELP YOU SELL MORE AND REDUCE COSTS

It's extremely important for process improvement specialists to think and talk in terms of money, especially in sales. Amid all the metrics and statistics, the financials actually make the business case for sales process improvement. As noted, both Lean and Six Sigma have been used to reduce costs in manufacturing, and they can do so in marketing and sales, too. If you reduce the number of non-value-adding activities in any function, you will reduce costs. But to grow your revenue and profits, you must be prepared to shift at least some of those expenditures to value-adding activities. Before you can do that, you must fully understand both your costs and your sources of profitability.

At HSBC, Jon Theuerkauf used activity-based costing (ABC) to define the costs of trading and services and, thus, the profitability of customers. As promised, I'd like to explain ABC and the value of a sales operating audit (SOA). The SOA is a tool incorporating ABC that I've developed and used with success.

Activity-Based Costing and the Sales Operating Audit

Given marketing and sales managers' intense focus on money, it's odd that they rarely relate the cost of specific activities to the financial results they produce. There's a black hole of aggregated sales expense. Yes, they know what they pay their ad agencies, direct marketing houses, and other vendors. They have budgets for travel, entertainment, training, and compensation. Yet they tend to calculate ROI only on direct marketing efforts, where the specific returns are obvious, and lump most other costs together.

The numbers game encourages such thinking: Bad leads, wasted advertising, and useless sales calls are all in the game. We have to climb a lot of bare trees to find fruit, and if only the fruit counts, why bother counting all those trees and what it costs to climb them? As a result, we deal with marketing and sales costs at gross levels. Meanwhile in manufacturing, cost of goods sold is a hard and fast number, and we know the exact value of the raw materials, work in process, and finished goods inventories. The corresponding number for marketing and sales—selling, general, and administrative expenses (SG&A)—tells us little, while the value of marketing and sales "inventories" (what it costs to produce leads and opportunities and customers) is literally unknown.

Actually, because of the rudimentary way most sales processes are defined, it *is* difficult to know which marketing and sales activities produced which results. It can be difficult even to know the cost of, let alone the return on, specific activities. What does it cost you to produce collateral material—aside from the printer's bill? How much time did your marketing director spend in meetings discussing it? How much time did your in-house copywriter spend writing it? While we're at it, what does it cost to conduct a sales presentation? To prepare a proposal? To close a deal? How much of your marketing and sales activity produces little to no results? What is the cost of waste in marketing and sales? What activities produce the biggest bang for the buck?

There are two solutions to this problem. One is to stick as closely as possible to the direct response model, which I'll discuss in Chapter 6. Don't worry: I'm not going to recommend doing only direct marketing. The key to using the direct response model is to understand how your sales process generates value for customers and to identify the actions customers take on the buyer's journey when they perceive or receive that value. Then you measure those actions to know the value generated for you and your customers.

The second solution is to get a handle on your costs with the sales operating audit. As I've noted, the SOA incorporates activity-based costing, which arouses controversy in some quarters, though it doesn't need to. The dollar figures all originate with the general ledger. ABC is just a method of allocating those dollars to activities, based upon the percentage of time that people spend on the activities. The percentages come from surveys of the people doing the work. Yes, people can be inaccurate or dishonest in accounting for their time. But I've found that the surveys generally yield extremely useful estimates. The goal is not to-the-minute accuracy. The goal is relative estimates of the percentage of time spent on an activity by people at specific salary levels. It's a good idea to explain the importance of the survey and to assure people that they won't be punished or laid off for their answers. (Some companies guarantee anonymity to all survey participants.) The resulting time-use estimates are one component of the SOA, and the fact that they are estimates is no reason to dismiss ABC as a source of information.

The Sales Operating Audit in Action

The SOA develops far more precise data on the cost structure of marketing, sales, and service than do budgets, variance reports, or financial statements. The SOA involves four steps:

1. First, on the basis of general ledger SG&A expenses and time-usage surveys, you allocate the expenses for a year to marketing, to sales, and to service.
2. Second, you calculate a total cost figure for each subprocess, which results in a cost-of-sales-operations statement, as shown for a technical services firm in Figure 3-7 (rounded to the nearest thousand).
3. Third, you analyze your cost drivers, as shown for the same company in Figure 3-8.
4. Fourth, this information can be used to model changes to the sales process, as shown in Figure 3-9.

FIGURE 3-7

Cost-of-Sales-Operations—Technical Services Corporation

Marketing	
Marketing Materials (collateral, Web site, etc.)	$109,000
Marketing Outreach (promotion, speaking, PR)	16,000
Prospecting	28,000
Network functions	24,000
Marketing Total	$177,000
Sales	
Partner relations	$43,000
New prospect sales calls with partner	11,000
New prospect sales calls without partner	41,000
Product demos and meetings	36,000
Proposal generation	32,000
Evaluation, close, admin. and contracts	34,000
Project planning and handoff	2,000
Sales Total	$199,000
Service	
Project management	$448,000
Specifications	226,000
Development and testing	267,000
Installation, data migration, and start-up	147,000
Training and support	168,000
Documentation	91,000
Account relationship management	155,000
Service Total	$1,502,000

To give you a look at part of an actual SOA, I'll walk you through these three tables.

Again, the amounts in Figure 3-7 result from allocating to marketing, sales, or service all general ledger SG&A expenses, including salaries allocated via ABC time-usage surveys.

With the cost of sales operations in hand, the next step is to identify the cost drivers, that is, the cost of developing leads of various types and of making sales, and to allocate the costs to their corresponding subprocesses. Figure 3-8 shows the cost drivers for Technical Services Corporation.

In developing the cost drivers, I defined the activities that pertain to lead generation (finding customers) and to selling and closing (winning customers). It turned out that the first activity in selling—partner relations—generates leads, so I included those costs ($43,000) in lead generation, although salespeople do the activity. This illustrates a key

FIGURE 3-8
Cost Drivers—Technical Services Corporation

Cost Driver: Generating Leads

		Leads Created	Leads Qualified	Leads Not Qualified	Percent of Leads Qualified
Marketing total	$177,000				
Partner relations	$43,000				
Lead generation total	$220,000	260	251	9	97%
Cost per lead		$846			
Total cost	~$220,000		$212,346	$7,614	

Cost Driver: Selling and Closing

		Total Opps.	Opps. Won	Opps. Lost	Opps. Close Ratio
New prospect calls with partner	$11,000				
New prospect calls without partner	$41,000				
Demos and meetings	$36,000				
Proposal generation	$32,000				
Close, admin., and contracts	$34,000				
Selling and closing total	$154,000	251	50	201	20%
Cost per opportunity		$614			
Total cost	~$154,000		$30,700	$123,414	

Rolled Throughput Cost

Number of opportunities		251	50	201	
Rolled-through cost per opportunity		$1,460			
Total rolled throughput cost	~$374,000		$73,000	$293,460	

Rolled Cost per Closed Opportunity

Number of deals			50		
Total cost	~$374,000				
Total cost per closed opportunity			**$7,480**		

point: Allocate the cost of activities to the process or subprocess, *not* the department.

Let's first look at lead generation, which finds customers. Technical Services produced 260 leads that year, at a cost of $846 per lead. It qualified and pursued 251 of those leads, meaning that it chased just about any prospect with a pulse. It cost Technical Services

$$\$220,000 \times 97\% \text{ (with rounding errors)} = \$212,346$$

to generate and qualify those leads. That means it wasted only $7,614 on "poor quality" leads, which sounds great—at first. Then why is the close ratio of these leads only 20 percent?

What would happen if we could change the process so as to flip those ratios around? Suppose Technical Services performed more rigorous lead qualification of the 260 leads. With a 21 percent conversion rate, you get about 54 sales opportunities. The marketing costs are the same, but it spends more money on deals it doesn't end up pursuing. Then suppose in selling and closing, it goes on to convert 94 percent of those highly qualified leads. (I know that is a high number, but stay with me and you'll see the point.) Because it isn't pursuing nearly the same number of deals, the amount and cost of sales activity decrease dramatically. The net savings equal about one full-time equivalent. Because Technical isn't spinning its wheels on all those low-quality leads, it has more time to sell correctly to the actual qualified prospects.

You could argue that Technical might have to spend more time on these deals because they are the ones that close. However, the company would save by getting the vast majority of those that they couldn't close out of the sales process sooner. In any case, the model would still be valid.

Now let's look at selling and closing, which wins customers. In Figure 3-8, Technical spent a total of $154,000 on sales efforts exerted on 251 leads. The definition of *sales efforts* here is inclusive in that it must include a lot of actual qualifying activity, and we can be sure that not all of these leads received demos and proposals. Yet that $154,000 divided by 251 leads translates to only $614 per lead, which doesn't sound bad.

What does sound bad—and is bad—is that they lost 201 of those sales opportunities. On a rolled-through, total-cost basis, Technical spent $293,460 developing and pursuing sales opportunities that it didn't win. (In Six Sigma terms, this is called the "cost of poor quality.") Its close

EXHIBIT 3-9
Projected Cost—Technical Company

Cost Driver: Generating Leads

		Leads Created	Leads Qualified	Leads Not Qualified	Percent of Leads Qualified
Marketing total	$177,000				
Partner relations	$43,000				
Lead generation total	$220,000	260	54	206	21%
Cost per lead		$845			
Total cost	~$220,000		$45,662	$174,193	

Cost Driver: Selling and Closing

		Total Opps.	Opps. Won	Opps. Lost	Opps. Close Ratio
New prospect calls with partner	$2,500				
New prospect calls without partner	$8,900				
Demos and meetings	$7,700				
Proposal generation	$6,800				
Close, admin., and contracts	$7,300				
Selling and closing total	$33,200	54	50	4	93%
Cost per opportunity		$615			
Total cost	~$33,200		~$30,750	~$2,460	

Rolled Throughput Cost

Number of opportunities		54	50	4	
Rolled-through cost per opportunity		$4,689			
Total rolled throughput cost	~$253,000		~$234,450	~$18,756	

Rolled Cost per Closed Opportunity

Number of deals			50		
Total cost	~$253,000				
Total cost per closed opportunity			~$5,060		
Original cost	~$374,000				
Projected savings	~$121,000				

ratio is only 20 percent, while its ratio of good leads to poor is 97 percent. Obviously, the more you have invested in something, the better it is to have a high probability of a return. So in that sense, its conversion rates are upside down. It should have a higher conversion ratio on selling opportunities than on leads turning into quotes.

Perhaps the most important number in Figure 3-8 is the total cost per closed opportunity: $7,480. Suppose the lifetime value (total lifetime profit) to Technical of this kind of customer was $50,000. While the sales effort might not be as efficient as you might like, you couldn't say it wasn't profitable. On the other hand, if the lifetime value of this kind of customer was $7,000, then the cost of acquiring customers clearly would be untenable.

If Technical had better qualification criteria and a better process for learning what it needs to know to qualify leads, could these numbers be substantially improved? The answer is yes. Consider the example shown in Figure 3-9, which takes the idea to the extreme to illustrate the point. The closer the sales organization can get to selecting the right prospects, the closer it can get to reducing its customer acquisition cost by:

$$\$121,000 \text{ projected savings} \div \$374,000 \text{ original cost} = 32\%$$

The total cost per closed opportunity falls:

$$\$7,480 - \$5,060 = \$2,420$$

Perhaps the more important realization is as follows. If that $121,000 in savings is reinvested in generating additional qualified leads and converting them to customers, the result is:

$$\$121,000 \div \$5,060 \approx 24 \text{ new closed deals}$$

The company would grow by almost 50 percent.

Companies that make this kind of shift in lead generation and selling efforts do so by paying close attention to the quality of the leads and opportunities rather than by chasing every prospect with a pulse. Often I've seen sales organizations resist this kind of approach because they like having a lot of prospects "in the pipeline." But when 80 percent of them don't buy, you have to question their value. You can do that only when you know what you're paying per lead and per sale, which is what the SOA enables you to know. Moreover, as changes are made to the process, this approach enables you to see the effects.

I have spoken with VPs of finance who wondered what they could do to assist their sales and marketing organizations. This information can help managers learn how the money is flowing in their sales and marketing organizations. It can help them prioritize their resources and get the most return for their investments in improving their sales process. It is bound to open lines of inquiry—and therefore possibilities—that have not been considered before.

WHY PIECING TOGETHER THE BIG PICTURE IS SO IMPORTANT

Regardless of your role in bringing process improvement to a sales organization, it's essential to link it to what marketing and salespeople are doing, to the results they're producing, and to the costs of the activities and results. By using figures from the general ledger and addressing financial issues, you ensure that sales process improvement has a financial impact that will be visible in the financial statements. That is what I've seen marketing, sales, and general managers take most seriously about marketing and selling the Six Sigma way.

At this point, we've seen how process improvement can be used in marketing and sales environments, and we've seen how it can help management identify what people can and cannot control. But we've also said that marketing and selling attempts to affect customers' behavior, in contrast to manufacturing, which aims to control the characteristics of materials, components, and products.

Can Six Sigma be used to improve yields and conversion rates? Can it rigorously examine the elements in an end-to-end sales process and improve that process—with measurable dollar returns?

The next chapter will answer those questions and introduce you to more methods and tools of Six Sigma.

S *pecial* **R** *esource*

What impact does your sales process have on your financial statements?

A few years ago, I presented a case study at a Six Sigma conference that illustrated how improperly defined sales processes are responsible for counterintuitive results in sales and marketing. I also showed how a properly defined sales process enables a company to establish clear cause-and-effect linkages to its financial statements. You can read this case study free by visiting *www.salesperformance.com/financial_impact.aspx*.

KEY POINTS

- The point of sales and marketing is to generate profitable revenue, not just revenue.
- Five basic principles are at work in any process improvement project, especially in sales and marketing:
  1. Give and receive value
  2. Insist on data and facts
  3. Understand cause and effect
  4. Erase waste
  5. Foster collaboration
- The traditional view of the sales funnel limits managers' insights into their sales process. Rather than accepting the funnel metaphor, managers should aim to design a sales process that
  - creates legitimate, verifiable value for customers;
  - organizes the company's resources, the workflow between people, and the work steps themselves; and
  - measures at least some of the actions customers take.
- A process approach enables you to identify bottlenecks and their effects, so you can prioritize your improvement efforts more effectively.
- A sales operating audit showing you where the money is going can help you prioritize bottlenecks on a financial basis.

4

AN END-TO-END SIX SIGMA PROJECT THAT INCREASED REVENUE BY 94 PERCENT

In Chapter 2, you learned that Lean applied when the problems and solutions of a process are already known, and that Six Sigma applied when the problem is known but the solutions are not. In this chapter, we'll take a deep dive into the latter with a walk-through of a formal Six Sigma project.

Although DMAIC (define, measure, analyze, improve, control) makes common sense, one of the things you quickly learn is that there is usually more to common sense than meets the eye. If this is your first exposure to Six Sigma, you may find some of the tools and techniques a little intimidating. I ask you to please stay with me, because what you'll get is insight into something quite valuable: a step-by-step approach (yes, a process) for improving your sales process.

Conversely, if you are a Six Sigma pro, you might find yourself asking, "Where are the rest of my tools?" Well, you'll find tools and statistical details in the Appendix. The nuts and bolts are in the back of the book so that readers without the benefit of Six Sigma training can begin learning about the approach in a more incremental way.

This chapter is based on a real project. The goal of that project was to improve the revenue from a Web site called Technical Résumé Group (not a real name). John Smith, founder of Technical Services, Inc., operates the Web site, a leading clearinghouse for technical job candidates and employers. I completed this Black Belt project with the assistance of Senior Master Black Belt Rob Tripp. Some technical issues have been deliberately simplified or omitted for clarity. However, the integrity of all the data has been preserved.

HOW THIS CHAPTER CAN HELP YOU AND YOUR SALES TEAM IMPROVE RESULTS

There's a real bonus in this example, which I didn't foresee when I began. The controlled environment of a Web site is ideal for illustrating a "pure" sales environment, because there's only one medium (a Web site) with a few sales pages, a direct response feature, and no salespeople. Although the purpose of this site is to generate sales revenue, what we learned applies equally to any sales process, whether we are generating orders directly, providing opt-ins to a white paper or newsletter, or personally presenting proposals to decision makers.

If you are a sales or marketing manager, an entrepreneur, or a senior executive, you may want to take your time working through this chapter. Because you have read this book this far, you have an idea of what Six Sigma means and how it applies to sales. Now you are ready to work through some of these steps for analyzing and improving a real sales process.

If you decide to study Six Sigma seriously, you'll probably find that it provides more analytical tools than you thought possible. In this chapter, I have simplified things by presenting only those tools required for you to understand this project. (Others are presented in their entirety in the Appendix.) At this point, don't worry about learning all the tools. Instead, focus on how the logical thought process helps you to spot errors in your knowledge and assumptions and how correcting these errors leads to dramatically improved results. By doing so, you'll learn to think through some crucial questions about your current sales and marketing operations (not just your Web site). In fact, what you'll learn is useful to any aspect of selling in a business-to-business environment, including marketing, promotion, distribution channels, and salespeople.

If you are already a process excellence or Lean Six Sigma manager and haven't applied the concepts of quality to sales and marketing before, you'll enjoy seeing how the principles of quality can be applied in these functions.

GOAL OF THE PROJECT: IMPROVE SALES RESULTS

Our goal was to achieve a breakthrough in the revenue of the Technical Resume Group (TRG). TRG charges a fee to employers who post job opportunities but not to candidates seeking jobs or posting resumes. TRG believed that more of the prospects who visited the Web site ought to be signing up for its services and didn't know why they weren't. Here's why they believed that:

- TRG had thrown the Web site up in a hurry and had not yet made any attempts to improve or optimize it.
- TRG knew of comparable Web sites that seemed to perform better.
- For reasons we won't go into, TRG's parent business had a Web site that drew quite a large amount of traffic. Clearly the orders from the TRG Web site were not proportional to the number of companies visiting the parent Web site, who were also likely to need technical employees.

Rather than take a shot in the dark by blindly trying different things, TRG wanted to use the Six Sigma approach. This meant that it would carefully analyze the situation and make only the changes most likely to produce the desired results. This chapter describes how Six Sigma was used to scope out the possibilities and zero in on the solution. In this chapter you will:

- see how the DMAIC steps—define, measure, analyze, improve, and control—apply to a sales process;
- learn about some of the tools that come into play at each step in a "live" situation; and
- gain proof (in case you are a skeptical reader) that Six Sigma can improve a sales process.

WHAT GENERALLY HAPPENS IN A
SIX SIGMA PROJECT

Remember those tricky word problems that frustrated many of us in high school math courses? Well, Six Sigma treats an entire project as if it were a kind of sophisticated word problem. The idea is to define the problem or defect we want to change (called Y, or the dependent variable) and figure out which independent variables (called Xs) most directly affect it. Naturally, this can be expressed in terms of an equation:

$$Y = f(x1, x2, x3, \ldots)$$

Literally, this means, "Y is a function of these Xs." The key to understanding cause and effect is in puzzling out how that function works. The discipline of translating words into the logic of math is why Six Sigma has the reputation for being rigorous and complex. While the complexity is not always present, the ability to handle complexity enables Six Sigma practitioners to solve some pretty intractable problems.

Projects begin with descriptions and clarifications of the problem or Y (project charters, brainstorming, and other techniques) and the process (using process maps, more brainstorming). Then more brainstorming efforts (incorporating fishbone diagrams, SIPOCS, and other tools) are used to tease out potential causes for the problem (Xs). The goal is to be sure we have explored the universe of potential causes.

The Xs are then ranked and prioritized using matrix-style thinking tools for that purpose (called XY Matrices and FMEAs). The goal of all this is to be sure we have identified and taken advantage of everything everyone on the team knows about the potential causes and ruled out the ones least likely to be related to our problem. (Illustrations of how we applied these tools to this project are included in the Appendix.)

Sometimes just a few of these exercises are enough to identify simple but important issues that can be fixed easily. If these fixes are enough to achieve your goal, then the project can be finished quickly. It's similar to the situation in which companies apply Lean techniques, fixing known problems before they move into applying Six Sigma to solve less obvious problems.

If you are a practical executive who is concerned about the complexity of Six Sigma, this is good news. It means you can lead your team to a common understanding of key problems and solutions without getting into complicated math. (In fact, you'll find some of those kinds of problems and solutions described very clearly in Chapters 5 and 6.)

It will be a long time before most sales and marketing processes are defined and measured with the precision found in manufacturing applications. That means you'll be able to find low-hanging fruit and make progress, and profits, relatively quickly with process approaches. Even in well-defined manufacturing environments, projects often reveal fairly simple solutions. Of course, Six Sigma is robust enough for problems that require a deep knowledge of applied statistics, but we won't be getting into anything like that in this chapter or in this book.

Step-by-Step toward the Results You Need

While the steps of DMAIC are clear and straightforward when you are working on a project, the dividing lines between those steps often get blurred. As you learn more and clarify your process and your problem, you may find yourself working back and forth between the measure and analyze steps. As you try to develop and test a theory about how to create an improvement, you may have to go back and forth between the analyze and improve phases as well.

Using the tools of Six Sigma amounts to implementing the scientific method. The tools help you to distinguish between assumptions and facts. Most companies that rigorously practice Six Sigma make no improvements or changes without hard data to support the decision. Intuition and guesses are frowned on, because they can be wasteful and expensive when they are wrong, which they often are.

In companies without this discipline, people may not have the skill, knowledge, or patience to tease out the facts. Indeed, in environments where a company does not formally support this approach, people who try to do so can be criticized and even penalized. Yet although practice and patience are required, the results are worth it. That is why demand is so high for managers and executives experienced in the Six Sigma approach.

PART I—DEFINE PHASE:
WHAT'S THE PROBLEM?

Most seasoned businesspeople have learned what happens when their initial approaches to a situation are too simplistic. One of the first things they learn is the importance of defining a problem correctly. The define phase of a Six Sigma project is designed to address these difficulties. For example, these tools help ensure that

- the problem is real, not just someone's pet idea or perspective;
- the problem is discrete, being manageable and not too intertwined with other problems;
- the problem is solvable;
- the problem is important to the right people, which means your stakeholders and customers want it solved;
- the data needed to solve the problem exists or can be developed (without data, you can't really conduct a Six Sigma project);
- the team understands the problem, and the goals and expected benefits of the project are clear; and
- the resources to do the job exist or are available, and applying them to the project will produce measurable benefits.

In some early versions of Six Sigma, the define phase was assumed rather than explicit. This caused problems in later phases, so the define step was created to state the problem clearly enough to keep everyone on track.

Tools of the Define Phase

The define phase of this project employed the following tools:

- **Project charter**
- **Brainstorming**
- **Measures of the process**
- **Fishbone diagram**
- **XY matrix**
- **High-level process map**

- SIPOC diagram
- Failure modes and effects analysis FMEA
- **Screen shots of TRG pages**

The bolded items are the ones we will cover in depth in this chapter. The others have been omitted to simplify the material. If you would like to study examples of the other tools as well, you will find them in the Appendix.

Project Charter. The project charter is an important tool for getting a project off on the right foot. However, we've covered many of the important elements of a charter already. Accordingly, the charter for this project is shown in the Appendix.

Brainstorming. Six Sigma teams typically use brainstorming to generate ideas that help define the process and the problem. In fact, most Six Sigma projects use lots of brainstorming in the beginning. The goal of brainstorming is to generate a large quantity of ideas in a nonjudgmental atmosphere and then to decide which ones are useful.

You'll notice in the following paragraphs that the initially simplistic ideas from our brainstorming sessions kept getting refined. They were made more specific as we worked through the succession of tools. A hallmark of successful Six Sigma projects is that they drive clarity and precision in the team's use of language. In our project, we began by clarifying the project's goals and objectives. In this section, we're starting with the brainstorming around the measurements we could use in the measure phase.

Measures of the process. The define phase must specify how the process will be measured and how data can be gathered for the measure phase. If data cannot be gathered and measured, the project will typically fail.

Questions: How is the process currently measured? What current data are available?

- The process itself is not currently measured.
- Output is measured (in revenue dollars from employers who sign up).

- Although it has not been used, data is being generated by the Web site's traffic measurement software for such items as page views per time period and other technical measurements of server activity (e.g., gif and jpg file requests and IP addresses).

Question: How do we know that the process needs to be improved?

- Low financial performance, with revenue averaging less than $20,000 per month from employers paying $99 - $1,500 per order
- Significant opportunity to convert more visitors into customers, given the level of traffic
- TRG has had roughly 200 employers purchase its resume service in its first six months or so, yet meanwhile
  - TRG's main site has access to approximately 200,000 visitors per month;
  - considerably more than 200 people have been hired in the technical community in that period; so therefore
  - it is logical to conclude that, while TRG has access to a large potential market, it is not capturing much of that market.

Questions: What change will be considered improvement? What standards must be met?

- Any or all of the following will be considered improvement:
  - Increasing the number of visitors to the site (more customers at the current conversion rate)
  - Increasing the conversion rate (more customers at current traffic levels)
  - Increasing the average revenue per order (customers making larger purchases)

Questions: How will we test for changes? What will we measure?

- Map the current process (number of visitors, number that convert to customers, amount of revenue)
- Measure the process's capability to move visitors through its stages
- Test (survey) potential and past customers about why they visit, what they want to do, and what they want to know

- Compare the site content with the reasons that people come to the site
- Devise a site-design strategy based on what the data suggest
- Begin making changes according to best practices in Web site design
- Measure changes in the process's capability to move visitors through the stages

Questions: What results will constitute success? Will the results meet customers' needs?

- We set a stretch goal of doubling revenue for this project. In fact, we had no data on which to base this goal, yet it seemed reasonable given the size of the available market. As noted, we thought the goal might be achieved in several ways:
  - Increasing the conversion rate (turn more visitors into customers)
  - Increasing the number of visitors (at the same conversion rate)
  - Increase the size of purchases visitors made

At the outset of the project, we didn't know if it would be possible to increase the conversion rate. So Plan B was to increase revenue by increasing the traffic to the site. As it turned out, Plan B was not necessary.

Fishbone diagram. In identifying all potential causes of the low conversion rate (whether they were valid or not), we came up with the following factors, presented in Figure 4-1 in a fishbone diagram. Fishbone diagrams are really a slightly more sophisticated form of brainstorming, where ideas are organized in categories (the bones of the fish).

Like many Six Sigma tools, the fishbone diagram provides a logical, compact, visual way of organizing information. Fishbone diagrams are also called cause-and-effect diagrams and Ishikawa diagrams (after Kauro Ishikawa, who developed them in the 1940s). They are often used to depict the causes of a problem, which in this case is poor sales results.

The "bones" of the fish are selected to fit your environment. For example, manufacturing industries use the six Ms of machines, methods, materials, measurements, mother nature (environment), and manpower

FIGURE 4-1:
Fishbone Diagram

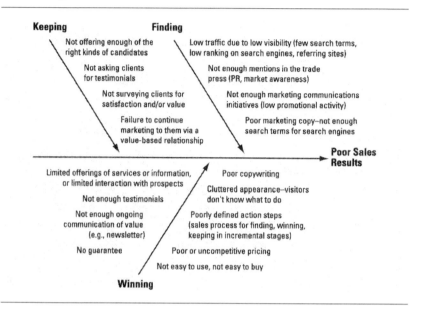

(people). Service industries use the four Ps of policies, procedures, people, and plant/technology. In working through cause and effect at a high level in marketing and sales, I typically recommend six bones: finding (marketing), winning (selling), keeping (servicing), managing people, managing systems, and managing initiatives. Because our project did not involve many people but instead the simple functioning of a Web site, we worked through the functional processes of finding, winning, and keeping, which amounts to three bones.

The fishbone diagram is a warm-up for the next step, an XY matrix.

XY matrix. An XY matrix is useful, because it organizes the causes and effects of the problem. We first listed the Ys or outputs—what the Web site produced in finding, gaining, and keeping customers (Figure 4-2).

These variables were Ys because they related to the site's visitors, and affecting those visitors was the purpose, or output, of the Web site. We ranked each Y on a 1–10 scale of relative importance. You can see that this caused us to start with the assumption that the Web site had to produce more than just revenue. In fact, after some discussion, we decided

FIGURE 4-2
Y Variables

Y Variables (Outputs)	Relative Importance
New Visitors	5
Repeat Visitors	6
Number of Members/Newsletter	7
Use of Value (Tools, Services, Info)	7
Number of Customers	8
Number Orders and Revenue	9
Number and Quality of Testimonials	10

FIGURE 4-3
X Variables

X Variables (Inputs)	Relative Importance
Site Ranking/Visibility	?
Proactive Marketing Communications Initiatives	?
Site Marketing Copy	?
Alignment of Visitor Problems with Site Offerings	?
Value of Offerings (Tools, Services, Information)	?
Ease of Using Services	?
Quality of Candidates Found	?

to give testimonials the highest ranking of importance, even higher than orders and revenue.

Then we assembled a list of possible Xs from the brainstorming (fishbone) exercise (Figure 4-3). These variables are Xs because they bring about the Ys.

To rank these in importance, they need to be compared to each of the Y's in turn on a scale of 1–10. For example, the importance of site ranking/visibility (on Internet search engines) in relation to the site's ability to produce new visitors is high, so it was ranked with a 9. Likewise, the importance of site ranking/visibility to the number and quality of testimonials is relatively low, so it was ranked with a 3.

Then we multiplied the value of the Xs by the output rating of the Ys and summed across (as shown in Figure 4-4). These calculations produced a ranking of the relative importance of the various Xs. Six Sigma tools often use this kind of method to prioritize alternatives, to familiarize

FIGURE 4-4:
XY Matrix

Date: 11/12/2003

Output Variables (Ys)	1 Site New Visitors	2 Site Repeat Visitors	3 # of Members/ Newsletters	4 Use of Value (Tools, Svcs, Info)	5 # of Customers	6 # Orders and Revenue	7 # and Quality of Testimonials	Rating	%
Output Rating 1 to 10	5	6	7	7	8	9	10	Rating	%
Input Variables (Xs)				Association Table					
Site Ranking/Visibility	9	7	6	6	4	4	3	269	12.7
Proactive Marketing Communications Initiatives	9	7	7	3	3	2	2	219	10.3
Site Marketing Copy	4	9	8	9	9	1	5	324	15.3
Alignment of Visitor Problems with Site Offerings	0	7	8	9	8	9	9	**396**	**18.7**
Value of Offerings (Tools, Services, Information)	4	8	9	8	8	7	5	364	17.2
Ease of Using Services	1	4	5	6	7	5	5	257	12.1
Quality of Candidates Found	2	3	4	5	6	7	9	292	13.8
							Total	2121	

the team with the problem and possible solutions, and to guide later data-gathering efforts. This method captures the knowledge and experience of everyone on the team and organizes them to support the best possible collective judgments. The key benefit of the exercise is that it creates actionable information. For instance, once the XY matrix shows which Xs are likely to have the most impact on the Ys, you can begin to measure those things. The XY matrix also provides a structured alternative to shouting matches and decision making driven by what the boss thinks.

The diagram revealed that the X with the most effect on the performance of the Web site was "Alignment of Visitor Problems with Site Offerings," which had a score of 396, accounting for 18.7 percent of the weight of all the Xs (highlighted in Figure 4-4). In this way, the XY matrix helped us prioritize which of the various Xs were most likely to deserve our attention.

You have to be careful about the preconceived ideas you bring to a project. For example, I had been exposed to a considerable amount of education on direct Internet marketing. Although some of those courses contained hype, others were very credible to me, especially regarding the importance of offering valuable information on Web sites to improve their "stickiness," encouraging visitors to opt in for further free information by way of building a relationship and marketing to them. Because our Web site lacked those features, I imagined that white papers and an opt-in newsletter were likely to be part of the solution to the sales problem. It made total sense.

Looking back, I can see that I was unconsciously jumping to a solution too quickly. Because I didn't even realize I was doing it, I couldn't have recognized the mistake without going through Six Sigma training. Toward the end of the project, I learned that while alignment of visitor problems with site offerings was indeed the key to improving the performance of the site, the actual solution was quite different from the one I imagined. In fact, had we implemented those white papers and the opt-in newsletter at the beginning, we would have wasted time and money without achieving much improvement.

Most students of Six Sigma go through this kind of experience. It is one of the biggest benefits of good Six Sigma training and one of the key reasons trainees must complete a project before they receive their certification. There is just no way to learn how these concepts apply in real life other than by applying them in real life.

High-level process map. A process map depicts the process and its subprocesses, activities, and results and the workflow and results. This helps the team and stakeholders to understand the process. Teams prepare these maps, which can be drawn in PowerPoint or with specialized software programs at various levels of detail.

Like any sales process, the TRG site must find, win, and keep customers. Instead of producing components and widgets, a Web-based sales process produces actions on the part of visitors and, thus, customers. For this site to produce those actions and customers, it had to give visitors something they wanted. This is, by the way, why this project applies to virtually any selling environment. Our success will be judged by whether our project actually increases the number of people who take the actions we want them to take (in this case, buy more resume services).

Finding potential customers on the Internet means attracting people to a Web page. TRG does this through a link on the Technical.com home page of the parent company, which attracts 200,000 visitors per month. Once people visit a site, something must prompt them to read the page and click through to other pages. This calls for quickly establishing trust and credibility. Visitors judge sellers based on their sites, just as they judge them on their marketing literature or salespeople. If visitors decide to investigate the site, the seller must then have a value proposition that persuades them to act. Once the visitor decides to buy, the transaction must be serviced through an ordering page that facilitates payment and delivery.

Figure 4-5 depicts this high-level process. Note that the value added in each step is demonstrated by an action on the part of a visitor on a specific Web page.

SIPOC (suppliers, inputs, process, outputs, customers). A SIPOC (*sy'pock*) diagram is a way of exploring the universe to ensure that you have identified all the things that might affect your process. You'll find the SIPOC diagram we used in this project in the Appendix.

FMEA (failure modes and effects analysis). Failure modes and effects analysis (FMEA) sounds more technical than it is. In fact, using the tool with a sales organization can be valuable because it prompts you to be thorough and systematic when thinking about what can go wrong in your process, how serious those problems can be, and how easily they can be detected. You'll find the FMEA we used in this project in the Appendix.

FIGURE 4-5
High-Level Process Map

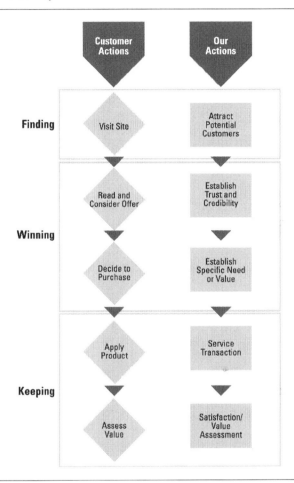

Screenshots of TRG Web pages. Given a Web-based sales environment, we had to examine the site's pages to understand the process that visitors and customers went through. The screens depicted in Figures 4-6 through 4-9 show how the Web site functioned before the changes were made. I have identified each screen's function in the process. If you like puzzles, you might enjoy studying the pages and making a list of the kinds of changes you think could cause improvement in sales conversion. Then you can check your list against what we discovered later in this chapter.

FIGURE 4-6

TRG Employer's Home Page. Function: Establish Trust and Credibility

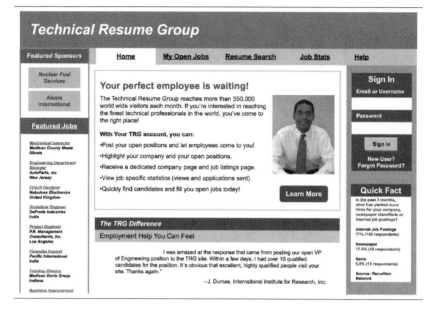

FIGURE 4-7

TRG Pricing Page. Function: Establish Specific Need or Value

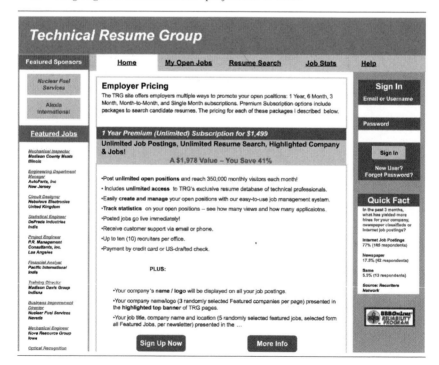

FIGURE 4-8

TRG More Information Page. Function: Establish Specific Need or Value

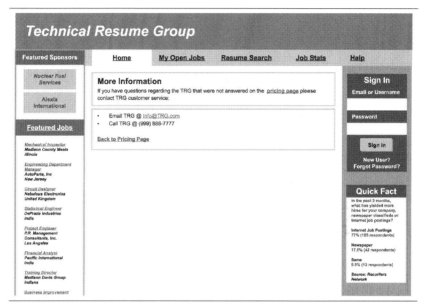

FIGURE 4-9

TRG Sign-up Page. Function: Establish Specific Need or Value

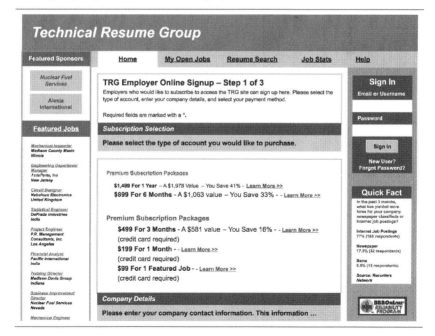

Observing the Flow of Visitor Traffic

Once visitors land on the home page, they are likely to want to learn more if they are at all interested in the service. Then, when they click on that link, they are taken to the pricing page, where they can learn about the account and pricing options. From there if they want more information, they go to a page that offers to help them send an e-mail so they can ask a question. The only other option is the Sign-up page itself.

Assess the Sales Pitch

With the project defined and the screen shots on the preceding pages, you basically know what we knew at the start of the project.

What do you think needs to be changed to improve sales?

There are many possibilities, including better art work, larger print, better pricing, or perhaps some advertising or Google ads. As noted, I thought that establishing an e-mail newsletter and putting some white papers on the site made sense. Which would you choose?

Don't answer that, because it is actually way too soon at this point in a Six Sigma project to be thinking about solutions. We need measurements of the process to ensure that we understand what's causing the current performance.

PART 2—MEASURE PHASE–PART A: WHAT WILL WE MEASURE, AND HOW?

As I mentioned earlier, Six Sigma projects often move back and forth between the measure and analyze steps, as was the case with this project. The team usually formulates and tests hypotheses in an iterative way to validate the variables as they're identified. To help you follow the logic as it developed, I've organized both the measure phase and the analyze phase into two parts, which I'll cover in the sequence in which they occurred in the project.

- *Measure: Part A.* We identified the defects, opportunities, and metrics of the process; prepared a detailed process map; identified the measurements we wanted to take; and developed a data collection plan.
- *Analyze: Part A.* We analyzed the performance of the process, the process map, and the initial measurement data. On the basis of this analysis, we decided to conduct a Voice of the Customer survey.
- *Measure: Part B.* We conducted a Voice of the Customer survey of visitors to the site.
- *Analyze: Part B.* We analyzed the Voice of the Customer data and discovered what could be improved.

Tools of the Measure Phase—Part A

Part A of the measure phase of this project employed the following tools. As in the previous section, we will cover only the bolded items in detail.

- **Defect, opportunity, unit, and metrics**
- Detailed process map
- **Data collection plan**
- **Data table**
- **Process measurement charts**
- **Situation assessment**
- Process capability

Define defect, opportunity, unit, and metrics. We operated from the following assumptions about the "defects" that were producing low yields:

1. Defects in promotion and marketing communications produce fewer visitors.
2. Defects in the ability to generate trust and credibility cause visitors to leave or not to buy.
3. Defects in the ability to establish a compelling value proposition cause visitors to leave or not buy.

We identified these assumptions so we could better evaluate the data we would be measuring, and know when, if ever, the data contradicted our assumptions. We decided to measure the yield of people through these stages by page views.

The logical process would be for visitors to start from the Employer's home page and then visit the Pricing page, but this sequence isn't enforced by the site. For example, if visitors had the URL for the Pricing or More Info pages, they could probably visit them before seeing the Employer's home page. However, the page view counts (shown in Figure 4-10) show that such a sequence is not common. The data supports the idea that the primary flow of traffic is from the Employer's home page to the Pricing page to the Sign-up page, although a few people check out the More Information page.

Detailed Process Map. A detailed process map for this sales process is contained in the Appendix.

Data collection plan. Lack of good data is the most common reason that Six Sigma projects fail. Come to think of it, it is the reason for a lot of failures in business. Figuring out how to gather the data you need is essential, especially in marketing and sales, where good data may be harder to come by than in manufacturing. You must know what you need to measure and have a plan for gathering the needed data. Here are the questions and answers we used to develop the data collection plan for this project.

Questions: How is the process currently measured? What current data is available?

- Site traffic is tracked in server logs and can be monitored and reported with site traffic reporting software.
- On the basis of extensive experimentation (outside the scope of this chapter), we will use page views (the number of times a page is viewed per week) as the primary data for measuring traffic.
- We will assume that page views are a good substitute for the number of unique visitors looking at each page. There will be more page views than visitors. However, unless visitors are extensively refreshing the same page, which is unlikely, page views should be fairly representative of the number of visitors who saw each page.

Questions: How will you test for changes? What will be measured?

- To measure the performance of the Web site itself, we need to be able to measure the input to the process as well as the output.
- The measure of outputs from the Web site is the number of orders and their value by week.
- Because they are the only reasonable metrics available, we will measure page views per week and orders per week as follows:
  - Home page
  - Pricing page
  - More Info page
  - Orders per day

Questions: What results will constitute success? Will they meet your customers' needs?

- Our goal is a 100 percent improvement in the number of orders, which will effectively double revenue. We know this is a stretch goal, yet it might be attainable, and we want breakthrough, not just incremental, improvement.
- We assume that a significant increase in revenue will reflect an improved capability of the site to meet customers' needs.

Data table. Data tables are an important tool in any Six Sigma project. In fact, the data alone, with very little in the way of analysis, often indicates what is really happening in the process. Figure 4-10 shows the weekly totals of page views and orders for the nine weeks beginning in March of the year the project took place.

The data shows an average of 567 opportunities (employers visiting the TRG home page) per week, which generate just over 32 orders and, thus 535 defects:

567 visitors – 32 orders = 535 defects (94%)

Ninety-four percent defects is a -0.07 process sigma. This low level of performance is common for this kind of process. Hold on to this point, as we'll come back to it later.

FIGURE 4-10
Page Views per Week (Before)

Week	Employer's Page	Pricing Page	More Info Page	Sign-up Page Customer Information	Orders	Average Order Value
7-Oct	669	214	61	48	28	$185
14-Oct	507	189	19	81	35	$119
21-Oct	715	361	20	82	26	$128
28-Oct	556	320	78	87	28	$176
4-Nov	332	200	75	46	41	$161
11-Nov	645	340	57	80	32	$172
18-Nov	583	273	68	82	38	$153
25-Nov	574	350	46	54	29	$177
2-Dec	549	230	82	41	39	$151
9-Dec	524	310	78	48	32	$151
16-Dec	727	300	36	93	27	$90
23-Dec	555	318	34	59	36	$100
30-Dec	629	336	30	47	29	$211
6-Jan	532	225	37	35	40	$129
13-Jan	539	325	62	41	25	$153
20-Jan	531	203	23	74	36	$204
27-Jan	577	232	16	69	37	$132
3-Feb	385	210	41	46	34	$93
10-Feb	687	277	52	59	32	$127
17-Feb	569	250	64	80	34	$115
24-Feb	519	303	79	59	40	$189
3-Mar	553	247	20	69	18	$175
10-Mar	483	240	79	69	29	$214
17-Mar	660	347	19	87	33	$143
24-Mar	636	296	40	96	32	$99
31-Mar	636	268	44	64	32	$111
7-Apr	572	280	68	48	36	$154
14-Apr	588	352	120	36	16	$399
21-Apr	580	288	32	64	40	$109
28-Apr	444	216	16	56	28	$99
4-May	392	168	16	40	36	$99
12-May	576	288	52	84	36	$132
19-May	76	20	2	2	6	$170
Average	**~567**	**~275**	**~49**	**~64**	**~32**	**~$152**
		Yield = .485		Yield = .233	Yield = .50	
					RTY = .056	

In the data table, note the yield calculations at the bottom. We'll examine those yields in some detail in the next section.

Process measurement charts. The data tables enable us to create a model of the current performance of the process. First, take a look at the yield calculations in the table. The yield of the Employer's home page to the Pricing page is:

$$275 \div 567 = 48.5\%$$

The yield of the Pricing page to the Sign-up page is:

$$64 \div 275 = 23.3\%$$

The yield of the Sign-up page to the Orders page is:

$$32 \div 64 = 50\%$$

Why didn't we calculate the yield of the More Info page in this figure? Well, at first we did. However, once we reviewed the before and after data tables (you'll see the after data table in the improve phase), the pattern that emerged revealed that this page wasn't actually part of the process flow.

Rolled throughput yield (RTY):
RTY   = yield of Pricing page × yield of Sign-up page
        × yield of orders
      = 0.485 × 0.233 × 0.5
      = 0.056

Process financial model:
Average visitors/week = 567
Average order value = $152.65
Revenue = visitors/week × RTY × average order value
        = 567 × 0.056 × $152
        = $4,826/week

The yields at these various stages are depicted in the rolled throughput yield diagram in Figure 4-11.

FIGURE 4-11
Baseline Rolled Throughput Yield

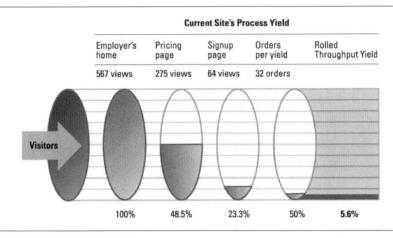

Current Site's Process Yield

Employer's home	Pricing page	Signup page	Orders per yield	Rolled Throughput Yield
567 views	275 views	64 views	32 orders	
100%	48.5%	23.3%	50%	**5.6%**

Situation assessment. Based on the data assembled in the data table, we prepared process behavior charts. These are also known as run charts (without the upper and lower control limits) or ImR charts (with the limits). The charts showed the following information:

- Employer home page views per week
- Order page views per week
- Close ratio per week

These charts are shown in Figure 4-12. They present the data in a context that makes it easier to understand the numbers. Furthermore, a statistical calculation provides upper and lower control limits (the horizontal lines along the top and bottom of the charts). These limits indicate the boundaries within which the process can be reasonably expected to perform in the future. In other words, they account for normal variation in the process. If the data showed points outside these limits, it would indicate that something other than normal variation was occurring, that perhaps some external factor was affecting things, and that the process would not be predictable. As it stands, these charts reveal that the process is fairly stable.

The data and the charts show that the visitors to the Employer's home page and the Pricing page as well as the number of orders per week

FIGURE 4-12
Process Behavior Charts

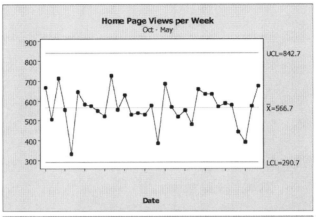

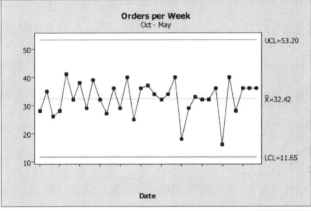

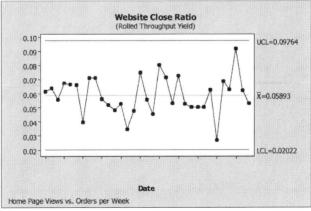

have been fairly steady. In other words, the data reflect the general stability of the process.

The close ratio for the TRG site (orders per week/employer home page views per week) is an important measure, because that is what we are trying to improve. We'll come back to this in the Improve section of this chapter.

Process Capability. A statistical process capability study of this data is presented in the Appendix.

ANALYZE—PART A: WE MOVE INTO ANALYZING THE SITUATION

With the data we have so far, we can do some analysis (so technically, this is the first segue into the Analyze phase). The goal here is to establish a clear performance base line. We also want to uncover what else we need to know to narrow down the independent variables (Xs) until we only deal with the ones most likely to have the desired effect.

Tools of the Analyze Phase: Part A

- **Analysis of value addition in the Web pages**
- Root cause diagram
- **Key input variables**
- Result of analyze phase: part A

Value-adding and non-value-adding process features. Our process should prompt customers to take actions, and customers take actions to obtain that which they value. So we examined the Web pages for value to the customer, using the Voice of the Customer (VOC) data to determine whether the process delivered what prospects said they needed to know. The screenshot with callouts in Figure 4-13 identifies those elements that have value or don't have value for customers (that is, employers). Note that a lot of content is neutral or of no value. Some of it, such as the sales copy in the middle of the page, is supposed to be helpful, yet we don't really know how helpful it is.

FIGURE 4-13
Screenshot with Value Callouts

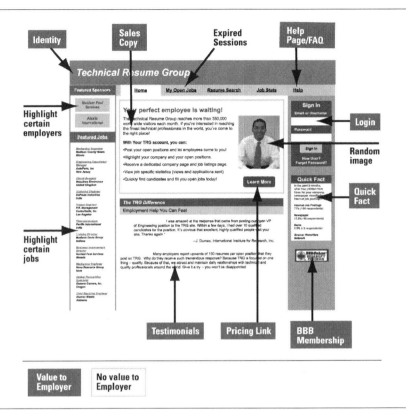

Determining key input variables. Tools such as the XY matrix (Figure 4-4) and root cause diagrams (see Appendix) help to clarify and prioritize the variables we believe are most likely to affect our problem. Briefly, here are the variables we were narrowing in on at this point.

- *Finding stage: getting visitors to come to the Employer's home page.* Key issues (input variables) affecting visits to the home page are:
  - Visibility of links to our Employer's home page on the parent company's technical Web site
  - Market visibility (number and location) of external links to the page
  - CEO's conversations with people about the site
  - Other external promotions informing people about the site

- *Winning stage: getting visitors to read the Pricing page (or the More Info page)*. While the finding stage was important, we were most interested in improving the winning stage. The XY matrix in particular had showed "alignment of visitor problems with site offerings" as the variable most likely to affect our output. As we worked through these, however, a different way of describing this emerged. See the bolded items below. Key issues affecting visits to the Pricing and More Information pages include:
  - **Trust and credibility generated by the home page**
  - **Perception of need or value generated by the home page**
  - **Number of repeat visitors generated by the home page**
  - Amount of employers' interest in and need for technically qualified job candidates
- *Winning stage: getting visitors to the Orders page*. The amount of trust and need these Web pages can create could be influenced by many factors, such as testimonials or guarantees, and the clarity of their message. Thus, in the Improve phase we will consider the use of more testimonials and other best practices of Web-based marketing. Key issues affecting visits to the Orders page are:
  - Trust generated by previous interactions with TRG
  - Need and urgency perceived by the visitor
  - Perception of value generated by Pricing and More Info pages
  - Risk eliminated by the pages and their clarity (Pricing, More Info, and Sign-up pages)

RESULT OF ANALYZE PHASE—PART A: WHAT DO WE REALLY KNOW NOW?

While these key input variables made sense, we had no direct evidence to support their validity. We have a great baseline of the Web site's performance, and we have verified that it is a stable process. But we also need information on causes, that is, answers to questions such as:

- Why do people visit the site?
- What are visitors thinking or seeking when they click here or there?

Unfortunately, we can't learn much more about the reasons for people's behaviors just from the information about site traffic. To get that kind of information, we need to know more about the customers themselves. This prompted us to conduct a Voice of the Customer (VOC) survey explained in the next section, Measure Phase—Part B. The VOC enabled us to assess the validity of our theories about the key input variables, and it was the best source for answers to questions such as those above. To get the answers, we followed these steps:

1. Conducted a telephone survey to validate our assumptions and get initial feedback
2. Created and conducted a Web-based survey for visitors and customers based on what we learned in the interviews
3. Analyzed the data from the survey to see if it indicated changes we might make to improve the process

The results of the Voice of the Customer survey guided our efforts to

- prioritize the potential improvements that we would be considering; and
- determine how to measure the process before and after the improvements.

Various technical considerations arise in gathering data. For example, you should seek some expert assistance if you have never conducted a VOC survey because experience is needed to avoid skewing the results inadvertently by the way you ask the questions. In general, the primary goals in this kind of data collection are to

- ensure that your sample is representative of the whole population, because you can rarely measure every instance. This involves testing the validity of the sample size with respect to the population.
- understand exactly what you are measuring and what conclusions you can and cannot validly draw from the data.

In this project, we did have some issues relating to sample size, given our rather small sample of data. Yet we were able to draw valid conclusions and make useful changes to the process.

MEASURE PHASE—PART B: LISTENING TO THE VOICE OF THE CUSTOMER ABOUT THE SALES PROCESS

Part B of the Measure phase of this project employed the following tools:

- **Voice of the Customer description**
- **Concerns before becoming a customer**

Voice of the Customer

Voice of the Customer (VOC) is often used in quality improvement methodologies to gather information on customers' wants, needs, and behavior vis-à-vis the process. On the basis of the VOC, you can determine the results that the process must deliver—and what you might need to change to improve the process.

VOC has no set formula or format. In any given project, it may employ one or more of the following techniques: surveys, personal and telephone interviews, focus groups, customer complaints, observations of customers' behavior, sales and service reports, and customers' product or service specifications. VOC is meant to be proactive rather than reactive. It hinges on learning about and meeting customer needs rather than responding to complaints or playing catch-up.

In this project, the VOC survey began with an outline of questions for interviews with existing customers. These interviews dramatically improved our understanding of customers and what they were seeking. For example, having never worked with people in the job search business before, I underestimated how much people already knew (and assumed their suppliers knew) about the business and what they needed. This showed me that my initial assumptions about providing white papers and an opt-in newsletter would not fill any need.

Moreover, it helped me to understand what employers and recruiters were looking for as they searched for job candidates and their alternatives for finding resumes. The insight gained by talking with just a half dozen or so people completely changed my perspective on the kinds of questions we needed to ask in a broader survey. So we went back to the drawing board.

Details about the survey itself are included in the Appendix. For now, it is enough to say that there were no significant differences in the way that customers, prospects, recruiters, or corporate employees responded to the questions. Rather than go through the entire survey, I'll just highlight the results that impacted the improve phase of the project, specifically visitors' concerns.

Concerns Before Becoming a Customer

While we learned a number of things from the detailed VOC survey, the data showed that the single most important question on the survey was this:

As you consider buying from TRG, what reservations or concerns are going through your mind? What information do you want to know?

Below is a list of possible concerns people might have or information they might want when deciding on a service like TRG. Please rate these on a scale of 0–10 where 0 indicates *not important at all* and 10 indicates *definitely important.*

Figure 4-14 shows the set of questions that were asked and the ranked responses that participants provided. The survey compared responses of customers (open circles) with those of prospects (crosshatched circles) for each question. The responses are similar.

The list of these 13 questions reflecting concerns was gleaned from the earlier interviews with TRG customers. Interestingly, none of the information they cited as important was available on the original version of the TRG Web site!

ANALYZE PHASE—PART B: WHAT'S CAUSING THE PROBLEM?

With the VOC data in hand, we needed to analyze some other information. The baseline performance measures of the performance of the

FIGURE 4-14
VOC Survey Question Response

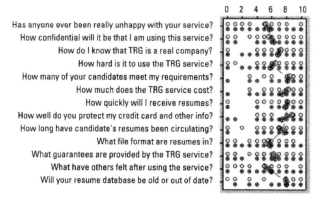

process did not give us clues on how to improve it, as happens sometimes. However, the VOC did give us a clue. To determine if the change would be worth maing, it is critical to calculate the *cost of poor quality.*

Tools of the Analyze Phase—Part B

- *Cost-of-poor-quality calculation.* The cost-of-poor-quality calculation is important, because it will tell us the potential value we could receive if we make the changes indicated.

What the VOC Suggested about Improvement

The VOC survey included many different questions. The answers to some of these pointed toward changes we could make to the information about the resumes on the site, to the sorting and presentation of that information, and to payment options (for instance, a more automated credit card processing device). However, those improvements would require an investment in reworking functions of the basic system.

In addition, none of these other indications were directly linked to our most likely key input variables, which were those affecting alignment of visitor problems with site offerings:

- **Trust and credibility generated by the home page**
- **Perception of need or value generated by the home page**
- **Number of repeat visitors generated by the home page**

Similarly, the ranking of the 13 "relative concerns buyers had before becoming a customer" was important because

- it provided concrete evidence of the relative importance of those issues to visitors;
- none of the issues was ranked below a 5, which meant that they were all relevant to some degree;
- the results confirmed our theories about what would cause people to decide to buy (see the Appendix for the root cause diagram: market visibility, awareness of value, trust, and need); and
- the information visitors cited was not available on TRG's Web site, and thus this data implied a simple, potentially valuable improvement: add sales copy addressing these concerns.

The data seemed to indicate that if we answered the questions on visitors' minds as they read our Web pages, our conversion rates might increase.

Ways to Achieve Improvement

We knew that to improve the revenue from the process, we must do one or more of the following:

- Increase the number of visitors to the site
- Increase the conversion rate of visitors to customers

To increase conversion, we must increase visitors' desire for our offer by:

- Increasing the perceived trust and credibility
- Increasing the perceived need or value

Clearly, the VOC survey had suggested a potential way of improving the site's ability to convert visitors to customers. However, before we get ahead of ourselves and jump into ideas for improving the site's perform-ance, we need to ask another analytical question: If we improved the process, how much would the results improve?

The goal: 100 percent increase in orders. Because we had data only on results, we could not precisely define a potentially achievable in-crease in either the conversion rate or the resulting orders. So we started with the goal of doubling the order volume. Working backwards, we could estimate rolled throughput yield (RTY) as follows:

Current:

$$567 \text{ employer's home page views per week}$$
$$\text{converting to } 32 \text{ orders per week}$$
$$32 \div 567 = 0.056 \text{ RTY}$$

Goal:

$$567 \text{ employer's home page views per week}$$
$$\text{converting to } 64 \text{ orders per week.}$$
$$64 \div 567 = 0.1129 \text{ RTY}$$

For simplicity, we rounded up to 0.113, meaning 64 orders per week.

Process financial model:

$$\text{Revenue} = \text{visitors/week x RTY x average order value}$$
$$= 567 \text{ x } 0.113 \text{ x } \$153$$
$$= \$9,802.86$$

Determining the amount of improvement possible. To justify any investment in improving the Web site, we needed to estimate the potential revenue increase and calculate a potential return on investment. Would our proposed change to the sales copy enable us to achieve the goal?

No realistic way existed to conduct a pilot program to gauge the in-crease without making the actual changes to the site's pages. However, information from the survey allowed us to make a plausible projection: 49 percent of the respondents to the VOC survey acknowledged a need for technical candidate resumes. This figure jibed with the percentage of visitors who had visited the Pricing page. If only 25 percent of those who expressed a need for candidates could be converted to customers,

FIGURE 4-15

Projected Yield (Based on Implications of VOC Survey)

Projected Yield Based on Survey Responses

Employer's home	Pricing page	Signup page	Orders per yield	Rolled Throughput Yield
			32 orders	
Visitors				
100%	49%	25%	50%	**12%**

the RTY would be 0.12, or just over 100 percent improvement. Because we had no reason to believe that TRG is uncompetitive in the industry, this goal did not seem unreasonable.

Admittedly, we were making an estimate. Yet, as mentioned earlier, we had little else to go on. Perhaps we could have revised the survey to ask additional questions that would have shed light on the number of respondents who might order the service, but given limited time, we went ahead with our recommendation based on judgment. After all, this situation didn't hold much risk.

Figure 4-15 illustrates the projected process yield based on these assumptions. I must tell you that, in some companies, this level of information would not be acceptable and more VOC research would be required. However, TRG approved the decision, because they wanted to move relatively quickly and making changes to the sales copy would not be costly.

Cost-of-Poor-Quality Calculation

With these projections for gauging potential improvement, we were also able to calculate the cost of poor quality, a key concept in process improvement. The cost of poor quality quantifies the money lost as the result of defects and problems. It's essentially the cost of the defect or

FIGURE 4-16

The Cost-of-Poor-Quality Calculation

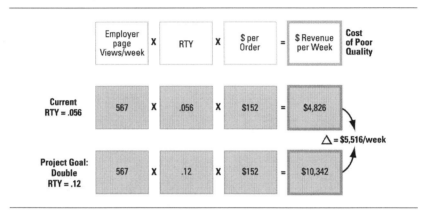

problem that's been identified in the process. More broadly, it also refers to the overall cost of whatever defects are present in a process.

Here the cost of poor quality is the cost of not having the improvements, illustrated in Figure 4-16. Because the cost of the problem was potentially $5,516 per week in forgone revenue and the cost of implementing the change would be far less than that, the improvements clearly were justified.

The cost of poor quality provides the justification for making investments to improve the process by quantifying the unseen cost of operating the process as it currently performs. This data is crucial, because many people tend to think things are optimal the way they are and resist investments to change things.

SUMMARY OF MEASURE AND ANALYZE STEPS

With the define, measure, and analyze steps completed, we are now—and only now—positioned to improve the process. At this point, the rigor and "rocket science" of Six Sigma should be a little more (perhaps painfully!) clear to you. In fact, some readers may be thinking, "You went through all this to come up with the idea of changing the sales copy?"

The answer is yes.

Fact is, many, many marketers and Webmasters would not have thought of improving the copy or known how to improve the copy, particularly if they hadn't conducted a VOC. (Never mind if they had written the copy themselves.) In fact, one school of thought is that advertising is more about images and white space than copy.

The VOC identified what visitors wanted to know that the Web site was not communicating. Without the benefit of Six Sigma, many marketers and Webmasters would have undertaken potentially complex and costly programs of search engine optimization, Web-based publicity, partner and affiliate arrangements—all to boost traffic to a site with suboptimal sales copy.

We did conduct this as a Black Belt project and to showcase Six Sigma in a sales environment, yet the benefits went well beyond the academic. The project identified low-cost improvements with a high probability of improving results.

Would simple copy changes work? It was time to find out.

PART 4—IMPROVE PHASE: WHAT CHANGES WILL FIX THE PROBLEM?

In the improve phase, we plan and implement the changes that will prevent the problem or defect from occurring in the future. Teams must resist the urge to implement improvements earlier in the process. That said, particularly in marketing and sales, the rigor of each step should be proportional to the costs and risk involved once you've identified the cause of the problem. In this project, the rigor—in the form of the number of tools employed and the extent of the research and analysis—was partly determined by the fact that this was a Black Belt project.

Tools of the Improve Phase

- **Brainstorming potential solutions**
- Selecting an improvement strategy
- Mapping the potential process
- Employing failure modes and effects analysis (FMEA)
- Planning for iterative process changes
- Defining results measures

Brainstorming potential solutions. When brainstorming, an obvious potential improvement appeared. The VOC survey revealed 13 questions that were on visitors' minds as they read the pages of the Web site yet were not answered on the site. It even provided the questions' order of importance. So adding information to the site that would answer these questions struck us as an obvious improvement.

While there were other potential improvements, this one was consistent with our first impressions of what might be wrong: "Alignment of visitor problems with site offerings." Furthermore, although my first interpretation of this was that we needed to improve stickiness by adding white papers and an opt-in newsletter, our VOC work had revealed something else entirely. People who were visiting the site already had a good education about the industry. Therefore, what they wanted to know was more specific to TRG's business and offerings.

Why not put those questions and their answers in front of a copywriter and add a page to the site that told visitors what they wanted to know? This was much less expensive than were other options, such as spending money to promote the site or changing the database functions to store and sort additional information about candidates.

One unusual aspect of this project is that, at the outset, we had data only on results. We formed a theory about visitors' behavior but had no process data to prove that theory. That's also why we had no data from which to project an achievable revenue improvement. Aside from past yield and revenue data, all we had was the VOC information. So, as noted, to measure the resulting changes in performance, we had to change the site itself. First, we brainstormed possible changes, then selected an improvement strategy and tested it. In Six Sigma, you approach the test of a strategy as just that—a test or an experiment that will produce results you must evaluate carefully. As it turned out, our test proved successful. But if it hadn't, we would have had other options.

For the sake of simplicity, and because the story does have a happy ending, let's zero in on the changes we made. (A more detailed description of the various alternatives is included in the Appendix.) Figures 4-17 through 4-19 illustrate the changes made to the sales copy on the Web site. You'll note that we eliminated the More Info page and added a Frequently Asked Questions page (FAQ) to answer all 13 questions that surfaced in the VOC survey.

FIGURE 4-17
Employer's Home Page

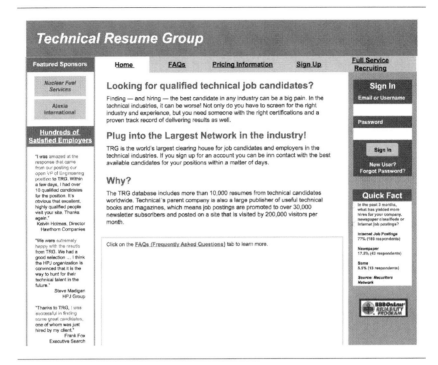

Figure 4-17, the Employer's new Home Page. Note that we removed the picture and added text (contrary to what many graphic designers would recommend).

Figure 4-18, the FAQ Page, shows the layout and content for this new page.

Figure 4-19, the Pricing Page, shows a prototype of the changes intended to improve the performance of that page.

Results of Process Improvements

Figure 4-20 shows the data table for the 18 weeks after we made the changes to the Web site. For comparison purposes, you may want to refer back to Figure 4-10, Page Views per Week (Before).

FIGURE 4-18
FAQ Page

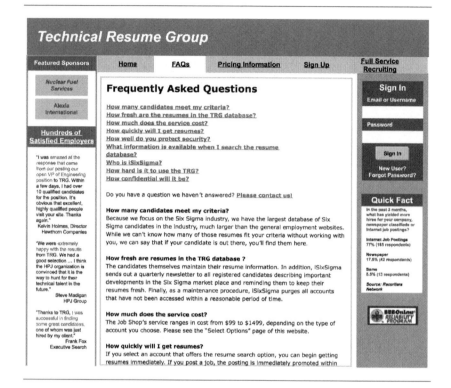

The results data reveal the following:

- The visitor traffic to the site is essentially the same before and after the change.

- The rolled throughput yield (RTY) jumped from 5.6 percent to 8.4 percent, an increase of 50 percent. A detailed analysis showed that no factor other than changing the Web site could be responsible.

- Because the only change made on the Web site was the sales copy, nothing else could account for the increased conversions to orders. This idea is also borne out by analyzing the yields: Before the changes were made, only 23 percent of the visitors to the Pricing page visited the Sign-up page, while after the change, 36 percent did. Because the primary change was the new sales copy on the FAQ page in 2005, the evidence supports the idea that the FAQ page readied more people to buy.

FIGURE 4-19
Pricing Page

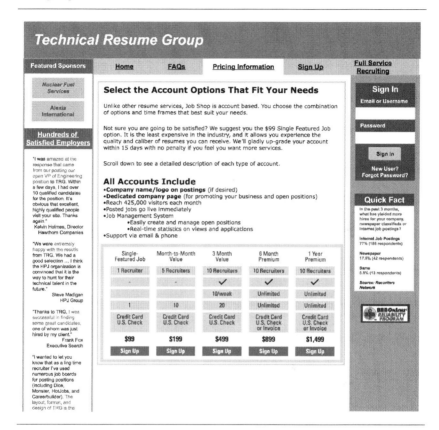

- In the measurement period, revenue per week almost doubled, from an average of $4,862 to $9,408. ($4,862 = $152 average order x 32 orders per week, and $9,408 = $196 average order x 48 orders per week.) Statistical analysis of the order values indicated neither a significant difference in the mix of new versus repeat customers nor in the value of orders from new versus repeat customers.

The results indicate that while we did not double the performance of the site with our sales copy change, we went a long way toward achieving it. Figure 4-21 compares the performance of the original site, the goal we set, the resulting actual performance, and the amount of improvement.

FIGURE 4-20
Page Views per Week (After)

Week Ending Date	Employer's Page	FAQ Page	Pricing Page	More Info Page	Sign-up Page	Orders	Average Order Value
6/02	716	118	264		56	60	$166
6/09	552	96	204		84	56	$163
6/16	660	78	280		76	48	$224
6/23	692	292	960		348	56	$363
6/30	500	64	184		64	48	$132
7/07	564	124	292		76	60	$197
7/14	536	96	204		68	48	$216
7/21	524	108	208		80	28	$153
7/28	444	104	212		80	60	$252
8/04	608	108	260	·	96	60	$211
8/11	548	92	172		72	32	$184
8/18	436	80	180		52	32	$111
8/25	792	136	352		136	44	$108
9/01	424	132	248		104	44	$324
9/08	636	132	252		144	52	$176
9/15	564	64	180		92	36	$188
9/22	560	84	184		88	52	$190
9/29	504	72	172		44	40	$169
Avg	**570**	**~94**	**~267**		**~97**	**~48**	**$196**
			Yield = 0.468		Yield = 0.363	Yield = .495 RTY = 0.084	

FIGURE 4-21
Performance Improvement

	Original Performance	Goal	Actual Result	Improvement
Rolled Throughput Yield (RTY)	0.056	0.12	0.084	50%
Average Order Value	152	152	196	N/A (not a goal of the project)
Revenue per Week	$4,826	$10,342	$9,408	94%

Incidentally, analysis of the traffic flow through the pages in Figure 4-22 is instructive. Visitors might naturally follow the sequence of home page, FAQ page, Pricing page, and finally Sign-up page. If so, the volume of page views would probably decrease as people "leaked out" of the sales process on each successive page. But the page view data doesn't support this theory. After an initially high number of visitors to the home page, a significantly smaller number of people visit the FAQ page. Then the volume of visitors to the Pricing page significantly increases, while the volume declines again on the Sign-up page. So people are not moving in lockstep to the FAQ page.

I believe a better theory of the traffic flow is this. About half of the initial visitors to the home page are sizing up TRG's offer, including getting an idea of the costs. That's why the Pricing page has the second highest number of page views. Then those visitors who are serious about buying return and spend time on the FAQ page. At that point, a very high percentage of them go on to the Sign-up page sequence.

Viewing these before and after graphs is instructive. Clearly, the volume of page views showed no increase in the input variable. The average number of visitors per week is almost the same. Yet the number of orders per week has increased from 32 per week to 47 per week, and the close ratio has increased as well.

If you measured results only, you would detect the increase in orders, but you would not know why they increased. You would be tempted to come up with a theory that explains the behavior. Perhaps that new marketing manager is making a difference, or a new channel partnership is bringing dividends. As a reasonable businessperson, you want explanations for such things. Yet you would have no evidence on which to base an explanation, unless you took the steps designed to produce that evidence.

Future Steps

Although we did not double the conversion rate, the VOC data revealed information that could be used to improve conversion and to improve the value of the product itself (the information provided to customers). Other steps could also be taken. However, we have substantially achieved our goals for this project and have proven that we can use the Six Sigma approach to improve a sales process.

FIGURE 4-22

Before and After Process Behavior Charts

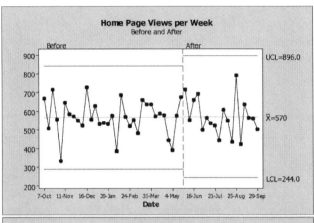

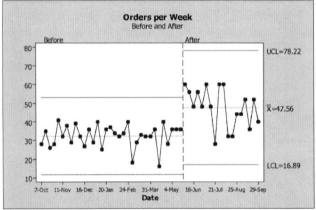

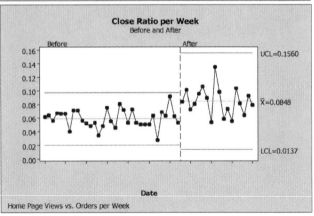

PART 5—CONTROL PHASE: HOW DO WE LOCK IN THE CHANGES?

In the control phase, the project team and process owners locked in the changes that improved the results. In a Web-based environment, especially one with a small range of offerings and customers, this phase is relatively straightforward. In environments with a sales force and various sales channels, marketing programs, and product lines, the control phase becomes far more complicated. Yet, straightforward or complicated, the control step is essential. This step generally entails developing a control plan—a plan for institutionalizing the changes—and defining the measurements that will tell management whether the process is performing as it should. Typical control plans include the following:

- Control plan for maintaining the gains identified through the project
- Documentation to ensure that other people can easily understand the changes that we made and why
- Monitoring to provide a way to keep current and future managers informed on the performance of the process and to alert them if it starts to go out of control
- Response plan that indicates what to do if performance begins to drift
- Training plan to instruct future process owners about the process and how to manage it effectively

TRG is a small enterprise with a few employees and a service delivered largely by automated systems. Therefore, the control plan centers on establishing an automated means of collecting and analyzing data with respect to the process. Given this, the control plan does not involve a lot of training or document preparation, which many plans must include because of the size and complexity of the operation or function.

Basically, our control plan was a recommendation to establish an automated way of maintaining the data tables and process behavior charts developed in this project. Also, rather than measure the performance of a page, make a change, and measure it again, we recommended an approach that incorporated split testing, a commonly used approach in advertising, whereby two alternate versions of a Web page are tested at the same time. This approach would speed up improvement of the site considerably.

SUMMARY AND LESSONS LEARNED

This TRG project followed formal Six Sigma procedures for defining, measuring, and analyzing the process; making limited changes to improve results; waiting for the changes to take effect or not take effect; and analyzing the results. It was a superb learning experience for me, one that organized and formalized my understanding of practices and tools that I'd been acquainted with—and in many cases using—for years without having conducted an end-to-end Six Sigma Black Belt project.

Aside from everything that you've read in this chapter so far, what else can be learned from this experience?

Recall that I am a sales professional first and a quality professional second. From that dual perspective, here are some lessons I think might be valuable:

- *Rigor has its rewards.* The Six Sigma steps and tools truly minimize the effect of politics, and even opinion, on management decisions. Figures don't lie. Yes, there are qualitative judgments, for example about potential causes and solutions, but even these are settled by a vote by the team members and tested with data. Also, I came to the project with some very definite ideas for improving the conversion rate, including by adding information and services to make the site sticky to keep visitors browsing longer. However, I learned that this functionality was not high on the list of things visitors wanted.
- *It's a team effort.* Speaking of team members, no one does a Six Sigma project alone. The process owner and other stakeholders, including prospects or customers, are always involved, because you gather information from them. You always have at least one process improvement professional. This team approach provides checks and balances and a rich variety of viewpoints, enabling the best ideas to surface and survive.
- *Pick and choose your steps and tools.* Unless you're in a formal project, you must explicitly decide how deeply to go into any one step or

tool. That decision will affect the resources you'll require for each step and for the project as a whole. This TRG project called for touching all the bases. But there's a cost-benefit ratio to everything, and most marketing and sales projects do not demand the rigor of this project.

- *Lack of measurement systems is a root cause of problems.* Unfortunately, most Six Sigma and Lean projects in transactional environments run into the precise problem we ran into: A lack of data for measuring activities and results, and a lack of systems to easily gather and present that data. Although the Internet is supposed to be the most measurable of all media, almost none of the traffic-reporting software systems we investigated could create a simple run chart from the data without special configuration and coding. The same is true for most business application software, including Customer Relationship Management (CRM) systems. This reflects the lack of process knowledge on the part of most people in the information technology world and in the larger business world. Hopefully, this attitude is changing as people gain more understanding of process improvement.

- *Yes, Six Sigma works in sales.* Best of all, the project achieved its purpose, which was to increase TRG revenue. It did so by increasing the conversion rate *and* increasing the average size of orders at minimal cost in terms of changes to the process.

- *The improvement needed was pretty simple.* Looking back on it, it is easy to see that the site was not giving people the information they needed to make buying decisions. However, at the time we were deciding what needed to be done, adding a FAQ was just one of any number of potential changes. Now that we have proven that this change worked and have an example, it is easier to look at other Web sites and spot the same problem.

- *What's the Six Sigma of it?* It will be tempting for some to say, "We do these kinds of improvements to Web sites too. What's so special about Six Sigma?" The answer is, of course, that Six Sigma is a process for improving the process. Given just about any situation, Six Sigma could be used to figure out how to fix the problem. Although other people may well have relevant experience, unless they are systematically taking into account all the factors in a situation, their approaches may be shots in the dark. In fact, relying on gut feelings and guesses instead of on facts and data is exactly what's wrong with most sales and marketing management consulting today.

Of course, Six Sigma becomes more challenging when you are working not just on sales copy but also trying to influence salespeople's behaviors. Fortunately, however, Six Sigma offers tools for dealing with that too, as will be explained in Chapter 5.

KEY POINTS

- A Six Sigma project consists of five steps: Define, Measure, Analyze, Improve, Control. Each of these contains tools that assist in understanding a problem and its causes in depth, in helping to identify solutions, and then in validating those solutions.
- A key to this kind of project is a rigorous focus on data, and not on what we think is the solution. Each step of the DMAIC approach generates data that is required in the succeeding step.
- To get to the bottom of complex problems, you sometimes have to go back and forth between the Measure, Analyze, and Improve steps until you find the right solution and the data to prove it.
- The key to measuring the right data in a sales process is to understand the value perceived by the customer in each step. This enables you to understand the customer's behavior, which is a prerequisite for solving sales problems.
- While DMAIC has in-depth tools and can sometimes require an intimate knowledge of applied statistics, do not make problems more complex than they need to be. In functions such as sales, which have typically not had their processes formally analyzed, projects tend to be more like "Define, Measure, Work things out," or even "Define, work things out." This is fine and is a necessary step for upgrading people's level of understanding and the consistency of the sales process. In fact, the learning that takes place this way is a prerequisite for more thorough implementations of Six Sigma that might be needed later on.

5

TOOLS FOR ALIGNING MARKETING AND SALES FUNCTIONS

In Chapter 4, we improved the performance of a simple sales process. In fact, it was so simple that it took place only on Web pages and involved no salespeople except, perhaps, when someone called the company to ask a question. So how relevant is that example to the problem of improving the sales and marketing functions of an entire organization, with various experts going about their tasks?

Before I answer that question, let's consider that selling was once done mainly by traveling salesmen (yes, they were usually men in the early days), presenting their wares personally to customers. This was the case whether those customers were housewives needing carpet cleaners or company presidents needing machine tools. Selling directly worked, but it was expensive. Therefore, companies began experimenting with catalogs, direct mail, and advertisements in newspapers and magazines. They learned that these techniques could often work as well. Although it required knowledge and skills somewhat different from those of the salesperson, it required some insight into the customers wants and needs.

So experimenting with different ways of selling started long ago. In the 1990s, companies began selling successfully with telesalespeople rather than outside salespeople—even for expensive, complex products and services such as computers and software. Today, people are experimenting quite successfully with the Internet as a sales medium. There is nothing magical about using salespeople or various channels or media to get prospects and customers to act. The same basic principle applies: people have free will, and they will take action only if they have a reason to do so, that is, only if they see the value to themselves. So I would say, yes, the lessons learned in our Web site project are highly relevant to a larger sales and marketing organization. Indeed, it would be difficult to say whether our improvements resulted from better "marketing" or better "selling."

This chapter and Chapter 6 will focus on the fundamental issue of value creation in marketing and sales. This is important because the different ways marketers and sellers work versus how manufacturers operate make it more difficult (at first) to translate the principles of process improvement from one to the other. This chapter and the next will provide insights and tools that directly apply process improvement to your marketing, sales, and service functions. Then, in Chapters 7 and 8, we will deal with more specific issues around bringing Six Sigma into the organization.

CONSEQUENCES OF THE MARKETING VERSUS SALES DISCONNECT

Earlier I mentioned that marketing and sales typically operate as separate silos. One major cause of this is the composition of the sales and marketing functions. Jeff Watts, vice president of account services at Creata, put it this way:

> When you look at the roles of people [in sales] who are doing lead generation, account management, and account development, or a sales engineer or a closer, they all sort of think the same way, even though they wear different hats.
>
> When you come into marketing, you have a product marketer, a public relations person, a media buyer, a creative or messaging designer, and perhaps a merchandiser. The experiences of these people are really very isolated and don't overlap nearly as much as in sales. As a result, the skill sets of marketing folks are more specifically and departmentally defined.

The cure for this is process thinking, that is, examining the end-to-end chain of activities in terms of how the pieces fit together and the cause-and-effect relationships within that chain.

Indeed, the lack of process thinking sometimes causes executives' strategies to backfire. I've mentioned examples where management thought its problem was one thing, but it turned out to be another. Although the following example is from a sales department rather than from a marketing department, it provides another vivid illustration. In their book *Managing Major Sales*, Neil Rackham and Richard Ruff present a case where a company hired a new head of sales to improve sales results. The new sales manager needed to increase the productivity of the company's sales force quickly. He soon learned that although management assumed salespeople were making three or four sales calls per day, the actual average was less than two calls per day. This was disturbing news, but it presented an obvious solution: push the sales force to make more calls.

The assumption, of course, was that more calls would equal more sales. On the face of it, this assumption seems plausible. After all, for many simple products, especially those sold in one call (perhaps even door to door), that assumption could be proven true. In these cases, a direct correlation exists between the number of calls and the resulting sales. However, in this company the product was complex and expensive. Success depended on the quality, not the quantity, of salespeople's interactions with customers. They had to be good at identifying needs and locating and qualifying decision makers and at proposing the right solutions at the right time.

Under increased pressure for more call activity, salespeople began focusing on smaller, simpler deals that required less preparation time for calls and for closing deals. The result was a larger number of transactions but a sharp decline in the average size of the transactions. As salespeople ignored larger accounts and overworked smaller ones, the pipeline dried up. In addition, tracking the increased activity dramatically increased paperwork. The move also alienated the best salespeople, who objected to the new targets and controls regarding their behavior. The sales results were not at all what the new sales manager or senior management had expected.

The case shows the futility of trying to make decisions and manage activities without really understanding the causes and effects involved.

That understanding is what process thinking brings to the table. Executives relying on traditional financial and sales activity reports have difficulty diagnosing sales problems and developing effective solutions. It would be useful, for example, if those reports revealed the true process costs, such as those identified by a sales operating audit as discussed in Chapter 3. Even if they simply showed where revenues were coming from (from current customers, new customers, new products, or market share gains from competitors), the reports would be better diagnostic tools. Unfortunately, most companies' information systems are not set up to gather the necessary data. Furthermore, because marketing, sales, and service have separate charters and different goals, it's difficult to see how they affect each other or when they are getting in each other's way.

Yet marketing and sales (and service) could not be more interrelated. If marketing doesn't find prospects, then salespeople will have to find them as well as convert them into customers. Likewise, if sales cannot convert the good prospects found by marketing into customers, then marketing's efforts have been wasted. And if service cannot keep customers, then marketing and sales will have to spend a lot of effort replacing customers who should not have been lost in the first place.

It takes all three functions to generate customers now and in the future. Therefore, without an understanding of how they interact and of cause and effect within the process, there's no way to see what needs fixing. Without this understanding, one cannot gather useful data, because there are no useful definitions of measures or how they relate to one another.

The all-too-common debates between marketing and sales reflect this. You have well-intentioned, hardworking people pulling in different directions, partly because that's what they're paid to do and partly because each of their solutions makes the most sense from their point of view. So marketing argues for more investment in the brand, while sales wants more feet on the street. Marketing lobbies for a promotional campaign, while sales puts in for sales training. There's no reliable way to tell which party is right, so the one with the loudest voice or most clout wins the day. This is how the usual fixes come about, and we will address the issue of these fixes—and how to apply them correctly—in Chapter 7, once we have clarified the structure of a true process approach.

BRIDGING THE MARKETING VERSUS SALES DISCONNECT

The divide between marketing and sales is a huge problem but one that a process approach is ideally suited to solving. After all, a process approach calls for examining all the activities that produce a certain result, and marketing and sales produce customers.

Many companies have tried to align their marketing and sales functions, and almost as many have failed. In fact, alignment between marketing and sales is almost impossible to achieve by the usual methods, which are to adjust the organizational structure, issue mandates, or both. Why? Because people will tend to conduct marketing and sales activities the way they always do—more or less independently of one another and from their parochial points of view—unless the activities are tightly linked in ways that people experience as real. Marketing and sales people have to see that the things they do and their respective inputs and outputs depend on one another. Moreover, people have to be working toward the same goal, and that goal has to be made very concrete. For instance, even the goal of creating value for the customer won't be concrete enough unless marketing and sales share a precise understanding of what customers value. Even then, *value* must be translated into concrete and measurable actions (of the seller and the buyer alike) that everyone understands.

People don't come to share a precise understanding of anything unless they work at it. The tools covered in this chapter enable marketing and sales people to develop a precise understanding of what customers value, not for its own sake but so they can create products, marketing campaigns, and sales methods that enable the company to find, win, and keep customers. Once they understand what customers value, they can develop better ways of delivering and measuring that value and that is the heart of sales process improvement, regardless of how formally or informally it is applied.

MARKETING = ANYTHING THAT MAKES SALES EASIER

I've uttered the words in this headline for many years, and they are true. Peter Drucker put it like this: "The aim of marketing is to know and understand the customer so well that the product or service fits him and sells itself." However, neither statement is a sufficient definition of marketing. For that, I'd like to refer, again, to Jeff Watts:

> Marketing identifies profitable market needs (market research), designs products and services that meet those needs (product development), communicates the value of these products (marketing communications and promotional campaigns), and makes these products easily accessible to the prospects who are most able and willing to buy them, and it does all this by the most effective and efficient means possible.

As noted, the people in these various roles are narrowly focused. Rarely does a field salesperson cross over into the marketing department, and very rarely vice versa. Product developers are unaware of how (or even if) their products will be promoted. Having never worked in a customer's business, copywriters and channel managers may be unaware of the real problems customers or channel partners face or how the products and services might solve those problems. They are forced, in effect, to do their best with what they can learn secondhand. And, as the company gets larger, more people come between each marketing person and the customer. This does not make sales easier but makes them harder.

As a result of the marketing and sales divide, and the tendency of companies to focus on their products instead of their customers, marketing departments often produce generic, product-oriented communications and promotions. Talented people work hard to produce newsletters that may go unread, leads that might be ignored, and collateral material that may not be used. In fact, one estimate of the American Marketing Association indicated that as much as 90 percent of marketing collateral goes unused by salespeople. Meanwhile, salespeople invent their own messages and value propositions, sometimes to the detriment of the company and the customer.

Note that Jeff's definition of marketing does not have *sales* in it anywhere. In fact, the marketing department's proper relationship to the sales department should be similar to the relationship between the engineering department and the production department within manufacturing organizations. Marketing must find needs and develop products and the means of selling those products as efficiently and effectively as possible. This implies a responsibility for the efficiency and effectiveness of the overall production system. It also implies automating all that can be automated and involving salespeople where the process can't be automated.

Of course, marketing activities can and should be measured. They comprise a long series of interdependent processes, whose causes and effects can be known through many kinds of tools and measurements. Even the effect of brand awareness campaigns can be measured though surveys, at least to some extent.

Among the most important tools for targeting marketing efforts are market research, Voice of the Customer, and customer value mapping.

CUSTOMER SATISFACTION VERSUS CUSTOMER VALUE

One mistake has undermined many a market research and Voice of the Customer (VOC) initiative: Failing to focus on the full context of customer value. Remember that value is what people will take action to obtain. Discovering what the customer values means answering questions such as these: What are our customers trying to accomplish? What stands in their way? What problems are they trying to solve? What means do they use to work around those problems? What does it cost them to do so?

This information differs from the kind of research emphasized in business school marketing courses such as demographics, income levels, and product preferences. It also differs from the product feature orientation of many VOC initiatives. Those help you understand markets and product requirements perhaps, but we need to understand the customer on a deeper level. What are people spending their time and money on (whether or not they want to)? Why and when do they think about what we sell? What is it that they really want from our product or service?

VOICE OF THE CUSTOMER (VOC)

VOC initiatives are a major component of Six Sigma deployments. VOC is a technique for gathering structured, systematic data about customer needs and wants. It employs surveys and interview data to validate hypotheses and discover new information about the customer's situation and needs. To elicit useful responses in surveys and interviews, you must carefully consider and phrase questions with the aim of translating soft customer perceptions into hard, actionable data and metrics that will drive improvement projects.

Because marketing and sales are the company's "eyes and ears," those functions shouldn't simply participate in VOC initiatives; they should manage and measure the VOC process for the entire organization. However, in many companies the quality department initiates and runs VOC efforts. In these cases, the quality department's lack of familiarity with marketing and sales often causes it to focus on product details and ignore what customers want and need from the marketing and selling process itself.

Typically, VOC initiatives rely on either passive or proactive sources of data or a combination of the two. Proactive sources include interviews, focus groups, surveys, or direct customer observations. Passive sources include customer complaints, technical support calls, warranty claims, or Web page traffic. The resulting data is expressed as customer needs that can be translated into a list of issues that are Critical to Quality (known as CTQs) or Critical to Loyalty. These needs are carefully validated and used to define product and service requirements.

Unfortunately, these efforts usually focus on specifications for engineering and features for product development rather than on actual customer needs. Those specifications and features are useful, but many other issues have a major impact on the customer's business, including these:

- Pricing
- Packaging
- Distribution channels
- Training and support
- Complementary or ancillary services
- Ordering mechanisms

- Customer service and support
- Marketing and informational services
- Selling services

These beyond-the-product characteristics all have value to customers and should be identified, analyzed, and improved with the same intensity as product features.

Yet most VOC initiatives that do go beyond product specifications and features extend only to customer satisfaction. Yes, customer satisfaction is important, but it's not as important as customer value. People drop services and products they are satisfied with all the time if they find something of greater value instead. Customer value mapping, which we'll discuss in the next section, can provide valuable guidance with respect to uncovering the customer's broader context and identifying the right questions to ask.

One cure for many of these problems is to get your salespeople involved in your VOC initiatives. In fact, if you have difficulty getting them involved, the initiative itself might be off track. Try to find out why. If your salespeople see the research as complicated and irrelevant, your customers may share that perception. If the salespeople see no value in the effort, ask them what you should be trying to learn instead. Also, ask them what *they* would want to know about the customers' views and experience of your company's products and services *and* its marketing and sales process. Mature, knowledgeable salespeople can play a valuable role on any team that conducts VOC research.

One criticism I have heard of involving salespeople in VOC efforts is that they might be in the habit of "always closing" and so may not add much value to a VOC effort. Yet everyone, from product managers to salespeople to marketers to Master Black Belts, needs education and awareness around the way questions should be asked of customers. Without this, real needs and wants may go unexpressed, while expressed needs and wants may miss the point.

Finally, when you gather customer information, know what you will do with it. Begin with the end in mind and carefully define the information that you really need for what you are trying to accomplish. To be as specific as possible, ask yourself these questions:

- What, specifically, do you want to know?
- Why do you want to know it?
- Who do you want to know it from?
- What do you plan to do with the information?

Note that these considerations weighed heavily in our Web site improvement project in Chapter 4. In fact, we were conducting VOC on customers themselves, indirectly asking them what they wanted to see on the Web pages. Your company can do these kinds of things as well. There really is no substitute for accurate, useful information about your customers.

CUSTOMER VALUE MAPPING

Customer value mapping helps you learn what your prospects and customers truly value about your products and services (as well as your sales process); then that knowledge is used to create powerful value propositions. In her book *Selling to Big Companies*, Jill Konrath defined a value proposition as "a clear statement of the tangible results a customer gets from using your products or services." Customer value mapping enables you to identify those results for everyone your product or service affects in the customer organization. I have found it to be an invaluable step in designing sales processes and sales tools in over 70 client engagements in the last ten years.

Identifying the impact of your product or service on various people in the customer organization is essential for two reasons. First, in business-to-business sales, "the customer" is rarely one person, or even one function. Second, the results and effects of your product or service will vary depending on which customer is using it. A product or service often affects upstream and downstream departments. This complicates the task of understanding what the customer values and thus the task of crafting value propositions.

For instance, a client of mine that sold to pharmaceutical companies wanted to increase sales of an ingredient for tablets and capsules. This ingredient could be formulated to dissolve when the pill reached specific locations in the digestive tract, a key consideration in some medications. The company prided itself on the technical expertise of its salespeople, who often held advanced degrees in research chemistry. These salespeople called on formulation chemists at pharmaceutical companies but felt uncomfortable dealing with other functions and with senior management. After all, given that the product's value appeared to be its technical superiority, what value could they offer to those parties?

In the pharmaceutical business, it's often one thing to develop a formulation in small quantities for research purposes but something else to scale up to production batches. The client's product had certain competitive advantages when used in larger batches, one of which was greater stability at varying temperatures. However, dealing with the problems involved in scaling up was the province of the process engineers, not the formulation chemists.

So the salespeople had more than a reason to call on people other than the formulation chemists; they had an imperative. The value to the production department could be significant, but unless the need was established at the outset of a project, the production people intended to ignore it. Given their products' high margins, production costs were not a major consideration to them. But time to market was, so the production people's interest lay in identifying at the outset anything that might reduce problems in scaling up formulas. Thus, the salespeople had a value proposition to present to the process engineers.

What value proposition would justify a call on senior management? Well, the interests of the formulation chemists and process engineers did not intersect at lower levels, but they did at higher levels. The vice president of pharmaceutical development would have a real stake in these benefits, and my client had a solid value proposition for this senior executive. Not only would more precise delivery of the compound within patients maximize its effectiveness, but time to market could be reduced by minimizing problems in scaling up to production quantities.

How did we develop these ideas and demonstrate them to the salespeople? How did the salespeople become comfortable making those sales calls and presenting these value propositions? How did we implement the coaching and training that made all this possible? With customer value mapping. Like standard process improvement tools, customer value mapping helps you develop and organize information and draw conclusions and present their implications in a systematic way.

FIGURE 5-1:
Sample Pharmaceutical Development Organization Chart
(Shaded positions are impacted by the product)

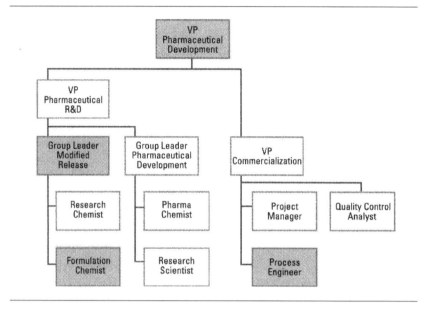

Customer Value Mapping in Action

In this section, I'll walk you through the customer value mapping process for this company.

First, you identify everyone in the customer organization who is potentially impacted by your products or services. To cast wide net, I usually start with an organizational chart of the company or division. Figure 5-1 illustrates a (highly) simplified organization chart for a pharmaceutical development function.

In this case, people potentially impacted by the product included the formulation chemist, process engineer, group leader, and vice president of pharmaceutical development. Once you've identified these positions, it's time to learn about the concerns of those in these positions. Those concerns will point you toward what they value. For this task, you need input from knowledgeable salespeople, sales managers, marketing or product managers, customer service representatives, and, ideally, someone from the customer's environment or with experience in it. For prac-

FIGURE 5-2

Customer Value Map for a Formulation Chemist

Constituencies/ Relationships	Objectives/ Responsibilities	Metrics
Discovery group	*Design of drug delivery system to meet specs*	*Meeting deadlines on budget*
Analytical quality control group	*Develop formulation as quickly as possible and patents*	*Produce a scaleable formulation*
Process engineer group		*Develop patentable innovations, intellectual property*
Regulatory group		
Purchasing		

Strategies		Issues and Challenges	
Internal	**External**	**Internal**	**External**
Staying current with technology	Cultivate vendor relationships	*Staying current with technology and education*	Gaining recognition through publications, presentations, and patents
Project management, prioritizing	Professional associations	*Gaining recognition*	
Politics		Working on successful projects	
Maximizing success to achieve advancement		Getting assigned to the best projects	

tical reasons, that last point of view may be difficult to obtain, but it's invariably worthwhile if you can get it.

When we mapped the values for the formulation chemist and process engineer, we came up with customer value maps similar to those shown in Figures 5-2 and 5-3. Note that developing these maps entails identifying what the person is trying to accomplish, *leaving aside your products and services*. This objective approach is crucial, because it goes beyond your concern, which is the product or service, and opens you to all of the customer's concerns, which extend far beyond your product or service. This approach helps you see opportunities for, and impediments to, sales that you would otherwise miss. As Figures 5-2 and 5-3 illustrate, you want to identify customers' concerns in the following areas: constituencies and relationships, objectives and responsibilities, metrics (which they evaluate, or on which they are evaluated), strategies (both internal and external), and issues and challenges (that they face, again, both internally and externally).

FIGURE 5-3

Customer Value Map for a Process Engineer

Constituencies/ Relationships	Objectives/ Responsibilities	Metrics
Formulation development group	*Scale up the formula into volume production*	*Successfully completed projects*
Analytical quality control group	Complete validation trials	*Lead time to completion, achieve milestones*
Regulatory group	Leverage existing production infrastructure	*Production efficiency*
Purchasing	*Design, specify, and purchase process equipment*	Maximize existing production equipment
Director		
Manufacturing group		
Marketing		
Packaging		

Strategies		Issues and Challenges	
Internal	**External**	**Internal**	**External**
Distributed manufacturing vs. central	*Research and qualify vendors of production equipment*	*Not having tech transfer and scale up research completed on time*	Complying with regulatory and validation requirements
Outsourcing vs. in-sourcing		Completing trials on time	
Identify problems		*Troubleshooting*	
Training		*Making things foolproof for operators*	
Safety		Training	
Optimizing workflow		Documentation, lot traceability	

With those concerns identified, you then highlight those where your products and services might have an impact. In Figures 5-2 and 5-3, the elements we could impact are highlighted in italicized, bold, underscored text.

Seeing the customer's entire world gives people in marketing and sales an authentic view of the customer's situation and of the role your company can play in it. The more highlighted items, the more impact your company might have, even to the point of that customer's outsourcing the function to you. The fewer highlighted items, the less impact you'll probably have on that customer. Remember, however, that in most business-to-business situations, multiple individuals affect the sales process and its outcome.

FIGURE 5-4
Value Proposition Table for a Formulation Chemist

We can help the formulations department to:

Do What?	By:
Design drug delivery systems that meet specs	Applying our extensive knowledge to the customer's formulation requirements
Develop formulations as quickly as possible	Providing tailored formulation recommendations that maximize the chances for success
Produce a formulation that's scaleable to production quantities	Offering feasibility studies and other lab services
Meet deadlines on budget	Providing extensive technical support globally
Stay current with technology and developments in its field	Presenting at industry events; contributing intellectual material to the industry
	Hosting annual workshops
	Providing in-house technical presentations at its request
Maximize success to achieve advancement	Using a consultative sales approach and applying our expertise where the department needs it most
Gain recognition	Helping it formulate successful products

The next step in customer value mapping is to articulate value propositions. By definition, the highlighted items are things that the person in that role values. A value proposition answers the question on every prospect's mind: "How can your product or service deliver what I value?"

Figures 5-4 and 5-5 provide examples of value proposition tables. These tables link the outcomes sought by the customer to the value created by the products. Note that while these are strong value propositions, they rarely mention the product or service. Some companies will add a column to the right of these tables labeled "How?" They use that column to link the features and capabilities of the product to what the customer values. This extends the value proposition well beyond the features-and-benefits approach typical of most marketing and sales efforts.

Now that we have defined value to the customer and our impact on it, we are ready to move into the most important aspect of customer value mapping: developing questions to uncover what the customer needs and values. If salespeople are to create value in the way they sell, they must know their subject deeply. The best way to apply that knowledge is by asking questions. Decades of research and experience have

FIGURE 5-5
Value Proposition Table for a Process engineer

We can help the production engineering department to:

Do What?	By:
Scale up the formula into volume production	Providing on-site assistance and broad expertise in the scale-up trials
Design, specify, and purchase process equipment	Recommending proven suppliers of appropriate equipment
Research and qualify vendors of production equipment	
Achieve successful completed projects	Being available for on-site assistance and troubleshooting
Achieve production efficiency	Helping formulators design formulas that are easier to produce
Troubleshoot	Applying our extensive knowledge to their formulation requirements
	Providing extensive technical support globally

proved that the most effective salespeople rely more on asking questions than on telling people what they know. Every prospect wants salespeople to understand and respect his or her unique situation. Demonstrating that understanding and respect is crucial to building trust. Salespeople can understand the prospect's situation and build that trust only by asking questions and listening to the answers, thereby creating a dialog. Moreover, questions stimulate the customer's thinking as well, which can be highly valuable.

Start by asking yourself: "What questions do our salespeople need to ask to discover whether a prospect has the kinds of problems we can solve?" Probably a number of general questions need to be answered, either through research on the Internet or other resources. For example:

- Where does the (customer) company stand relative to others in its industry?
- Why do *its* customers buy from it?
- What are its primary objectives and its strategies to achieve those objectives?
- What key issues and challenges may inhibit the company from achieving its objectives or implementing its strategies?

Many more general questions may be appropriate in a given situation, and many sources list such questions. Examples of such resources include Miller and Heiman's *Conceptual Selling* (1987, Warner Books), Shonka and Kosch's *Beyond Selling Value* (2002, Dearborn), and Nick and Koenig's *ROI Selling* (2004, Dearborn). Examining customer value maps enables you to develop a much deeper knowledge of the customer's situation with regard to your industry and your products and services. Figures 5-6 and 5-7 provide some examples of these questions in connection with our pharmaceutical supplier example. Customer value maps, value proposition tables, and question lists enable you to capture the knowledge in people's heads and make it available to everyone who can use it. Or they may reveal blind spots where you need additional research. Either way, they are extremely useful tools.

That said, the questions developed from the value maps must be used skillfully. Inexperienced salespeople may try to use them in a formulaic way, asking the questions as though they were taking a survey. That won't work. In fact, questioning and listening skills are fundamental to most sales training courses. Questions like the ones in these examples are more like conversation starters. They help newer, inexperienced salespeople do what seasoned pros do instinctively. For that reason, strong value propositions and incisive questions provide an excellent basis for training and marketing materials, sales aids, presentation guidelines, and other devices that make salespeople's jobs easier and easier to master.

These templates are meant to convey an idea of what you might accomplish with customer value mapping in your business. The technique has been used successfully in over 70 companies, including long-distance carriers, farms, kitchen cabinet makers, manufacturers, financial institutions, hospitals, and software developers. These templates also show product development and marketing communications people how they can help salespeople sell. They do this by providing an ideal template for helping product developers as well as copywriters and messaging designers to work through the value propositions in depth. Customer value mapping enables them to devise the details of a sales process, such as whom to call on (or promote to), what questions to ask, and what value propositions to offer those individuals, whether in person, in print, or via electronic media. Including value maps in launch kits enables the sales process to be tested and proved prior to launching the product itself. While customer value mapping is hard work, I have never seen a case

FIGURE 5-6
Questions for the Formulation Chemist

Formulation Chemist

Consider what you know, and what you might like to know, about the formulation chemist's objectives, issues, and challenges. Although you may not be able to ask these questions directly, what you might like to know include the following:

- Which projects pose the most challenges to you at this time?
- What kind of requirements and specifications are provided to you for a given project?
- Which departments down the line do your decisions most affect? In what way?
- What factors make creating a formula that is scaleable most difficult?
- What are the most time-consuming aspects of your job?
- Which parts of your job pose the greatest risk to completing projects on time and on budget?
- In your view, what are the most important factors that affect the scalability of a given formulation?
- If we could wave a magic wand and create a new technological innovation in your field, what would it be?
- What is your view of the potential for timed-release coatings to affect your business?
- How does your work impact other departments, such as process engineering, production, and so on?
- What has been your experience with timed-release ingredients (versus other release formulations)?
- How important is gastrointestinal targeting in the projects you are working on right now?
- What patents and technological advantages has the department achieved in the last few years? Who was involved in those developments?
- What is the best way for you and other formulation chemists to stay current with developments in your field?
- How do people go about getting assigned to winning projects?

---

where it didn't significantly elevate the team's insight into the customer. In fact, developing a product or a marketing program without the benefit of customer value mapping strikes me as potentially futile.

PRODUCT VALUE MAPPING

Another type of value map I often help clients develop is called a product value map. It is similar to the feature-and-benefit-style maps that

FIGURE 5-7
Questions for the Process Engineer

Process Engineer

Consider what you know, and what you might like to know, about the process engineer's business. Although you may not be able to ask these questions directly, what you might like to know include the following:

- Which projects are most important to the scale-up department right now? Why?
- What kinds of things cause the most difficulty in scaling up a formula for production? How do you address those challenges?
- How critical is the process equipment to successfully scaling up a formulation?
- What is the protocol for determining when new equipment is needed and for selecting and acquiring that equipment?
- What equipment limitations and capabilities must you consider?
- What has been your experience with timed-release coatings (versus other formulations)?
- If you could wave a magic wand and create a new technological innovation in your field, what would it be? Why?
- What is the one thing the research chemists could do that would make your job easier?
- What might the validation and production departments wish your department could do for them?
- In what ways do you interact with other departments in the company?
- What challenges do you face in dealing with various vendors of production equipment?
- What kind of troubleshooting gives you the most difficulty?
- What aspects of production have the most effect on production efficiency?

---

many marketing and sales functions employ. The format of these maps is quite simple with three columns, one each for "Features," "Benefits," and "So What?" The So What? question prompts you to articulate why the benefits would be important to the prospect. In other words, "What would the prospect try to do that would make that benefit important?" This last question is similar in intent to those derived from customer value maps.

Although this is a simpler kind of map, as with customer value mapping, the exercise of creating it with your team is beneficial. It is helpful for people to explicitly understand what constitutes a feature versus a benefit and to try to articulate the related value propositions for various people in the customer organization.

DEVELOPING QUALIFICATION CRITERIA

With your sales process defined and measurements established (and incorporated into your CRM system), you can measure the quantity of leads, opportunities, and deals with some precision. (We'll discuss measurement in more detail in Chapters 6 and 7.) At this point, the key issue is measuring their *quality*. This resembles measures of the quality of raw materials, work in process, and finished goods in a manufacturing plant. Purchasing brings raw materials of a certain kind into the company, and production adds value to them until the product is ready to ship. Similarly, marketing brings people of a certain kind into the company, and sales adds value to those prospects until they are ready to buy.

All too often, however, salespeople are left to develop their own qualification criteria. This results in highly individualized criteria, which are in neither the company's nor the customers' best interests. Allowing salespeople to decide what type and amount of effort is allocated to which opportunities generates far more inefficiency, waste, and unpredictability than allocating sales efforts on the basis of internally developed, standardized measures of the quality of a lead, prospect, or customer. It's not that salespeople can't qualify their prospects. It's that they can do so only on the basis of their unique view of the marketplace, which is a view through a "soda straw." A preferable process would collect all those individual views, roll them up, and enrich them with those of marketing and service people.

There's far more to qualification than most businesspeople realize. In fact, developing sound qualification criteria is one of the most seriously underused techniques in sales process improvement. In my view, no lead, prospect, or opportunity should be in the sales funnel without an assessment of its quality, measured along three dimensions:

1. *Value to the customer.* What benefits will the customer realize? Cost savings? Increased revenue? Faster cycle time? Improved control?
2. *Value to your company.* What benefits will you realize? Money earned? Improved competitive position? Future revenue growth?
3. *Selling challenge.* What are the barriers to the sale? Do we have coaches in the right departments? Are gatekeepers blocking us? Do we know which issues decision makers will raise in internal discussions?

To illustrate how these concepts work in practice, Figure 5-7 provides a sample qualification assessment that a company in the paper distribution business uses when recruiting distributors.

These characteristics can be set up as statements or questions on hard copy or electronic forms. Then a salesperson can assess each on a scale of, say, 1–5 or -5–5, the scores subtotaled for each characteristic and the subtotals summed to a single score. This simple assessment tool improves sales results in four ways:

1. There's the Hawthorne Effect, in which improvement occurs simply because people know management is monitoring something more closely. The effect, named for the Hawthorne plant of the Western Electric Company where research first documented the phenomenon, is usually temporary, yet it's very common.

2. Improvement occurs anytime you reduce or remove a source of unwanted variation in a system. For instance, with standard criteria, salespeople will pursue fewer unqualified opportunities and more qualified ones. This reduces the variation caused by salespeople individually deciding which opportunities to pursue. Helping salespeople more consistently prioritize their efforts minimizes the time wasted on low-quality opportunities.

   For instance, a manufacturer selling an engineered product though distributors boosted its close ratios using qualification criteria. One major sales cost was time spent by the engineering staff estimating each unique configuration. By asking distributors to fill out a simple qualification form, the company was able to prioritize those engineering efforts more effectively, and the close ratio improved immediately. In addition, the cost of sales declined because fewer engineering hours were spent preparing quotes for low-quality opportunities.

3. Salespeople see what they need to do to increase their chances of closing the sale. For instance, the qualification assessment will sometimes score an opportunity lower than the salesperson would, especially in the early stages of using the new system. When salespeople examine the factors that cause the low scores, they can modify their approach to the opportunity accordingly. Does the prospect really have the kinds of problems we can solve? Do we have coaches in the right departments? Do we need to obtain more in-

FIGURE 5-7

Sample Qualification Assessment for Distributors

Account name:	Salesperson name:
Project name:	Date:

Characteristic	Qualification Issue (1 = Low → 5 = High)	(1 → 5)
Value to them—extent to which they have problems we can solve (product fit)	Focused on our application market	
	Need and value technical support	
	Value our ability to train their people	
	Have gap in their product line	
	Have strong relationships in a growing sector	
	Want to reduce their number of suppliers	
	Value our technology reputation	
	Subtotal:	

Characteristic	Qualification Issue	(1 → 5)
Value to us	They value disciplined forecasting	
	Creditworthiness	
	Annual volume (rating of 1 = $100k/year, 5 = $5 million/year)	
	They value a reduced number of suppliers	
	They handle smaller accounts well	
	Professional and committed to the industry	
	Offer local service and repairs	
	Have value added engineering/integration services	
	Can qualify accounts and opportunities well	
	Subtotal:	

Characteristic	Qualification Issue	(1 → 5)
Selling challenge (relationship qualification)?	Amount of publicly available data we have	
	Degree to which we have an insider's perspective on departmental issues	
	Degree to which we understand what objectives and issues the decision maker(s) might raise at a staff meeting	

FIGURE 5-7

Sample Qualification Assessment for Distributors (continued)

Characteristic	Qualification Issue	(1 → 5)
Alignment with influence	Another (competitive) supplier is aligned with the key decision maker.	
	Someone influential in the company or on the decision maker's team has had a negative experience with us and still holds a grudge.	
	Consultant is making the recommendation.	
	One or more of the individuals with specific expertise to influence this decision is in our camp, and we can articulate why.	
	We have had at least one successful business meeting with the decision maker(s), and this person(s) said things that clearly support us.	
Strength of coach network	Our contacts can articulate the company's objectives, strategies, obstacles, projects, and budget items.	
	We understand the [general manager's/sales manager's] objectives, the manager is a coach, and we grasp their business and personal reasons to share information.	
	Our coaches will encourage us to gain access to senior-level management and guide us to the best way of doing so.	
	Subtotal:	
	Total:	

formation on the upstream or downstream impact of our product? Assessment scores can point toward effective account development strategies and help ensure that salespeople take the right steps to close the deal.

The manufacturer mentioned above experienced this. The engineers saw some funny numbers coming in on the qualification assessments. They discovered that some distributors were afraid that low qualification scores would result in their not getting a good price. (Those distributors believed that if a prospect had a low score, the engineering company wouldn't bother to prepare a quote.) As a result, some distributors were motivated to fudge their assessment scores to try to improve their odds of getting a decent quote and the deal. This created an opportunity for the engineers to sit down with the distributors and discuss things rationally. "Look, Frank," they would say, "do you really think you can close this business if you don't know whether they have the kinds of problems we can solve, or if you don't have coaches in the right departments?" Everyone had assumed that the distributors were implementing good selling practices. The qualification assessment helped to ensure that they were in fact doing so.

4. Institutionalizing the use of assessment criteria permanently elevates the performance of the sales process. Qualification criteria measure the closeability of a given prospect at the beginning *and* end of the sales process, improving sales forecast accuracy, a competitive advantage itself in many industries. Also, changes in qualification criteria scores over time can help you gauge the health of the market. For instance, the scores of prospects for a product early in the product's life cycle differ from those of prospects later in the cycle. This helps companies more accurately predict revenues and profits. For example, in high-tech industries, customers who buy early in the product life cycle typically rate very highly on the what's-in-it-for-them criteria; they have a huge need for the product and will derive tremendous value from it. This usually justifies higher prices and more one-on-one selling than for prospects later in the cycle.

Developing sound qualification criteria and an accurate scoring system delivers other benefits. The national accounts sales force for a major hotel chain found a different, more effective way to segment, and thus prioritize, customers. That improved the salespeople's ability to allocate their time to high-potential accounts, improving revenue. With regard to sales forecasts, comparing the scores of deals that close with those that don't can show you how to improve forecast accuracy. Also, because assessments can change between the salesperson's initial contact and the final score (with the deal won or lost), tracking those changes can reveal salespeople's strengths and weaknesses. Similarly, comparing the scores of prospects produced by various marketing campaigns will indicate their relative effectiveness. Market segments also can be compared. How many times does a company target the sales force toward a market segment only to find no improvement in revenue a year later?

Qualification assessments work like a ship's rudder. You can change the scoring system to motivate certain behavior changes to take place, thus ensuring that decisions are actually carried out. For instance, once you have data to support it, you could specify that only leads meeting certain threshold scores receive in-person sales calls and those below the threshold are referred to a telemarketing unit where they can be nurtured effectively.

SMASHING THE SILOS

While customer value mapping and qualification criteria are not standard Six Sigma tools, they do bring marketing people and salespeople together and enable them to do their jobs better. Whether they are applied in rather sophisticated industries like the ones presented in this chapter or in simpler applications, these tools bring principles of process improvement to marketing and sales by helping people to structure their thinking and measure what is happening. They focus everyone on creating value for the customer and helping them to recognize waste. They help people to define a lead, a prospect, and an opportunity and to measure their quality. And they foster collaboration.

Implementing tools of process improvement like these and others is a participant sport. You can't have the vice president of marketing and the director of communications sit down and draw up their own customer value maps and value propositions. That would defeat the purpose. Moreover, as salespeople will tell you (if you insist on a candid answer), when tools created by other people are handed to them, they usually look them over, place them in a pocket of their briefcase, and leave them there until they buy a new briefcase and discard them.

In creating these tools together, marketing and sales professionals recognize and accept the validity of the tools and of one another's mission. They see what they are all trying to accomplish, and they make the tools as accurate and as useful as they can be. In contrast, most management efforts to align marketing and sales amount to ordering them to "start talking to one another" or "play nicely together." Or management searches in vain for the organizational structure that will somehow force people to work together. What is needed instead are vehicles for getting them to work together and to communicate in productive ways. These tools are those vehicles. The need to use them is driven by the need to get customers to take action, which I'll discuss in more detail in Chapter 6.

Special Resource

For a further explanation of customer value mapping, download Michael's popular article "Customer Value Mapping: A Key to Making Sales Easier." This article contains another example of value mapping in a manufacturing industry. You can find it at *www.salesperformance.com/cvalue.aspx*.

KEY POINTS

- Selling techniques have been evolving for many years, from door-to-door sales to advertisements and direct mail, to radio and TV, and now the Internet.
- Although many people treat marketing, selling, and servicing as separate functions, in fact they are highly interdependent.
- A process approach is the best way of bridging the disconnect that typically exists between marketers and sellers.
- Marketing is anything that makes sales easier. This includes:
  - *Market research*. Identifying profitable market needs
  - *Product development*. Designing products and services that meet those needs
  - *Marketing communications*. Communicating the value of these products
  - *Channel management*. Making them available to those most able and willing to buy them
  - Doing all of the above in the most effective and efficient way possible
- Some powerful tools for translating marketing knowledge into actions include Voice of the Customer, customer value mapping, and appropriate qualification criteria.
- Customer value mapping identifies who within the customer's business is impacted by your products and services, and then
  - defines their objectives, issues, and strategies;
  - identifies which of these your offer could affect;
  - articulates that impact; and
  - determines questions that your salespeople should ask to uncover that value.

- Qualification criteria development provides assessments of the three key dimensions of the relationship with your customers:
  1. Value to them
  2. Value to you
  3. Selling challenge

6

DESIGNING A SALES PROCESS THAT WORKS

Marketing and sales professionals generally see their job as getting prospects into the sales funnel and then pushing them through it until they become customers. As a result, marketing throws as many prospects as possible into the funnel because, according to the numbers game, the more prospects you throw in, the more customers come out. So a lead is often anyone with a pulse. This tends to leave salespeople, who also usually want to maximize the number of prospects, to deal with rejection and objections from prospects while constantly trying to close the sale. (Indeed, some sales training methods take the acronym ABC—Always Be Closing—as their mantra.) This approach to marketing and sales sets up a dynamic in which salespeople ask prospects to take steps in the sales process before the prospects are ready. The prospect's resulting behavior is seen as rejection and resistance, which salespeople must deal with and overcome. That's why sales trainers recommend that salespeople deal with rejection by not taking it personally and overcome resistance by continuing to "sell" in spite of it.

Here's an alternative approach. Instead of viewing everyone as a prospect, doing things that generate resistance, and then trying to overcome that resistance, why not do things to prompt real prospects to identify themselves, then gradually lead them to become customers by giving them what they need to help solve their problems at the various steps of their buying process?

Let me state this bluntly: ABC is nonsense, unless you believe in one-shot, high-pressure selling. Yes, it works for some salespeople on some prospects in some industries. But I'm assuming that you want a sales process that doesn't require high pressure and a never-ending supply of new people to bamboozle. Any sensible person who is asked to do anything before he or she is ready to do it will display resistance, whether it's accepting a marriage proposal, taking up an offer to go rock climbing, or enrolling in an advanced calculus course. Yes, people can be rushed into bad marriages, dangerous pastimes, or confusing courses, but a positive payoff rarely results for anyone.

The process approach—adding value to prospects and customers until they are ready to buy (or not)—doesn't generate resistance. Or, perhaps more accurately, in the context of a process approach resistance ceases to be a useful way of describing prospects' behavior. The question shifts from "How do we deal with rejection and overcome resistance?" to "Are we attracting people who have the kinds of problems we can solve— that is, genuine potential buyers?" and "Are we giving those people what they need/value at the appropriate points in their problem solving/buying process?"

The marketing and sales process exists to attract those people and to give them that value. If the process isn't fulfilling those two purposes, then the process itself is flawed. All too often, however, management fails to see those flaws and instead blames the salespeople.

WHY SALESPEOPLE MAY NOT BE THE PROBLEM!

When I've talked about rigorous prospect qualification criteria (as in Chapter 5), I've often heard sales managers say, "If we use that kind of criteria, we won't have enough prospects."

That is a problem and a serious one. But it is not a sales problem. It may be a problem with the product, price, or definition of the market. It may be a marketing problem, such as ineffective advertising, promotion, or lead generation. But blaming salespeople for a lack of potential buyers is akin to blaming production workers for a lack of raw materials.

Yet many companies see a lack of prospects as something salespeople can fix. That's understandable. In fact, you could design a valid sales process in which salespeople generate leads, convert poorly qualified into strongly qualified prospects, and work with sales opportunities in various ways until they close. Early-stage companies often have salespeople (usually the founders themselves) who "do it all," as do many small companies and professional firms. Their deal flow may come from past relationships. Their ability to convert prospects may come from their vast knowledge, experience, and track record. Yet unless they can clone themselves, this business model is not scalable.

The same problem often exists when senior executives say, in effect, "Prospecting is the salesperson's problem, and they should be able to handle it." Yet the sales forces of many companies who take this position struggle to find enough qualified opportunities, which means that this approach may ignore a potentially serious problem.

The marketing function exists to make selling easier, and it does so in three main ways:

1. Engaging in the design of overall sales and marketing processes and monitoring their performance
2. Generating leads, the raw materials for salespeople to convert into customers
3. Automating any part of the sales process that can be automated

In this chapter, we'll look at how these functions are executed. First, however, let's recognize that failure to do these things—designing the process in the first place, lead generation, or appropriate automation—is not a sales problem but a marketing problem. Then there are product problems, pricing problems, and so on. Yet because salespeople enjoy a challenge and tend to see sales as an exercise in overcoming resistance, they often accept blame and even blame themselves when they can't launch a new product, crack a new market, or just bring in more business. However, if they are working in a broken sales process, they are neither responsible for the problem nor positioned to fix it.

Who is responsible for fixing it? Who is positioned to fix it?

Why management, of course.

Let's start by looking at a sales process that really works.

HOW A HOMEBUILDER BECAME NUMBER ONE

Here's an example of a sales process in which marketing and sales each do what they are supposed to be doing and which, as a result, adds maximum value for customers and for the company. It shows how well a company's marketing and sales process can be linked to its production function. It also demonstrates the Lean concept of adding value for the customer as well as the practice of matching your sales process to the buyer's journey, which I mentioned in Chapter 3.

Linking the Production and the Sales Processes

Bellevue, Washington, homebuilder Quadrant Homes has revolutionized itself since 1998, when it started scheduling production of homes before they were sold and offering these homes at attractive prices and with specific move-in dates. This strategy did away with the "spec house" approach, which can leave a builder with inventory that may not match customers' demands, and gave its customers a reliable date for moving into their new home. To make this change, Quadrant took a Lean approach to production *and* to marketing and selling.

As part of this effort, Quadrant decided to establish an integrated system of marketing, selling, and production. This is still not the norm in the homebuilding industry, although more and more builders are moving in this direction. Indeed, even when houses are built to order, after the contract is signed many builders send customers around to various stores and suppliers to select from a limited set of color schemes, flooring materials, lighting fixtures, and appliances. This creates delays, difficulty, and frustration for all parties while adding no value for customers.

After a customer has visited one of Quadrant's new home communities and selected a lot and the sales representative has guided the home buyer through the choices of exterior and interior finishings and household appliances, the order is scheduled for construction. It takes a mere 54 working days from scheduling to completion. Customers experience a predictable building process instead of the stop-and-start frenzy of most construction endeavors. The design of this sales process makes sales easier for both Quadrant and its customers, so let's examine it in detail.

How Selling on a Schedule Makes Money

In 1998, at the beginning of its transition to Lean, Quadrant asked its sales force to sell one home per day, a target that the company was able to raise to two per day in 1999, three per day in 2001, and four per day in 2002. In 2004, the company reached a rate of six homes per day (the ultimate goal is nine per day). This daily sales schedule generates two interrelated benefits:

1. It enables the company to "pull" materials and labor at a predictable rate that lowers costs and improves quality.
2. The lower costs enable the company to build large homes at extremely competitive prices, ensuring a steady flow of customers.

Has it worked? As noted in Chapter 3, Quadrant has become the number one homebuilder in Washington, was voted "Best Company to Work For" by *Washington CEO* magazine in June 2004, and enjoys referral rate four times the national average for homebuilders.

Consider the four steps Quadrant took in its Lean approach:

1. It looked at what customers valued: high square footage and quality at a competitive price, with minimal hassle and a predictable construction process (and move-in date).
2. It streamlined both the production process and the sales process—and added value for customers—by offering one-stop shopping in a permanent showroom, featuring a large, online selection of floor plans and finishing options.
3. It achieved an even, predictable workflow by scheduling a set number of sales and housing starts per day, which increased by one per day in most years to reach six per day in seven years.
4. It knew that to build large, high-quality homes at competitive prices, they had to streamline the process of sourcing materials, which they did by offering the customer a huge choice in the controlled environment of the Web site and the showroom under a salesperson's guidance.

This example shows the value-laden, win-win nature of process improvement at its best. The company gives customers a large choice and high quality while streamlining and increasing its control over its sales and production processes. True, by opting for steady growth at a set number of homes sold and started per day, the company might have missed a few sales during periods of peak demand. However, in the long run that steady strategy helps the company avoid the roller-coaster pattern of most home construction operations. As a result, Quadrant gradually ramped up to become the state's largest homebuilder, able to both generate and capitalize on demand.

Lean and Six Sigma's focus on value to customers brings discipline to the pursuit of customer focus. One of the sad truths about business is that many companies (and many individuals within those companies) view the customer as someone else's problem or at best a necessary evil. We've all been at the receiving end of this when we've been kept waiting for the privilege of paying for something, when we've been astonished at a company representative's lack of concern about our problem, when we've stopped doing business with a company and nobody even bothered to call us to ask why. Conversely, managers in those same companies are wondering how to get enough profitable customers.

Process improvement, with its definitions and measures of value, can help management put a process or parts of a process in place that will keep everyone honest when it comes to adding value for customers. Value for customers stops being a slogan on the cafeteria wall and starts becoming a way of life.

HERE'S HOW TO LEAN YOUR SALES AND MARKETING OPERATION

As the case of Quadrant Homes shows, applying Lean in marketing and sales can greatly benefit both sellers and buyers. The fundamental idea behind Lean manufacturing, as pioneered by Toyota and documented by Womack and Jones in *The Machine that Changed the World: The Story of Lean Production,* comes down to doing more with less while giving customers exactly what they want. The six basic steps of Lean, which has become widely accepted in supply-chain management, are to

1. implement basic 5S housekeeping principles;
2. identify customer value and map the value stream;

3. remove waste, which is anything the customer would not pay for;
4. reduce batches to the smallest possible size and ensure smooth handoffs and production flows;
5. have customers "pull" the product rather than pushing it on them (key to just-in-time methods); and
6. pursue perfection by continually reducing errors, mistakes, and waste.

A word about 5S. It stands for Sort, Straighten, Sweep, Schedule, and Sustain. It is a set of housekeeping principles that enables rank-and-file production workers to achieve a cleaner, safer, more productive environment where they know exactly what is expected of them. In the sense of being organized and disciplined, the spirit of 5S applies directly to sales and marketing. It implies that people's workspaces, including their computer screens, files, and databases, are thought out and structured in a way that makes it easy for them to do their work. It also implies consistency in how sales and marketing people pursue leads, opportunities, and deals and respond to variables.

Managers have dramatically improved production operations by re-thinking their design from the customer's perspective and asking questions such as, "What value is created for customers by maintaining huge inventories in remote areas of the plant?" and "How does the customer benefit from our having complex machinery that requires extensive setup and maintenance?" The answers to both are "Very little," which is why most Lean manufacturers discontinue such practices. Once manu-facturers saw that certain methods detracted from customer value *and* cost them money, they redesigned their processes to match customer de-mand, with short lead times and minimal work in process. Often the re-designed processes utilized crosstrained employees and simpler machines with lower costs. These companies typically reduced overall costs while better serving customers, thus increasing the value added by the process for both the company and the customer. We now need to do the same in our marketing and sales processes.

Lean Lessons That Are Creating Wealth in Companies Today

How do Lean principles apply to marketing and selling? Quadrant Homes looked at the usual homebuying process and asked: Where's the value in sending customers around to various suppliers? Where's the value in limiting their choices? Where's the value in unpredictable completion dates? How can we maximize what customers value most in the house itself—high square-footage and distinctive features—while maintaining competitive prices and healthy profits? How can we make the most of the prospects we generate while squeezing waste, including wasted time for us and the customer, out of our sales (and production) process?

Another approach is to consider what your marketing and sales professionals do—advertising and promoting products, writing collateral material and tending the Web site, conducting sales presentations and preparing proposals, and delivering service and support—and then ask: Which of these activities would be valuable enough that a customer would actually be willing to pay for them (with time or money)?

The harder it is for you to answer this question, the more your marketing and sales functions will benefit from Lean. Why would a customer want to read your company's advertisements? Is a visit from one of your salespeople valuable enough that a customer would pay for the privilege? People buy products and services because they believe they'll receive value from them. But it costs them time and other resources to deal with your company during their buyer's journey. So what value do they derive from your marketing and selling activities? In other words, you have to map your value to your customers and prospects clearly enough that you can help them to

- Become aware and educated about causes of their problems
- Decide which problem to address and when to address it
- Identify alternatives for solving the problem
- Understand the pros and cons of the alternative solutions, including the financial ramifications
- Assess the risks and the upstream and downstream effects of various solutions
- Trust the information on which they are basing their decision

- Reconcile the opinions and agendas of other people in the company
- Implement the solution in a smooth and timely manner

Those are just a few of the questions that customers need help answering. They value that help and they welcome, rather than resist, companies that provide it. Your marketing and sales process creates value by providing that help. Delivering that value transforms the work of your marketing and sales professionals from a numbers game and a battle of wills to an exercise in finding and helping people with the problems that your company solves.

If not enough people have those problems, your company has to find other problems to solve. This doesn't mean that you should move into an entirely new business—although it may. Usually it means looking upstream, downstream, and elsewhere in your customer organizations or in new markets for problems that you can solve or developing better methods of addressing those you now solve. If no such problems or methods exist and you want to stay in the buggy whip or vacuum tube business, then the size of your diminishing market is a fact best faced squarely.

TO MAKE MILLIONS, MIMIC DIRECT MARKETING!

Okay, I'm kidding with that headline—half kidding, that is. However, the direct response model from the world of direct marketing, together with Lean practices and giving customers what they need on their buyer's journey, can help you design a sales process that adds value for customers and for your company. Before discussing ways of matching your sales process to the buyer's journey, I want to spend a moment discussing the direct response model.

The direct response model comes from the world of direct marketing, mainly direct mail, although television has proven quite effective in consumer sales. (Try though we might, who can forget the Ginsu Knife?) And of course, the Internet represents the newest direct response sales medium. Essentially, the direct response model requests an action on the part of the customer. That action may be placing an order or requesting a bit of information, a discount coupon, a complimentary analysis, a sales call, a newsletter, or membership in a group. (The latter has been used very effectively by pharmaceutical companies, which create affinity groups of people on certain medications or suffering specific maladies.)

Effective marketing and selling recognizes that people act in their self-interest. The best marketing and selling prompts people to act—to read something and respond, to accept or return a phone call, to allow a salesperson to visit, to consider a proposal, to place an order—by appealing to their self-interest, which means offering something of value to them. Good copywriters (and salespeople) influence their prospects by speaking to *their* needs and demonstrating what's in it for *them*. Yes, they sometimes get carried away and make outlandish promises in their headlines or copy. But they know they must speak to readers in terms of their needs and interests. Professional sales copywriters eschew product-focused explanations of capabilities in favor of vivid descriptions of the results you'll get and the way you'll feel—if you act now! They write that way because it generates a better response from their target market.

The direct response model is predicated on exactly that—direct response. You put the marketing piece out there, whether it's a letter via snail mail or a sales page at your Web site, and you either get or don't get the desired response. You don't worry about things like "impact," "recall," or "awareness." You worry about whether you got enough good leads or sold enough product to justify the cost of the mailing, the Web page, or the campaign. You either did or didn't. It's a very disciplined world, this direct response business.

Direct marketers have been measuring their sales processes and testing various ways of prompting prospects to act for decades. Indeed, direct mail outfits routinely conduct split tests, in which they change a feature—envelope color, message on the envelope, headlines, sales copy, configurations of the offer, prices, and so on—and then measure the results against those of a control mailing. If the tested version beats the control, it becomes the new control and the one to beat.

These methods work. If you've ever wondered why so many direct mail packages contain "involvement pieces," such as little stamps that you stick in a box on the subscription request form, it's because they pull in more sales for that product than do mailings without involvement pieces. These marketers have proven that enough grown men and women would rather move a sticker that says "Yes!" from a piece of paper to a little card than to check off a box that says "Yes!" (And they don't have to look for a pen.)

The point is that many businesspeople who view junk mail as an unsophisticated backwater could benefit tremendously from the tests and improvements that direct marketers implement.

Obviously, the words and phrases that cause thousands of people to order diet pills would not motivate CFOs to buy Treasury services. However, the same principles apply. You will find the message that matches your market systematically through experimentation and measurement. (Sounds a little like DMAIC, doesn't it?)

Keep the direct response model in mind when you design your sales process. Always ask yourself: What action can we ask the prospect to take to receive the value we offer at this point? These actions are not at all mysterious. They are simply what we ask prospects to do: visit our Web site, request our white paper, opt in for a newsletter, take our phone call, see our salesperson, share information with us, or request a quote. How these actions are prompted, sequenced, and measured will determine the success of your sales process.

CREATING A SALES PROCESS THAT CREATES VALUE

Good marketing and selling is inherently Lean because it focuses on customers and their needs. Poor marketing and selling isn't Lean. Instead, it generates waste by targeting the wrong prospects, allocating resources to things customers don't care about, and engaging in activities that don't help them in their buying process. Many companies leave decisions about prospects, resources, and activities up to individual marketing and sales staff. These companies need a sales process that guides marketing and salespeople's decisions in these areas. One way to begin to design such a process is to identify the steps that your customers take on their buyer's journey and then develop sales tactics to assist them at each step. This process is depicted generically in Figure 6-1.

Recall that buyers make a journey from being unaware of the problem to acknowledging the pain it causes or can cause to defining their needs until they make the purchase and engage the seller to solve the problem. As Figure 6-1 indicates, the steps in the buyer's journey correspond to the finding and winning parts of the sales process. (The keeping part comes after that journey is complete.) At each step, the seller

FIGURE 6-1

Matching Sales Tactics to the Buyer's Journey

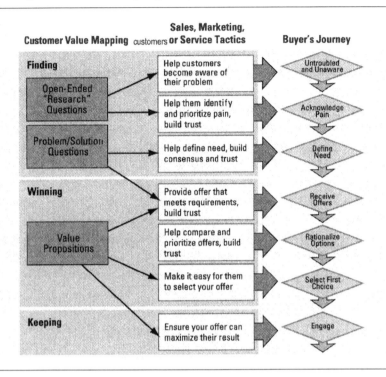

can supply something of value to the buyer: information, expertise, analysis, a free bonus, a guarantee, whatever the buyer needs. You start designing a sales process that buyers will follow by identifying that "something of value" at each step.

How? As the figure also indicates, customer value mapping, covered in Chapter 5, will indicate many of these things. In the finding stage, you must help the prospect become aware of the problem, understand the potential pain it could cause, give priority to the problem, and start defining the prospect's needs vis-à-vis the problem. All of this leads the seller to qualify that prospect (or not). The questions that you develop in customer value mapping enable you to engage the prospect in these steps. Similarly, in the winning stage the buyer considers offers and options, selects an option, and makes the purchase. The value propositions that you developed in the customer value mapping exercise enable you to engage the prospect in these steps.

Figure 6-1 reflects a generic buyer's journey and generic selling tactics. Every company must define that journey and those tactics for its own customers and organization and thereby develop its unique sales process. Then marketing and sales can match its questions and value propositions to the value that buyers seek at each stage. You may find it useful to compare the sales process diagram in Figure 6-1 to the sales process map back in Figure 3-1. The selling tactics in Figure 6-1 are analogs for the process steps in Figure 3-1. Each buyer's stage in Figure 6-1 is actually the intended outcome of the related process step. In other words, you want the prospect to take the next step. Not all of these outcomes are easy to measure. Therefore, it's useful to define some measurable action the buyer must take to indicate they should be classified as a lead, such as making an inquiry, opting in to a newsletter, requesting a video, or paying a small fee of some kind. Then a salesperson can qualify the lead according to the company's qualification criteria, which should be as clear and action-oriented as possible.

Matching the Sales Process to the Buyer's Journey

As I've noted, marketing often aims to generate the highest possible *quantity* of leads, then leaves sorting them out to salespeople. Those salespeople are then evaluated on the amount of sales activity they engage in and how much they sell. So they try to make as many sales calls and close as many deals as possible. Dealing with the rejection and overcoming the resistance that this engenders becomes the biggest part of their job. Indeed, the fact that most companies focus on their own activities and goals rather than on buyers' interests and needs helps to create a situation in which sellers and buyers repel one another.

This situation is portrayed in Figure 6-2, which depicts the divergent interests of buyers and sellers. Over the course of their journey, buyers traverse a path that begins with their being untroubled and unaware to their acknowledging the problem and the attendant pain to defining their need for a solution and so on until they finally engage a supplier to solve the problem. Meanwhile, in their quest for revenue, sellers focus on activities and goals such as prospecting, scheduling sales calls, making presentations, conducting demos, generating proposals, and taking orders.

FIGURE 6-2

Buyers Are from Venus, Sellers Are from Mars

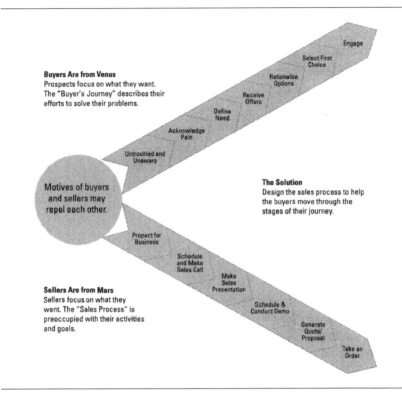

Buyers Are from Venus
Prospects focus on what they want.
The "Buyer's Journey" describes their
efforts to solve their problems.

Untroubled and Unaware
Acknowledge Pain
Define Need
Receive Offers
Rationalize Options
Select First Choice
Engage

Motives of buyers
and sellers may
repel each other.

The Solution
Design the sales process to help
the buyers move through the
stages of their journey.

Sellers Are from Mars
Sellers focus on what they
want. The "Sales Process" is
preoccupied with their activities
and goals.

Prospect for Business
Schedule and Make Sales Call
Make Sales Presentation
Schedule & Conduct Demo
Generate Quote/Proposal
Take an Order

The sellers' preoccupation with activities and goals distracts them from, and can even blind them to, the buyers' interests and needs. This sets up the dynamic of buyers resisting sellers' activities and thwarting their goals, and of sellers attempting to overcome resistance while failing to meet buyers' real needs.

To do away with this dynamic and to design a sales process that creates value for customers, you must understand your buyers' journey. Then you can match your process of finding, gaining, and keeping customers with that journey. You must deliver value at each step of the journey, which means helping prospects and customers through the steps of becoming aware of the problem, acknowledging the problem and the pain, defining their need for a solution, and so on.

FIGURE 6-3
Helping Prospects Solve Problems

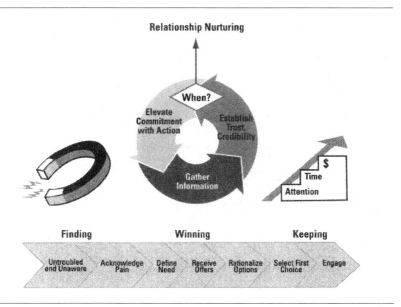

As Figure 6-3 shows, this process is a continual, cyclical one of establishing trust and building credibility, gathering information on the prospect's situation, and prompting the prospect to elevate his or her commitment by taking an action—moving to the next step in both the buyer's journey and your sales process.

ADDING STEPS CAN MAKE THE JOURNEY EASIER

At every stage of your sales process, you want to do something that will enhance trust, increase your store of information, and elicit an action that elevates the prospect's level of commitment. What about prospects who don't want to elevate their commitment? We'll get to them in a minute.

First, however, consider the approach taken by an enterprise software company with a $100,000 product. This company found it difficult to close sales, mainly because it hadn't clearly defined the steps its

FIGURE 6-4
Delivering Value at Every Step of the Process

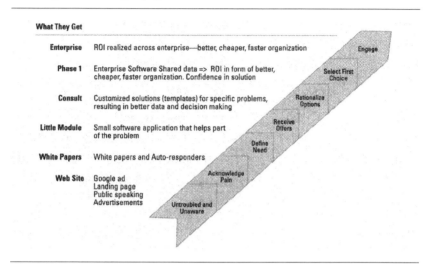

What They Get	
Enterprise	ROI realized across enterprise—better, cheaper, faster organization
Phase 1	Enterprise Software Shared data => ROI in form of better, cheaper, faster organization. Confidence in solution
Consult	Customized solutions (templates) for specific problems, resulting in better data and decision making
Little Module	Small software application that helps part of the problem
White Papers	White papers and Auto-responders
Web Site	Google ad Landing page Public speaking Advertisements

(Diagram labels: Engage, Select First Choice, Rationalize Options, Receive Offers, Define Need, Acknowledge Pain, Untroubled and Unaware)

customers had to take on their buyer's journey. In effect, the company was asking prospects to take steps that were just too large. As Figure 6-4 shows, the answer was to establish additional smaller steps—and to deliver something of value to prospects at each of those steps. So they studied their buyers' journey and then used Google ads, public speaking, and a Web site to make people aware of the problem this company could solve. The company used white papers to help potential customers see the effects and acknowledge the pain of not solving the problem. It developed a minimodule of the software to help people solve part of their problem and better define their needs.

All during their process, the company is building trust and credibility, gathering information, and asking the prospect to take a baby step on their buyer's journey and in the sales process. To access the white paper, prospects must give contact information. To obtain a 30-day free trial of the minimodule, they must provide information about their business and contemplated applications. To keep the minimodule beyond the trial period, they must pay a small fee. The contacts developed by this low-risk approach provided opportunities for the company's professional sales and service people to learn about these customers' businesses. From there, they could build relationships that sometimes provided an inside track to proposing small (and not so small) consulting engagements. These engagements enabled the company to learn more about a prospect's business problems at higher levels, so it could propose customized solutions that incorporated its enterprise software applications. At every step, the company nurtures a relationship based on give-and-take and exchanges of value and information. In the process, the prospect benefits and learns more about the solution and the potential return on investment.

This software company's experience is not atypical. In many situations, particularly in complex, high-ticket, business-to-business sales, a company can benefit its customers and its salespeople by introducing additional, smaller steps into the sales process. Just be sure that each step requires a measurable action on the customer's part.

One key difference between this approach and the one often found even in today's well-run sales organizations is that most outfits leave the designing of baby steps, qualifying, and follow-up to the discretion of individual salespeople rather than designing and implementing a set of proven approaches. Again, management's job is to design the sales process; the salespeople's job is to implement it.

MAXIMIZE YOUR ROI BY NURTURING THE RIGHT RELATIONSHIPS

Now, what about prospects who just aren't ready to take the next step? If they are truly not qualified and never will be, they should be routed out of the sales process. If they are simply not ready but might be cultivated or might become qualified in the future, they should be routed to a continuing contact function. That function ensures that they remain aware of developments that might increase their pain and of your ability to reduce or remove that pain. This is a marketing function, one best fulfilled by newsletters, articles, white papers and executive bulletins, seminars, speaking engagements, membership groups, and other low-maintenance (often media-based) methods.

Note that this approach is low maintenance, not no maintenance. You have to invest in staying in touch, but if you are working with high-quality leads (because you are using sound qualification criteria), then the investment will usually be justified. And when it isn't, you will have metrics that will tell you why. These tactics put your sales process miles ahead of that of the average company and probably way ahead of where you are now.

You might think of this nurturing function as one of maintaining the prospect at a comfortable stage in the sales process. You continue to maintain and nurture the relationship via "drip" or "wave" marketing to stay on the prospect's radar. Occasionally, you prompt action toward the next step. This way, you can involve salespeople only when the prospect is worth their time and effort. When that time comes, you'll have earned the salespeople's attention and respect.

The many benefits of this approach include the following:

- Most companies don't have to invest a lot of money or do a lot of things differently to implement this kind of sales process. Nothing is revolutionary about Web sites, newsletters, white papers, membership groups, trial offers, complimentary situation analyses, and so on. Indeed, many people point out that Six Sigma itself is not all that new. What's new is the purpose and discipline, and the management environment, in which these tools are applied.

- Selling is no longer a battle of wills pitched around resistance but a way of guiding prospects through a process that benefits them. If prospects see no benefit, then you are working with the wrong prospects, or you are giving them the wrong information or support at the wrong time—or giving them less than your competitors. If so, you must change your process to address those shortcomings.

- Continuing to nurture prospects who aren't ready to buy minimizes the number of times your company educates prospects only to lose them to competitors. Such situations infuriate salespeople, who feel betrayed when they've worked with a prospect for weeks or months, only to lose the sale and later learn that the customer bought elsewhere. Instead of blaming the prospect, however, it's more useful to assess our possible role in this outcome. Did we try to force the prospect to take the next step? Did we understand the prospect's problem and craft a true solution? Did we fail to establish trust? Prospects don't buy elsewhere to spite salespeople. They do so because they see it as being in their own interest. Yes, maybe they used your salesperson and then bought from his or her brother-in-law, but that's not the way to bet. Brothers-in-law just aren't that popular.

- By examining the buyer's journey, you can better determine what marketing should be doing to make sales easier and what sales should be doing to help marketing automate the sales process. Most companies make decisions about marketing on the basis of cost rather than value to customers. (Can we afford new product literature? Are enhancements to the Web site in the budget?) Or they base decisions on some desired level or frequency of activity. (When did we last do new product literature? What's the Webmaster done for us lately?) I am not saying that costs are of no concern. I am saying that management must establish mechanisms by which salespeople tell marketing what's going on in the field so that marketing can adjust its part of the sales process in light of costs and potential value. Those leads were great? Terrific, we know where to get more of them. Prospects think the Web site's hard to navigate? Let's learn what they want, then make those changes. It takes us too long to generate proposals? We can streamline that process. You can't do everything at once, but you can at least know what needs doing and set priorities based on projected costs and benefits.

Transferring sales activities to marketing by means of automation is key to designing an effective sales process, so let's look at this more closely.

SELLING ON AUTOPILOT

In the long run, and often much sooner, transforming sales activities into marketing activities by means of automation will pay off. Automation, like marketing itself, is a "wholesale" rather than "retail" proposition. Indeed, a standard definition says that marketing is directed toward groups while selling is done one-on-one. Here's a great rule of thumb from Jeff Watts, vice president of account services for Creata Promotion: "If something happens five times in sales, it has to become part of marketing." Any part of the sales process that can be automated should be automated, and salespeople should be doing the parts that cannot be automated. That's an excellent rule of thumb for sales process design. Here are some others:

- When you design a sales process, think about ways to get prospects to "raise their hands" and identify themselves. That way, you don't have to look as hard for them.
- Marketing can potentially supply a huge amount of *useful* information to customers in order to save salespeople's time and labor. To be useful, information must be supplied when the prospects need it, which is when they'll pay attention to it. For example, explaining the workings of your regulatory compliance software to a senior executive who hasn't given a thought to regulatory compliance, let alone to the risks of noncompliance, won't be useful. But if you can save your salespeople time and effort by automating the explanation or showing how it works, perhaps by means of a demo, then you need only deliver it when the prospect is ready.
- Look at ways to automate parts of the sales process that *the customer* must now deal with—research, needs assessment, comparison shopping, and so on. These customer activities can create bottlenecks that seem to be out of your control but may lie within it. For instance, Quadrant Homes saw an opportunity when it realized that most builders sent customers around to various suppliers to choose their décor and finishes. By making those features accessible online and having salespeople guide their customers, Quadrant greased the skids that led to sales. By the way, to help customers with comparison shopping, some companies' Web sites offer links to competitors' sites. (Talk about a trust builder!)

Again, Jeff Watts says: "Marketing's goal is to automate as much of your sales process as possible. I want salespeople to go into a meeting with the first hour already taken care of. I want the prospect to know who they are, know what they sell, and have a positive opinion of them." In that first hour and at every other point in the sales process, potential buyers need help, information, expertise, and solutions. Success is a matter of putting the sales and marketing teams together to help buyers at those points in the buyer's journey. In general, the greater the extent to which help, information, expertise, and solutions can be delivered automatically, the better and more cost effective the process.

One caveat, however, warrants mention: do not isolate your salespeople from prospects and customers. In some cases, building "touches" into the process helps salespeople to develop relationships with prospects.

For example, consider the enterprise software company's approach described earlier in this chapter. In today's busy and demanding commercial (and consumer) environment, touch may be less necessary than it once was; few prospects have much time to schmooze with salespeople. However, those who value personal touches should by all means receive them and with e-mail, teleconferencing, and videoconferencing, those touches can be executed in highly cost-effective ways.

Finally, please know that designing an effective sales process becomes far easier and more precise if you first develop customer value maps, sales process maps, and solid qualification criteria for your business. Customer value maps and qualification criteria were covered in Chapter 5; sales process maps are covered in the next section. All of these tools usually lead marketing and sales teams to valuable insights, tactics, and strategies without formal Six Sigma or Lean training.

ENERGIZE, DON'T ALIENATE: CONDUCTING SALES PROCESS MAPPING SESSIONS

When done correctly, sales process mapping is another vehicle for bringing people from marketing and sales (and service) together productively. I say "when done correctly," because traditional process mapping focuses on "how work is done," and this focus is not needed, at least at first. Instead, sales and marketing teams need to begin with "why work is done." Sales process mapping, which I introduced in Chapter 3, prompts teams to step back from the daily details of their job to examine the context of their work, often for the first time. In sales process mapping, they ask questions such as, "Why are we doing things the way we do?" and "What is the value to the customer?" In a sales and marketing environment, much of the detailed work often associated with traditional process mapping is a waste of time unless you have defined that context first.

In a typical sales process mapping effort, people write out their usual work activities on sticky notes, then organize those notes into categories. In doing so, they come to see the ways in which they define those categories and the underlying premises they bring to their job. For instance, some teams come up with categories like "dealing with the plant" and "entertaining" as key elements of their sales process. With proper guidance, they have a terrific opportunity to discuss why they selected the categories they did and the implications of that thinking. They also have an opportunity to adopt value to the customer as their organizing principle. Inevitably, when teams see this alternative, they start developing a simpler, stronger process map that they all see as relevant.

Useful sales process maps clearly define outputs in terms of measurable actions that customers take. Those action-level outputs will enable you to measure the quantity of production. The examples of sales process mapping in Chapter 3 (Figures 3-1 through 3-3) illustrate these points, and although every company must develop its sales process map in light of its own product, customers, and industry, these examples provide useful guidelines.

By the way, it's essential to prepare sales process maps before implementing sales training or CRM software. Doing so enables you to understand your sales process as a production system rather than as selling skills or a standard sequence of steps. This distinction is crucial: the sales process is not the same as "what salespeople do." The sales process describes the entire system for finding, gaining, and keeping customers. Sales training and CRM software support the overall sales process, but *they are not the sales process itself.* That fact can be obscured by the use of the term *sales process* by many sales training and CRM companies. What sales training and CRM software are composed of are not sales processes but rather, respectively, selling skills and sales information management systems. (At various points in this book, you may have wondered how sales process improvement would affect such tools as sales training and CRM and such activities as product development and pricing. Chapter 7 answers this question and describes how to get more from these and other tools and activities.)

Few companies are in a position to build their sales processes from scratch according to the principles provided in this chapter. Instead, they must work with the systems and people they have and adjust specific activities and subprocesses to improve results incrementally. Still, understanding how your company's ideal sales process would work is useful. That way, people see the direction that the organization must take and can identify helpful incremental changes. As more data is gathered, the bottlenecks and waste at various stages become apparent. As these are addressed, your sales funnel can flow increasingly faster, and you can, in the true spirit of process improvement, continually make your marketing and sales process more effective and efficient.

CREATING A SALES PROCESS THAT YOUR SALESPEOPLE WILL FOLLOW

What about salespeople and their infamous resistance to new methods? Let's start dealing with that now, although we'll take the subject up again in the next two chapters.

If your sales process truly creates value for customers, then those customers will follow that process. Sales resistance will be minimal, and when you have added enough value, prospects will take the next step. I realize that this description may strike some readers as an idealized portrait of the hurly-burly of selling. Not so, because none of this is easy. Finding good prospects, learning their needs, establishing trust, delivering value, and leading them to the next step are all difficult. However, this approach is easier and more effective than slapdash, unmeasurable, badly designed, push-them-through-the-funnel sales methods. If your sales process assists buyers on their journey, they will, with guidance and encouragement from skilled salespeople, follow that process.

When salespeople see that the process works, that prospects display less resistance, and that marketing is making selling easier, they start coming on board. In other words, when you design a sales process that your customers will follow, your salespeople will follow it, too. Will they initially resist the new process? Of course. Think back to the case of HBSC, where salespeople fought tooth and claw to hang on to trading accounts that were actually losing money for the bank. However, the payoff—more money than they had ever made, with half as many accounts—came in a matter of months.

Here's another short but illustrative example. In a business-to-business sales situation, a company's marketing campaigns produced leads at a highly variable rate. A volume of hundreds would slow to a trickle between campaigns. The company's salespeople would cherry pick their leads, working only the biggest opportunities. As a result, many of the smaller leads were never followed up on. The sales manager suspected, but couldn't prove, what was happening. The company was not making its business plan, which called for penetrating smaller accounts as well as the larger ones.

So management started to regulate the flow of leads a bit differently. Instead of distributing leads automatically as they came in, the leads were parceled out five to seven at a time to each salesperson. "Go work those leads," the sales manager would say, "and when you have feedback on them and are ready for more, I'll give you more." Did the salespeople like this? No. Did they express their displeasure? Yes. But they also understood the business rationale and accepted it—and developed the smaller opportunities along with the larger ones.

The result? The close ratio improved by 27 percent. Revenue per head count and profitability increased as well. This outcome may seem counterintuitive, unless you have lived in a manufacturing facility that implemented Lean production. In that case, you will have seen what can happen when production schedules are evened out.

Here is one more example of salespeople initially resisting a change in the sales process that they later came to embrace. The field salespeople at a manufacturer of high-tech testing equipment were used to getting a volume of relatively low-quality leads every month. A new vice president of marketing began using a software system to manage marketing campaigns more closely. She set up a three-tiered rating system for her call center agents and changed the process so that only A-quality leads were forwarded to salespeople. She then encouraged the call center agents to work harder to cultivate and qualify their B and C leads.

The volume of leads received by the field sales force plummeted, causing much concern. However, within a few months field salespeople saw a 30 percent lift in the close ratio on those A leads. At that point, their attitude changed. They learned to put their best efforts into every lead, because every lead was high quality. With the ability to analyze the performance of her lists and campaigns, the new marketing director was able to pare down less productive lists, refine the company's approaches, and help the inside sales team to do a better job of cultivating B and C leads. A year later, they were delivering more A leads to the field salespeople as well.

The key consideration in changing any part of a sales process is that it ultimately must help salespeople sell. Like most people, salespeople initially resist change, but also like most people, when they see the positive effects of the change, they drop their resistance. Indeed, after seeing the benefits, they actually would refuse to return to the former method.

IMPROVING A PROCESS FOR SELLING THROUGH CHANNEL PARTNERS

Sales process mapping can help you understand virtually any sales process. The tool applies especially well in business-to-business sales but will work with any multistep method of finding, gaining, and keeping customers. Sales process maps also work well for companies that sell through channel partners, such as dealers, wholesalers, retailers, and original equipment manufacturers (OEMs). Such selling situations are particularly challenging, because partners carry multiple product lines and juggle competing claims on their resources amid myriad considerations.

In a very real sense, when you sell through channel partners, you are selling to two sequential sets of customers—the partners and the end users—and must generate demand in both of those groups. From the end user's perspective, each channel partner must add more value than cost. Likewise, from the channel partner's perspective, a profitable process must exist for creating and servicing demand.

Sales process maps will help you analyze your sales process, your process for recruiting and working with channel partners, and even your partners' sales process. The power of these maps is demonstrated by the case of WaterFurnace Industries, a Fort Wayne, Indiana, manufacturer of innovative heating and air-conditioning systems under the WaterFurnace brand. These units heat and cool a house by means of thermal-exchange technology, which uses heat from the ground in place of fossil fuel or electricity. When I met Bruce Ritchey, the CEO, the marketing department had recently completed a promotion that had generated thousands of leads. These had been sent to WaterFurnace's dealers, never to be seen again. Given this frustrating experience, Bruce assembled his management team for a two-day session devoted to mapping the company's sales processes and identifying potential ways to improve sales.

Like many companies, WaterFurnace depends heavily on its network of dealers. The company's telesales efforts could bring in orders, but unless the customer, typically someone building a new home, lived in an area where WaterFurnace had an active dealer, the unit couldn't be installed and supported. These dealers, who did not stock inventory as a distributor ordinarily would, were almost always heating, ventilation, and air conditioning [HVAC] contractors. While a few dealers were successfully promoting the WaterFurnace line, the vast majority were not,

FIGURE 6-5
Consumer Sales Process Map

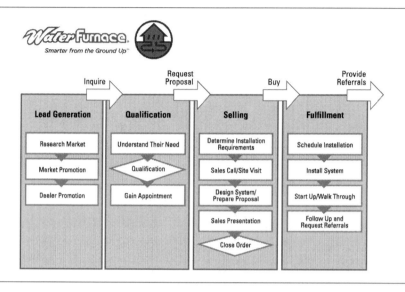

but instead were just passively fielding one or two orders a year. The service technicians at those dealers didn't understand the line, and their ignorance generated excessive customer service problems for WaterFurnace when they tried to service a unit or install one for the rare new customer. Yet a few of the dealers did quite well, selling millions of dollars of the line year after year. Why were some dealers so successful while others actually cost WaterFurnace money?

Sales process mapping proved quite illuminating. Figure 6-5 shows the first of the sales process maps that WaterFurnace completed—the consumer sales process map, which depicts the way orders come in from homeowners.

The first step in selling to homeowners was to qualify them as prospects. This meant determining their needs. If they met certain standards (such as an achievable deadline, the ability to pay, and a nearby dealer), they were offered an appointment with a salesperson, typically a representative from a local HVAC contractor. The sales call included a walk through the customer's site to explain the technical requirements and to ask the customer about his or her needs, intentions, and time frame. The dealer would prepare a proposal, hopefully resulting in an order, and

FIGURE 6-6
Dealer Sales Process Map

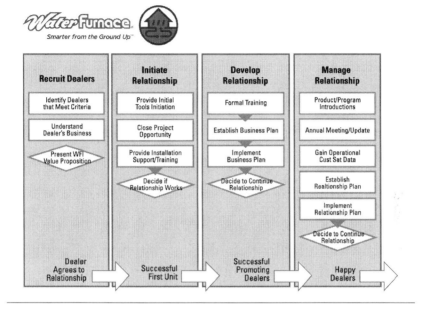

then scheduled the installation. If all went well, the salesperson was back on the premises collecting a testimonial and referrals a few months later.

As Figure 6-5 shows, the sales process is defined by the customer's actions. In areas where WaterFurnace had a local office, the company could conceivably perform all the functions shown in the map itself. Yet to grow at its desired rate and to capitalize on the full potential of this technology, WaterFurnace had to tap some of the thousands of outfits already selling, installing, and supporting HVAC systems. Recruiting and growing these channel partners had proven extremely challenging.

The WaterFurnace team mapped the dealer's sales process next, as shown in Figure 6-6. Note that WaterFurnace uses this process to recruit channel partners; this is *not* the partner's sales process for customers. As the figure shows, because WaterFurnace's sales process for channel partners aims to recruit new partners and manage existing ones, it focuses far less on managing specific orders coming through those partners. In other words, this process basically assumes that partners are originating and handling orders properly. However, as evidenced by the infrequent sales and frequent customer service problems at some part-

FIGURE 6-7

Combined Consumer and Dealer Sales Process Map

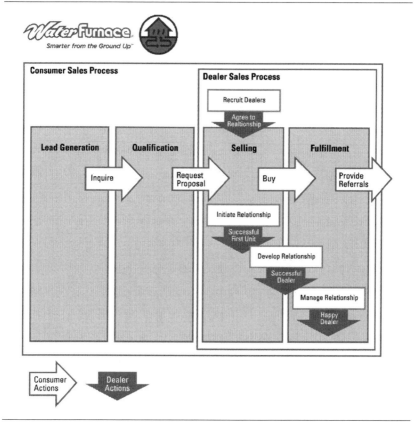

ners, not all signed-up partners were doing a good job of originating and handling orders.

During this analysis, WaterFurnace discovered that its consumer sales process and its partner sales process were complementary. In fact, they intersected, as shown in Figure 6-7, which combines the two sales processes shown in Figures 6-5 and 6-6 and strips them down to their essentials.

As a practical matter, WaterFurnace was able to generate and qualify leads but needed a local channel partner to sell, install, and service the unit. As Figure 6-7 shows, by linking the hand-off of customers with the recruitment and development of partners, the two processes could be combined to the benefit of WaterFurnace, the channel partner, and the customer.

In developing these maps, several people on the team saw a potential solution to WaterFurnace's problem. They knew that once a new dealer became comfortable with WaterFurnace products, acquired testimonials and references, and developed technicians who knew the products, the dealer's salespeople became enthusiastic about the line. It is, after all, low cost, low maintenance, and environmentally friendly. Those enthusiastic channel partners were the moneymakers for WaterFurnace and had been for years. Unfortunately, the vast majority of the channel partners Water-Furnace had signed up had never gotten comfortable. WaterFurnace realized that instead of spreading its support and incoming orders over numerous low-volume operators, it should select a few new dealers at a time, the best ones in a given market. It needed to give them not one or two leads but several orders and then provide superb support.

WaterFurnace decided to spend whatever it took to ensure those few dealers got comfortable and became enthusiastic about WaterFurnace. This meant changing its approach to investing in dealer relationships. Instead of playing the numbers game of signing up as many dealers as possible, WaterFurnace picked its best shots and worked to develop mutually profitable relationships. Both WaterFurnace and the channel partners saw more business as a result, and customers benefited from improved installation and support.

This was a radical change but one that CEO Bruce Ritchey championed. It was also the kind of breakthrough that happens only when you bring the right people together and pose the right questions. That's a key point: Simply getting WaterFurnace executives, marketing people, and sales technicians in the same room for a structured discussion about who does what helped tremendously. That discussion clarified what Water-Furnace represented to various dealers and to the customer, financially and otherwise. With that information on the table, the thinking about both the process and what the company should measure evolved.

Note that although this was not a formal, five-step Six Sigma project, it definitely helped WaterFurnace improve its sales process. As Bruce noted, "The mapping session we did made an impact and led us to a full commitment to roll out Lean throughout the office, sales, order fulfillment, and engineering process. We are using Six Sigma charts to track warranty and react to field quality issues more quickly than ever." Indeed, WaterFurnace was not ready for a formal Six Sigma deployment in marketing and sales, especially one that would subject people to classes on

DMAIC and statistical process measurement. It was, however, ready to map, discuss, and improve its sales process vis-à-vis their channel partners and customers by thinking through its processes in an objective, disciplined manner with tools that fostered such an approach.

VALUE STREAM MAPPING: SEEING THE FOREST *AND* THE TREES

A company usually improves its sales process in stages. A sensible first step is to organize marketing, selling, and servicing activities into a high-level sales process map. With that map, managers readily see that their processes can be made simpler and more effective by redesigning activities around value to the customer as shown in the WaterFurnace process maps. Then the company can begin implementing continuous improvement with value stream mapping and DMAIC.

WaterFurnace began its continuous improvement journey by rolling out a Lean manufacturing initiative throughout the company, including the sales force. During that effort, several people saw opportunities to improve parts of the sales process. For instance, Jill Miller, a respected territory manager who participated in the Lean training program, prepared a value stream map on the process for creating special quotes. Quoting is part of the Selling phase of the company's Consumer Sales Process Map (a subprocess under Design System/Prepare Proposal in Figure 6-5). WaterFurnace dealers sometimes encounter special pricing situations when preparing quotes for commercial projects or projects with unusual requirements. The process for generating this pricing is cumbersome and time consuming. In addition to working through complex configuration rules and getting a manager's approval, the dealer must document the quote so it is valid from commercial, technical, and contractual perspectives. Making customers wait during this process can lose the sale.

The original process at WaterFurnace was fraught with time-consuming problems and handoffs, as Jill saw when she listed the steps for creating a special quote. (See Figure 6-8.)

Next, Jill prepared a value stream map that depicted the overall time required for the process, identified value-added versus non-value-added steps, and opportunities for improvement (shown in the starbursts at the top of Figure 6-9).

FIGURE 6-8

Current State Process List for Special Quote Process

Process Step	Time Elapsed
Dealer meets with prospect and discovers need for special quote	1 hr
Phone call to territory manager	2 hrs
Return call to dealer	2 hrs
Handwrite order in phone log	10 mins
Wait time to get back to office	8 hrs
Type and send e-mail approval to regional manager	10 mins
Wait time for reply	1 day
Type up quote (look up all part numbers/pricing/account numbers—item by item)	3 hrs
Fax/e-mail quote to dealer	10 mins

Jill's calculations showed that the entire process required some 2,430 minutes, of which only 10 percent (or 4 hours and 10 minutes) were value-added time. Her goals for improving the process were to eliminate the requirement for management approval by standardizing guidelines for special pricing and to improve the quotation form itself by using a computerized form. (Another member of the sales force had programmed model numbers as well as pricing and configuration rules into a spreadsheet.) Jill proposed that all members of the sales force use this new form.

As shown in Figure 6-10, Jill's Future State Value Stream Map, the benefits of this new approach were clear. The total amount of process time decreased 66 percent to only 820 minutes, with significantly reduced opportunities for errors thanks to the computerized spreadsheet.

While rolling out a change like this requires salespeople to buy in and be trained in using the new form, the benefits to them will be readily apparent. Approaches such as this hold tremendous potential for salespeople, whose questions about "the way things are done around here" are often dismissed by managers as routine complaints. Process maps and value stream maps give everyone the same system-oriented perspective so they can see what's going on and then change the ways in which they work to reduce waste, make selling easier, and improve customer value.

FIGURE 6-9

Value Stream Map of Quotation Process

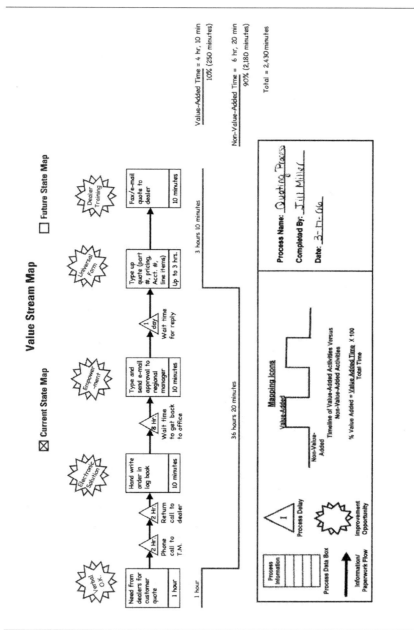

FIGURE 6-10

Future State Value Stream Map for Quote Process

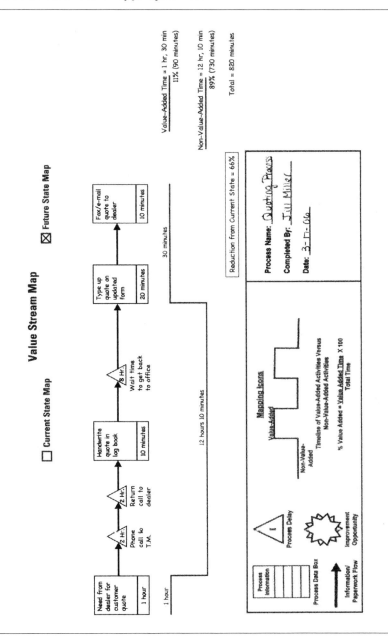

SALES PROCESS IMPROVEMENT WORKS
AND SO DOES SIX SIGMA IN SALES

Although many companies don't start their sales process improvement efforts with formal Six Sigma efforts, some companies do—and it works. For example a large camera and optical supplies distribution company experienced dramatic cash flow, productivity, and gross margin increases through a series of Six Sigma projects. Before implementing Six Sigma, its concept of customer focus encouraged branch managers to stock the lines they thought their customers preferred in each location. However, this occurred in the absence of information systems that could provide product movement and margin data by week and by store. Once that information became available, it contradicted what many longtime managers expected.

Serious study of the data drove a series of DMAIC projects. A project on buying patterns showed that customer requirements for certain kinds of industrial cameras could be addressed by stocking 5 models of cameras instead of 30, enabling the company to increase its gross margin on those lines. Other projects reorganized the store inventory around customers' needs rather than vendors' categories. The number of purchasing processes plummeted from 22 to 5, and the company streamlined distribution operations by reducing the number of hub locations. Responsibility for stocking decisions was removed from branch store managers (over their objections) and replaced by automated stocking decisions. The company reduced the number of distinct products from 90,000 to 30,000. Some of these changes were gut wrenching for the people involved, but they were undertaken on the basis of sound DMAIC procedure.

The result? In the first year, inventory was reduced by $14 million. Overall sales grew by double digits. Gross margin rose by two percentage points—almost unheard of in the distribution industry.

Sales process improvement, including sales process mapping and Six Sigma, definitely applies in channel partner environments. It can be used with processes for bringing on and supporting channel partners of all kinds, including resellers, brokers, and even retailers. Moreover, it can be used to map channel partners' sales processes, so that you can understand them, suggest improvements or useful metrics for them, or create your own metrics for evaluating them.

As noted, few companies have an opportunity to design their sales process from scratch, and few marketing and sales functions are ready for an all-out formal Six Sigma deployment (the characteristics and implications of which I'll discuss in Chapter 8). However, as this chapter and its examples and those throughout this book demonstrate, sales process improvement can occur incrementally. You can change the way you conduct and use Voice of the Customer and incorporate what you learn into your sales process. You can examine your prospects and customers in terms of the value they seek and build steps into your sales process that will deliver that value. You can change the way you find and qualify leads, and you can work in new ways with channel partners.

Moreover, by applying principles and practices of sales process improvement, you can get more than ever from vendor offerings such as CRM, sales training, and advertising as well as from activities such as product development and product and service pricing. Chapter 7 shows how to go about this.

KEY POINTS

- You can improve sales results by designing your sales process around steps that create value for prospects and prompt them to take some kind of action.
- Measuring the actions customers take enables you to apply Six Sigma methods to your sales process.
- Value to customers is evidenced by the actions customers take, so a Lean approach focuses analysis on the actions you can get the

customer to take rather than on the actions salespeople or marketing people take.

- Direct marketing practitioners use split testing to experiment with alternative approaches (such as headlines, sales copy, or offers) to determine which ones draw the best response from customers.
- Prospects attempt to solve their problems by searching for the right product or service in a process known as "the buyer's journey." Your sales results will improve if you design your sales process to help your prospects through that journey.
- To gain people's cooperation, sales process mapping should focus on the "whys" of the activities, which are to create value for the customer. Only then will you be able to define the correct "hows" within in the process.
- Market channels, such as independent representatives, dealers, or distributors, are actually another category of customer. For a sales process to work in a market channel, both that process and the product must benefit the market channel as well as the end user.

7

MAKING MARKETING AND SALES DECISIONS THAT GET RESULTS

Like every other function in an organization, marketing and sales employ various more or less standard initiatives to improve performance. I've labeled some of these, such as sales training and CRM systems, "the usual fixes," which is what they are when employed without careful consideration. Other efforts, such as advertising and product development, are ongoing activities in most sizable companies. All these play an important role in marketing and sales functions when managed as processes. However, the approach to them—and their implementation—will differ from what they would be without a process approach.

This chapter examines how these initiatives can achieve better results by taking a process approach to both the decision to use them and ways of using them. Not all of the examples in this chapter are based on Six Sigma projects, although they could be. If someone somewhere has not already implemented all of these as some kind of Six Sigma project, they will soon.

INFORMATION INFORMS

The basis for informed decisions is *inform*ation (data on activities, results, and cause and effect in the process). When you set out to improve your sales process, you will probably lack the right information. That lack of data precludes formal statistical analysis, and generating enough useful data for such analysis can represent a serious hurdle. Yet defining your process correctly (aligning your activities around value to the customer and clarifying your operating definitions) can create a clearer context for decision making even when data is scant.

Instead of gathering information, however, managers often make decisions about expensive initiatives on the basis of what they think they know without actually validating their assumptions. They act on gut instinct or intuition or in response to a vendor's presentation rather than on the basis of measurement, analysis, and rigorous assessment of needs. Please know that I grasp the rationale for these decisions. It's not irrational to say, "Our salespeople aren't closing enough deals. They need more training," or "When our salespeople call, people haven't heard of us. We need more advertising." But while not irrational, such statements hardly represent decisions based on cause and effect. Therefore, luck plays a role in whether these decisions have the intended result.

Sooner or later, to make truly informed decisions about marketing and sales initiatives, you'll need to measure the quantity and the quality of the leads, opportunities, and deals. That information will best position you to determine the cause and the solution for a problem, whether it's sales training, a CRM system, or any other initiative, and whether the fix worked. As you'll see in this chapter, however, other, less rigorous data can also improve your decisions immeasurably—or, I should say, measurably.

Consider the ways in which doctors diagnose illnesses. Sophisticated tools such as MRIs, CAT scans, and tests for antigens enable physicians to detect and treat illnesses more effectively than ever. If a physician prescribed a complex treatment for a patient who happens to be a sales manager without such tests, that manager would question the doctor's competence. Yet that manager will recommend an expensive initiative for a sales function on the basis of what amounts to a hunch.

Again, most sales managers see an increase in sales as the only result that matters. Yes, that's the ultimate goal of most marketing and sales initiatives. But sales results can be truly and permanently improved only when the flawed part of a sales process is fixed. Such improvement requires definition, measurement, and analysis.

To show how to achieve real improvement, this chapter examines ways of employing the following marketing and sales initiatives and activities in the context of a process approach:

- Sales training
- CRM systems
- Market research
- Advertising, promotion, and merchandising
- Pricing
- Product development
- Customer service and support
- Sales force management

How Does a Process Approach Help?

A process approach helps managers employ these initiatives by:

- Providing baseline measures of the process that point to the root causes of problems
- Calculating the expected ROI of decisions, based on expected costs and benefits as calculated from reliable data about sales operations. (Recall the sales operating audit in Chapter 3.)
- Enabling managers to measure—or at least consider—the productive capacity of the marketing and sales process, or of subprocesses, before and after a decision
- Showing how a decision about one area of the sales process might affect other areas (if you increase the flow of leads, you may need to increase sales' ability to handle them—and service's ability to service the resulting customers)

As I've pointed out, most companies lack both the data and measurements that deliver these benefits *and* the operating definitions needed to identify what needs measuring. For instance, you need to define the sales cycle—when it begins and when it ends—and the close ratio (particularly the denominator) before you can reduce the former and increase the latter. I'll discuss the hurdles that lack of data presents and how to overcome them in Chapter 8.

For now, let's just get this on the table: To make truly informed decisions about initiatives and efforts, managers need solid data and measurements on at least some of the interim stages of their sales process and the results. Unfortunately, most of them don't have it.

A WORD TO VENDORS, CONSULTANTS, AND THEIR CUSTOMERS AND CLIENTS

I've talked with numerous vendors of training, CRM systems, consulting services, and other means of improving sales results. Many of these folks would like to document the value of what they do for their clients. But most of those clients struggle to measure only gross data such as upticks or downticks in leads and sales (and have little ability to correlate the two). Further, they may not understand the value of spending time and money establishing processes or measurement. Worse, many senior executives resist looking at marketing and sales as a process without realizing it.

For instance, representatives from CRM firms have told me that few clients want even to think about redesigning their sales processes. The CRM firms would prefer to have an actual process in place, because it would increase their systems' chances of success. Yet without saying it, most clients simply assume "the salespeople will do what we tell them to. They'll just have to enter the data and do these administrative tasks. They can't be *that* busy. Then we can look at modifying this thing later." CRM firms find such statements hard to counter, especially when argument might get in the way of a making a sale.

However, unless they get lucky, only clients who see their problems in process terms can consistently choose the right solution, whether sales training, a CRM system, or a new pricing policy. Further, as pointed out by David Mansfield of Raptor International, a database mining software company, decision-making systems such as management scorecards, dashboards, or artificial intelligence strategies that depend on analyzing marketing and CRM databases are useless (at best) if their "data" has not been developed with proper operational definitions and if they have not been validated appropriately.

Clients who define their sales processes properly can measure activities and production results, exposing vendors and consultants whose products and services are ineffective. Likewise, this measurement will bolster the case for vendors and consultants with effective products and services. Indeed, the ability to measure the positive effects and ROI of an initiative by using the process approaches described in this book is essential to knowing where and when to apply these interventions and knowing whether they have worked and are worthwhile.

Let's look at individual initiatives and activities in this light.

SALES TRAINING: WHAT IS IT GOOD FOR?

The problem isn't that sales training doesn't work. It does, when used properly. The major vendors and many smaller firms generally provide solid training in basic selling skills such as establishing rapport, questioning, listening, and moving the sale along. Many firms also offer training in complex, multiple approval sales and national account management and are willing to tailor their training to their clients' needs.

The problem is that clients don't always understand their needs, and you know why: they haven't taken a process approach to assessing those needs. Salespeople may be doing so many different things that it is difficult to tell what is going on, much less which skills are the most crucial. When salespeople themselves become the bottleneck, everyone is dependent on them, which makes the situation even worse.

If companies don't know which part of the sales process isn't working, they don't know whether training is the solution. Moreover, if training is the solution, they often can't determine what specific training is needed. They rely on "tribal knowledge" or the judgment of the training department. As a result, even if salespeople receive useful training but they go back to work in a sales process that doesn't reward their new skills or is fundamentally flawed, any gains will be short-lived. Here are some examples of what happens:

- A sales manager had her call center agents trained in sophisticated selling techniques based on her notions about how selling would be changing in their markets. But her people rarely encountered the kind of prospect that required the consultative approach they'd been taught. When they returned to the field, the salespeople were expected to produce improved results within the same business environment as before, with the same mix of prospects. Predictably, they reverted to their previous sales methods.

- Another company trained its salespeople in a more consultative sales approach that took more time per sales call. Yet management insisted that the salespeople make the same number of sales calls per week as they had using the old approach, without giving the new approach time to prove or not prove itself. As a result, these salespeople also reverted to their former methods.

- A shipping services company trained salespeople in cold-calling techniques with the aim of generating more leads. However, the company was in a saturated market, and the issue was not finding leads. A business either needs shipping services or it doesn't; salespeople can't get the prospect to start shipping if shipping isn't part of its business. The problem was not a lack of leads or ways of finding them; the problem was the company's cost structure and its uncompetitive prices. The time and money spent on training in cold calling would have been better spent on developing ways to deal with costs and pricing or on ways of taking accounts from competitors, if possible.

Sales training, even when supported by mandates, cannot exert more force over salespeople's behavior than the sales process does, nor is training designed to address flaws in the sales process. The implicit assumption in most approaches to sales training is that the sales process doesn't need fixing but the salespeople do. In fact, sales managers tend to think of what salespeople do—qualifying leads, calling on prospects, conducting sales presentations, and so on—as the sales process, so that's what they try to change while leaving the actual sales process in place. Sales managers want to change the way people work but not how the process works. In contrast, process improvement seeks to change the process to change the way people work. That's why a process approach to sales is so important. You use *the process* to determine the behaviors that generate sales and to reward and reinforce those behaviors.

So if the problem is poor lead generation or salespeople trying to handle too many things, then sales training is not the solution. But does training people to cope with a broken process make sense? Wouldn't just fixing the process make more sense? Also, many salespeople who succeed in a broken sales process leave when they realize they can make more money with less hassle elsewhere.

Don't get me wrong. Training is important and necessary, and many salespeople don't get enough of it. Yet training is often poorly matched to the real needs of the company, or it is not reinforced by middle managers or not aligned with salespeople's performance or compensation requirements. In these circumstances, neither the trainers nor the trainees can connect its effects to the business process, so no accountability or cost justification can occur. Even with anecdotal evidence of the training's value, that positive impact can get lost if salespeople are so tied up in other duties, they don't have time or motivation to implement what they have learned. Training becomes just another of the many things executives may or may not need to implement to achieve their objectives. That's one reason training budgets get cut at the first sign of economic clouds.

Getting the Most from Sales Training

To get the most from sales training, it must demonstrably provide the skills salespeople need to be more effective with their customers. Once the process is defined correctly, both defining these skills and observing the effect of having or not having them becomes easier.

Basic skills, such as researching customers' businesses, asking good questions, and listening skills all can be taught and tied to steps and stages of the sales process. Their absence or their presence can be measured by the results achieved by the salesperson over time. More advanced techniques and business acumen can be measured the same way. The key is having a means of assessing the quality and quantity of leads, opportunities, and deals in addition to providing salespeople with the appropriate skills to deal with them.

Yet getting people's behaviors to change is never easy. Consider just some job pressures as the following from the salesperson's perspective:

- *Perceptions.* How immediate supervisors and peers think the job should be done and their expectations for performance.
- *Deal flow.* The quantity of leads, opportunities, and deals.

- *Quality.* How easily will those leads, opportunities, and deals convert?
- *Message to market match.* How effective are the company's messages in its communications and collateral materials? Do these augment or detract from the salesperson's ability to close?
- *Systems.* These can be estimating, credit, order history, CRM, or numerous other internal systems, often designed to make things easier for someone inside the company, not to help the customer or the salesperson.
- *Compensation and reward policies.* These may not be aligned with customer requirements, market needs, or even management expectations.
- *Reporting.* The data that management reviews on activities and results may not be aligned with customer requirements or market needs.

Improving sales skills requires self-awareness and even risk taking. It is best accomplished with the assistance of knowledgeable sales trainers who can provide the safe environment and coaching that people need when learning new behaviors. Yet salespeople's behavior ultimately will be influenced by far more than what goes on in a class. That's why good sales training focuses on more than just what salespeople do. It also focuses on sales managers, who must provide leadership and reinforcement of the new behaviors, and on elements such as aligning the CRM systems and marketing messages with the new skills. If these initiatives are accompanied by a sound production measurement system, the results will be better and more visible.

Affecting human behavior in an organization is inherently complex. Management must design its organization so as to create enough value for all parties involved. Trade-offs sometimes will be necessary, and sometimes the market will dictate that some parties get more or less value than they desire. However, the context in which people function, including the sales process they are expected to implement, needs to be constructed carefully, brick by brick, with a clear eye toward the buyer's journey and the actions you want buyers to take.

Many Six Sigma and non–Six Sigma companies have done work along these lines. They have defined broad campaigns incorporating descriptions of the skills and competencies that affect their sales processes, and they have implemented training programs that elevated skill levels and established a common language in the sales organization. These programs have often had a positive result, if only because they are improvements over the bedlam that existed before. Management must establish processes for their people so that better methods and behaviors can be identified, communicated, practiced, and rewarded. To the extent that sales training helps in this endeavor, it can be extremely valuable, as long as you work with a vendor who grasps your sales process and the role that your salespeople play in it.

CRM SYSTEMS: VISION VERSUS REALITY

Two disciplines, customer relationship management and information management, coupled—and gave birth to CRM systems. Their offspring seemed promising at first, and that promise has not died. But it has not been fulfilled, either.

The promise was to make useful information on customers available to everyone who could use it to do a better job. Salespeople could track everything from the names of customers' kids to the products purchased from other divisions. Marketing people would know everything from the source of a lead to next year's sales forecast. Management could measure everything from salespeople's productivity to account profitability. Many companies have adopted CRM systems, often at great expense, but most of these benefits haven't been realized. On the surface, this shortfall appears to be an information technology failure or another case of over-hyped technology. Look beyond the surface, however, and those simplistic explanations fade.

A while back, I conducted a Six Sigma conference workshop on using CRM systems to measure the sales process. Of the 30 companies represented in the room, only 1 claimed a return on their investment in its CRM system. None used their systems for forecasting. Most felt they were years away from emulating the use of computers in manufacturing operations. In one exercise, we reviewed a CRM system sales forecast report. The report covered expected revenue and projected close dates, and estimated a "percent chance of closing." It included no process or quality measures of leads and sales opportunities, instead focusing only on results. I had expected that someone in the room—from this self-selected sample interested in applying Six Sigma in sales—would have experimented with a more process-oriented approach to CRM, one where the quantity and quality (and yield) of earlier stages of sales production were measured. Unfortunately, no one had done so.

With apologies to Shakespeare: The fault lies not in our systems but in ourselves. In theory there's nothing wrong, and a lot right, about CRM systems. I'm all for data on customers. The question is which data and for what purpose? I'm voting for applications that help salespeople sell, meaning those from which "process-type" data (in addition to the current "customer-type" data) can be drawn to help manage the process.

CRM firms identified a real need—the need for better marketing and sales data available to multiple parties on a single platform—and the market responded. Unfortunately, the data turned out to be the usual data that managers use to manage salespeople (rather than process data). Salespeople saw that any data they provided could and would be used against them *and* that much of the data would have to come from them. Data entry tops the annual list of Things Salespeople Hate, placing ahead of filling out expense reports, sitting in traffic, and arriving at hotels after room service and the bar have closed for the night. So sales managers tell them to enter the data, or get data-entry clerks to populate the system, and then tell the salespeople to maintain the data. And then they don't. On top of which, key data from other areas generally isn't getting into the system. Data on products purchased from other divisions? Nope. Data on deliveries? Sorry. On service calls? Not in there. On problems open or resolved? Afraid not. Nor are sources of leads, previous company experience, and quality metrics in there. Of what use is a system that lacks the data that people require from the system?

The goal of a CRM system should be to make salespeople more productive. Many CRM systems have been bought and sold on this premise. Yet few organizations took the time to understand what salespeople were really doing—and should be doing—and how to help them do it. Note that relatively few CRM initiatives were driven by the sales function. Most represented an attempt by marketing or finance to get more "control" over customer data and salespeople. This approach more or less doomed these efforts for lack of salespeople's cooperation and lack of customer focus. Still, CRM systems can potentially play a central role in managing sales as a process.

Delivering on the Promise

We are still a good way from perfect CRM systems, and a process approach won't change that overnight. However, the following guidelines will help you maximize the effectiveness of a CRM system:

- Recognize that a CRM system is *not* a sales process. Many companies and vendors miss this point. The sales process is what the company does to find, gain, and keep customers. Most CRM software assumes that the "sales system" in the CRM software (based on contact information, record of sales calls, schedule of appointments, outcomes of follow-up, and so on) is the sales process. It isn't.
- Adapt the CRM system to the organization's sales process rather than the other way around. Why? Because the sales process must be built around helping customers through the buyer's journey, not around a system defined by CRM software (even if that system is flexible).
- Ensure that the CRM system interfaces with other systems, particularly order placement and delivery systems. A CRM system must be the system, or be integrated with the systems, for handling leads, tracking quotes and proposals, pricing products or jobs, and recording service calls. That way it can pinpoint bottlenecks, track the results of activities, provide customer data for product development, and so on. Too often, companies lack a practical, cost-effective way of getting data into the CRM system and making them accessible to all who need it.
- Design a CRM system that helps salespeople sell and that is easy for salespeople to use. They must get at least as much, and preferably more, out of it as they put into it. Otherwise, why will they use it? Because they are told to? That's not the way people, especially salespeople, work. Many a failed CRM initiative proves it.
- Incorporate consistent operating definitions into the CRM system. For example, an "opportunity" for one salesperson should mean the same to another salesperson. Otherwise, close ratios and other measurements are meaningless.

The point is to focus your company on the customer by aligning your sales process to the buyer's journey. This probably will change the work that sales and marketing people do, making it more directly relevant to customers and providing more immediate feedback. CRM systems should be designed to support and facilitate the work people do to help customers buy. They should make sales easier by helping to qualify and clarify the value to the customer, and they should remove administrative burdens (rather than add to them).

In the same way that production management systems in manufacturing plants help account for production inventory, CRM systems should help account for the inventory of marketing and selling. Just as operational definitions, bills of material, and routings define value added in manufacturing, so should operational definitions, sales processes, value maps, and qualifying criteria define value added in sales. CRM software is the ideal vehicle for tracking data about the quantity and quality of leads and their conversions to opportunities and deals.

Unfortunately, most CRM software designs contain major false assumptions about the sales process. For one thing, they assume you can assign an arbitrary percent chance of close to each stage in the sales process instead of using the system to help measure the actual yield of that stage. In fact, the entire concept of multiplying the dollar value of an opportunity by the percent chance of close is bunk, and the data this math produces is terribly misleading. I know this idea comes from deep in the culture of salespeople, but it is unfortunate nonsense. If ever there was a way to blind managers to what is actually happening in their field organizations, this is it. Real process improvement is based on clear-eyed measurement of the actual yield of the steps of the process, irrespective of the operator's (salesperson's) "gut feel."

Instead, the systems should address the real issues salespeople face. Of course these would vary dramatically by industry and company, but here are some examples. Suppose the systems actually helped salespeople make better decisions about how to spend their time by capturing the specific qualities of their opportunities (such as by automating the qualification criteria assessments from Chapter 5) and providing customized sales tools according to that data? Further, suppose they automated the means of nurturing the relationship over time by providing useful information in the form of free courses taken by e-mail or scheduling industry experts to call from time to time with valuable information. Or suppose they made it easy to provide immediate pricing alternatives while in the customer's office instead of having to go back to headquarters for approval days or weeks later. Of course, various companies are doing many of these things now, though they might not be included in a traditional CRM project. The point is to find where the production bottleneck is in your organization, then *change the process* so as to expand it. Make sales easier, and salespeople will follow you anywhere. Do it with computer systems, and you have the added benefit of being able to measure it.

Companies using CRM systems are in a position to use data the way baseball teams use batting averages and other statistics. Once these measurements are credible to its salespeople, the organization can begin establishing performance metrics that also are credible to them. The value of this kind of alignment is obviously huge.

Most CRM systems take monitoring salespeople's behavior as their major goal, without really helping them sell. That's why salespeople often don't support them. To help salespeople sell, the system must give them information that will help them sell. Solid customer and contact information is a minimum requirement. They also need information on the customer's needs, experience with your company (including service experience), current stage and next step in the sales process, and quality metrics. The better the information on activities and results, the better for sales, marketing, and management. Although these conditions are rarely in place, the basic issues are the benefits of change and the cost of change. When the benefits clearly justify the cost of making the necessary managerial, behavioral, and technology changes, then CRM systems will realize their full potential.

MARKET RESEARCH: WHAT DO YOU KNOW?

I discussed Voice of the Customer in Chapters 4 and 5, so I need not belabor the role of market research—or perhaps I should say *customer* research—in making process improvements. I would only point out several caveats.

The distinction between research into markets—demographics, psychographics, and income patterns—and research into customer needs is important. Demographics and psychographics have their place, but relatively little of that data is as actionable as research into customers' needs, problems, and views of your product. When you know what customers will take action to address, how they've tried to solve a problem, what it costs them to use those methods, what they're trying to accomplish, and what they really want from a company like yours, then you have actionable information. Think about your customer value map, value propositions, and qualification criteria (as explained in Chapters 5 and 6) and get information that will help you develop and refine those tools.

Also, avoid market research designed to justify a position that management has already adopted. The term *researcher bias* doesn't begin to describe this phenomenon. Voice of the Customer is aptly named: it's the customer's voice, not management ventriloquism.

Always consider the source—and purpose and objectivity—of any purchased market research data, including industry studies and surveys. Some extremely robust forecasts have never come true, thanks to faulty samples, leading questions, bad analysis, or data that wasn't verified or in some cases even factual. I worked with a company that launched a new plastics controller, and we relied on lists that corporate had sent us on facilities with injection molding machines. More than 40 percent of the data was dead wrong. The lists included plants that had been closed for years and some that never had housed the machinery, while the same lists also missed prime targets. In general, as often happens, the lists substantially overestimated the size of the market.

Before fielding any market research, ask a few salespeople to review the study design and survey questionnaire and to make suggestions. Test every survey with a sample of the intended respondents. Yes, this is standard operating procedure, but it warrants mention. Remember, too, you should know at the outset what you will do with the information.

Be sure to mine the data you already have on your customers' behavior. When well designed, your processes for finding, gaining, and keeping customers should provide reams of valuable "market research" data. This data will include information on the sources of your best prospects and customers, on value propositions that work and don't work, on prospects' quality scores and the outcome of related sales efforts, on who purchased which products to solve what problems, and on account profitability. With this information, you may well be able to reduce the amount of market research you do and more precisely target that which you do choose to do.

All of that said, sometimes even customers don't know what they want. The most striking case of this remains Citibank's market research in the late 1970s, which revealed that customers would *never* use ATMs. Respondents said they needed the interaction with the tellers, they would never trust their money to machines, they feared robberies (understandable, given New York City in the 1970s), and so on. Did they lie? No, they just didn't grasp the concept, let alone how they would use ATMs. Fortunately for Citibank and the rest of us, the bank pushed forward with ATMs anyway.

Discovering real needs and real solutions to real problems—whether customers know they have them or not—represents the most reliable way to create value. This goes double when it comes to new product development.

PRODUCT DEVELOPMENT: WHAT'S NEW?

Some 80 percent of all new products fail within six months or fall significantly short of their profit forecast, according to *How Customers Think* by Gerald Zaltman. While the use of customer data in product development is improving, it is, from a process improvement perspective, in its childhood. A Forrester Research Study of 50 of the 100 largest U.S. companies found that only 10 percent listed product development as a user of customer data. While that figure strikes me as understated, I'd like to focus on which data is being collected and how it's being used in product development.

Many major manufacturing companies, including Motorola, General Electric, 3M, and Johnson & Johnson, now apply formal Six Sigma to product development. Some apply it to certain parts of the process, such as product definition and design, others to the entire process. All use it mainly to minimize new product failures, a particularly frustrating and costly form of variation. Yet even most Six Sigma approaches to product development emphasize the engineering and technical aspects of products or focus on validating product features with their customers. "Validating features with your customers assumes that you have the right features," warns Sheila Mello, managing partner at Product Development Consulting, Inc.

Applying Six Sigma to product development is an entire subdiscipline of Six Sigma. Indeed, the quality movement sprang up to improve product quality by improving the processes that produce products. Major Six Sigma product development methodologies include Design for Six Sigma (DFSS) and DMADV (*de mad' vee*, define requirements, measure performance, analyze relationships, design solutions, verify functionality), among others.

However, from the marketing and sales standpoint, the tasks in applying Six Sigma to product development would be to:

- Obtain input, usually via Voice of the Customer, on customer requirements for a product and its performance (often stated as CTQs—customer requirements critical to quality)
- Verify that the actual potential market for the product is large enough to warrant investment in the development and production of the product, including by testing the market for, and pricing of, the product as well as its concept, design, and functionality
- Ensure that the potential customers can be reached through existing sales channels, or channels you can develop, at acceptable costs
- Design and test a *sales process* for the rollout and sale of the product

As noted in Chapters 5 and 6, business value maps, value propositions, and sales process maps can be particularly valuable in new product development, as can customer complaints, service records, and other experiential data.

Given the percentage of new product failures, it's wise to take Sheila Mello's advice and go well beyond validating features with customers and even beyond the usual means of gathering data on their needs. Sheila, author of the book *Customer-centric Product Definition*, recommends gathering "images" as opposed to asking about product features or even product needs.

You gather images by asking customers about the situations in which they use the product and their experience of using products of this type. Images reveal the context in which customers use the product and their real needs. Sheila uses the example of golf bags. Rather than asking about materials, compartment configurations, and features, she asked people about their experiences playing golf related to transporting their clubs, garnering three broad categories of responses:

1. *My golf bag doesn't really protect my equipment.* Comments about clubs and gloves ruined and about lost or stolen equipment
2. *My bag is a pain in the neck.* Comments about bags being unwieldy, oversized, airport unfriendly, and generally in the way
3. *My bag is confusing.* Comments about difficulty locating the desired club and about having to check too many pockets to find tees, tools, and ball markers

Such information enables you to understand what customers need the bag to be able to do. For instance, customers often felt that their play was hampered or that they looked bad or even silly as a result of confusion, dirty or wet clubs, or attempts to reach items at the bottom of their bags.

Then the team can translate the image statements from these customer interviews into clearly stated customer requirements. In the case of the golf bags, requirements came down to the following, among many others:

- Golfers want to focus on playing golf and therefore need to
  - find what they want in the bag quickly;
  - return things to their place in the bag easily; and
  - carry and move the bag with minimal effort and stress.
- Golfers want to emulate professional golfers and therefore want to
  - carry as many clubs as possible and anything else they need for the game;
  - keep their clubs clean and dry;
  - have a bag that looks good, even with rugged handling; and
  - be prepared for any weather conditions.

The challenge then becomes designing and producing a bag that meets as many of these and the other requirements that emerged from the images, in a practical, cost-effective manner.

When you set out to solve real problems, you harness the engine of growth for your company. Solving problems rather than developing meaningless, marginal product-line extensions, is the key to that growth. Innovations such as Sheila Mello's "images" go beyond active listening to probing the customer's actual experience. That can lead to real breakthroughs. When developing ATMs, Citibank knew that customers wanted ready access to their cash, even if the survey respondents didn't. But perhaps if researchers had asked customers about how they go about obtaining cash during nonbanking hours, the research would have turned out differently.

Finally, developing and testing the sales process for the product or service results in proper prelaunch preparation of marketing and salespeople. Prototyping the sales process amounts to a real market test rather than to an exercise in approving the product for rollout.

ADVERTISING, PROMOTION, AND MERCHANDISING: WHAT WORKS?

Advertising, promotion, and merchandising include a broad range of activities, and some are easier to measure than are others. The key, however, is to make sure that the advertising, promotion, and merchandising activities that you do use are consciously chosen, integrated into the sales process, and measured for effectiveness. Each activity should have a definite role in the process, meaning it should somehow serve the prospect on the buyer's journey.

In general, advertising makes prospects aware of a problem and your ability to solve it. (I am defining *problem* broadly, to include such situations as the lack of a Porsche or the need for more functions in a cell phone.) Advertising can be either direct response advertising, which aims to get prospects to buy or to identify themselves, or brand advertising, which aims to build awareness. Promotion aims to prompt purchase with discount coupons, special offers, tie-ins, and the like, while merchandising prompts buying action at the retail level through point-of-purchase displays, in-store demonstrations, free samples, and so on. I won't even get into Web-based, viral, and buzz marketing here, but every tactic, from the oldest to those yet to be invented, should be measured to the extent possible.

Motorola, as might be expected, has experimented with combinations of marketing tactics, including advertising, price reductions, promotions, events, sales rep visits, discounts, rebates, and incentives for retail sales associates. The experiments measure whether a tactic or combination of tactics achieves the desired result, such as a target ROI, a certain increase in sales, or both.

A Six Sigma tool known as design of experiment (DOE) enables marketers to test several tactics simultaneously by measuring results and using statistical analysis to determine which variable (which tactic) produced which effects. Chip Leon, corporate director of the Motorola Corporate Incentives Group, explains, "The goal is to determine what really causes lift, then to do more of what works and kill what doesn't. We need to know how each tactic affects the output, the effects of interactions among various tactics, and which tactics and combinations are most significant."

Toward that end, Chip's team fielded combinations of tactics to support sales of phones at various store locations. For example, Location #1 might combine an interactive point-of-sale (POS) demo with seeding (giving a sales associate a phone to use) and sales incentives for the associate. Location #2 might combine seeding and sales incentives but no POS demo, while Location #3 might employ the POS demo and the sales incentive but no seeding. Locations #4, #5, and #6 might employ only the POS demo or seeding or the sales incentive, respectively. And so on, with tactics such as advertising and price reductions in the mix.

When a large enough sample of data has been collected, that data is analyzed. Early results revealed that the POS demo and sales incentives each produced a significant lift in sales but actually produced less lift when combined. A price reduction alone produced lift. Product advertising produced less lift, but combining a price reduction with product advertising produced greater lift than did either tactic alone. This experiment also found that, at least at this point, seeding did not cause significant lift.

Subsequent iterations of this research, however, revealed that seeding with exciting new phones as opposed to older models produced the greatest lift and POS demos the second-best effect, while a special backing card for the product packaging produced no significant lift. Interestingly, combining these three tactics—seeding, POS demos, and backing cards—did not produce significant lift either.

Only rigorous experimentation and measurement enables marketers to determine accurately which tactics generate which effects on sales. Of course, this level of rigor may be unnecessary for many companies, but any company that invests heavily in advertising, promotion, and merchandising—or in any marketing effort—without tying the results to specific activities may well be wasting money. Equally troubling, such a company may be missing opportunities to increase sales with that money by allocating it to tactics that do work.

PRICING: WHAT'S IT WORTH?

Some companies practice value pricing, which is based on the value delivered to the customer. However, the more common practices are competitive pricing (which pegs prices lower, higher, or parallel to those of competitors) or cost-plus pricing (which sets prices to achieve target profit margins). While not every company can employ value pricing, when it works it can maximize revenues and margins—provided you deliver high value.

From a process improvement perspective, no pricing method should be used without first gathering data. Indeed, your company's current pricing method may be based on assumption, tradition, or standard industry practice. None of these is the way to go, which is why companies employing Six Sigma to grow revenues usually apply it to their pricing policies at some point.

For example, pricing was one of the earliest and most successful areas in which Service Master applied Six Sigma. You'll recall from Chapters 2 and 3 that ServiceMaster includes ARS (American Residential Services, HVAC repairs) and TruGreen ChemLawn, both of which compete with numerous independent small businesses. This competitive picture led many branch locations of these companies to discount prices to win and keep business. However, the Six Sigma project team found that discounting was unnecessary in both businesses.

ARS had a standard price book, but the local HVAC technicians with whom ARS contracted typically either discounted the standard prices or ignored them on the grounds that they "knew how to price jobs."

"Management really didn't control the discounting," says Mark Burel, president of ARS. "We let the technicians and our salespeople control it." The technicians discounted the price to close the sale quickly, but they lacked the data that the Six Sigma team had developed. Indeed, the team's Voice of the Customer surveys found very little price sensitivity among customers. Other drivers of customer satisfaction were far more important, including service people's arriving on time, fixing the problem the first time, and providing a written guarantee on their work.

So in addition to sharing this information with their people in the field, ARS standardized the task codes in the price book and established a procedure for pricing and acceptable reasons for discounts.

Mark explains, "We measured the heck out of compliance to the process. We audited invoices and produced monthly reports for the regional and divisional managers. We used scorecards for compliance and graphs to show actual versus book price, and we measured the variation. In the beginning, the variation was wide, but you could see it narrowing as compliance increased and discounting decreased."

As I'll explain in Chapter 8, in situations involving branch locations or external parties, compliance seldom comes about just by mandate. Yet it did come about at ARS. Mark points out, "This was a really big win for us from a revenue and profit perspective."

The Six Sigma team achieved a similar win in Service Master's Tru-Green ChemLawn business. John Crossmock, Six Sigma deployment champion, explains:

> Our senior managers knew that discounting at the branch level was too high, but we didn't have the metrics in place to deal with it. It was more of a feeling than a fact. So we put tools in place to provide the measurements. We did competitive pricing surveys and market-by-market analysis of our branches' pricing structure. We examined the competitive prices and then locked each branch's pricing structure—their price list—into the computer system. We provided reports to the branch management team that showed each sale at that branch, by sales rep, so they could see the discounts they were providing or allowing. We did weekly reports showing all the branches in the company and their position in terms of relative price discounting.
>
> All of this crystallized that, yes, discounting is a problem. Then we put the tools in place—price lists, discount procedures, and so on—and the branches ran with them. In the lawn care business, the sales rep at each branch makes the decision on how much discount, if any, to provide to make the sale. So we built the rigor around the measurements and then put the wheels in place for the field to take that rigor and make it happen. Then we gave them weekly feedback on how it was going. This had a strong, strong effect on our pricing structure. Over the course

of this project, discounting decreased from 11 to 12 percent off book prices to a bit over 4 percent.

So at ARS, the Six Sigma effort guided the company to adopt value pricing, while TruGreen ChemLawn stayed with competitive pricing but in a more disciplined way. Why did this occur? Homeowners have more at stake in their heating and cooling systems than in their lawns. So for ARS, having a technician show up on time in a clean uniform, with an explanation of the price and a guarantee on the work, adds substantial value. In the TruGreen ChemLawn case, even with a professional approach, lawn services are more of a commodity. Therefore, the survey of competitive prices in local markets proved invaluable. The key is that in both cases, the company made its pricing decisions based on research and data. Each company also worked closely with branch managers and salespeople to promulgate the new pricing policies (as we'll see again in Chapter 8).

Of course, we don't have room here to touch on many areas of pricing, including pricing of transaction-based services, new products, and products farther along in their life cycles, to name a few. Yet in pricing, as in all areas, the principles remain the same—make decisions based on objective data, experiment to see what works, and involve the people who will be doing the work in the process.

CUSTOMER SERVICE AND SUPPORT: WHEN DOES IT DO THE MOST GOOD?

Although the customer service and support function plays the essential role of keeping customers, I've said little about it so far. That's because I've chosen to focus on the largest problems in the sales process, and because most companies I've worked with and spoken with have applied Six Sigma mainly in marketing and sales. However, the service part of the sales process provides fertile ground for process improvement, for several reasons:

- Service is a subprocess composed of measurable activities and results, just like marketing and sales, and it can be managed as a process.

- Many companies generate data on these activities and results—for instance, on the number and nature of complaints, resolution of problems, and customers' satisfaction with the solutions—and often track that data electronically. Those that don't, could.
- Service functions offer potentially high returns on process improvements, in cost savings, and in revenue saved and earned by keeping customers in the fold. It's far less expensive to keep a profitable customer than to find a new one.

John Goodman, president of the consulting firm TARP, is doing some of the most interesting work in the area of quantifying process improvement impact in the service function. For example, John performs a simple but powerful market-at-risk calculation to help managers set priorities for quality improvement in service. He has kindly granted me permission to explain that calculation here.

As John says, "In many organizations, the problems that get attention are either those where a customer screams the loudest or gets to the CEO, or the problems that are most often reported. But neither 'screaming' nor 'problem prevalence' necessarily indicates the most serious— meaning potentially most costly—problems." To find those, you need to measure and analyze data on the problem's frequency and its potential damage to customer loyalty.

The market-at-risk calculation developed by TARP is as follows:

Overall % Experiencing the Problem	x	% of Specific Problem Frequency	x	% of Customers Not Likely/ Not Willing to Buy Again	=	% of Customers at Risk

TARP's method enables you to allocate customer service resources to the problems that have the greatest impact on customer loyalty and thus revenue. Figure 7-1 illustrates this method at work.

The data in Figure 7-1 shows that the top three most frequently reported problems at this company are back-ordered products (50%), delivery time (39%), and invoice accuracy (28%). However, although customers experience back orders nearly twice as frequently as inaccurate invoices, each problem places similar percentages of the customer

FIGURE 7-1

Market Damage Estimate for Top Seven Problems

Problem Experienced (42%)	Problem Frequency (%)[1]	Percent Who Won't Buy Again		Percent of Customer Base Potentially Lost	
		Will not[2]	Likely not[3]	Minimum[4]	Maximum[5]
Product on back order	50	22.2	55.5	4.6	11.7
Length of delivery time/ on-time delivery	39	28.6	28.6	4.7	4.7
Accuracy of invoices	28	40.0	90.0	4.7	10.5
Product availability within desired time frame	11	5.0	10.0	0.2	0.5
Ease of obtaining credits/adjustments	11	45.0	65.0	2.0	3.0
Availability of sales rep to discuss product failure	11	50.0	75.0	2.3	3.4
Sales rep informs you of new products/ enhancements	6	25.0	50.0	1.1	2.3

[1] Based on multiple problem selection
[2] Based on "will not repurchase" only
[3] Based on "will not repurchase" and "might not"
[4] = Column #1 (42%) x Column #2 (e.g., 50%) x Column #3
[5] = Column #1 (42%) x Column #2 x Column #4

base at risk. The percentage of customers potentially lost because of back-ordered products ranges from 4.6 percent to 11.7 percent, while the percentage due to inaccurate invoices ranges from 4.7 percent to 10.5 percent. The second most frequent problem, delivery time, puts only 4.7 percent at risk.

This means that although it's only the third most frequent problem, inaccurate invoices place as much of the customer base at risk as the most frequent problem, back-ordered products.

John points out that in prioritizing these problems for solution, management must also consider the cost of fixing each one. We can assume that fixing the back-order problem would cost more, given the probable need to expand inventories, than fixing the inaccurate invoice problem. Therefore, the third most frequent problem—inaccurate invoices—would be the one to fix first. John's work shows once again the value of data, measurement, and analysis in identifying and prioritizing problems.

Of course, this is only one small example of the kind of problem solving that a process approach enables in the service function. Other examples would include increasing the efficiency of call centers, identifying the most cost-effective ways of servicing customers, and identifying not only problems and bottlenecks but ways to fix them.

SALES FORCE MANAGEMENT: GET FOCUSED!

How would a process approach to sales management look to senior sales managers? If they wanted to improve sales performance, how would they think about objectives? Which data would they draw upon and share with regional and district managers?

To answer those questions, let's examine a Six Sigma project conducted by a major company. The company wishes to remain anonymous, so I'll call it Lumber Products, Inc. (The company is not in the lumber industry, but all other facts and data are unchanged.) Lumber Products, Inc. (LPI) began Six Sigma in 1999 as a companywide initiative. Six Sigma reached marketing and sales in 2003 in the form of a growth-and-margin project conducted in three divisions with the following two objectives:

1. Gain market share by improving growth
2. Improve margins

According to the fictitiously named Lee Anderson, LPI's Six Sigma leader, the first step was to develop operational definitions, the importance of which was noted in Chapter 3. The project team defined the following:

- *Focus group.* Sales reps who had the largest decline in growth (volume) or in margins from 2003 to 2004
- *Region growth.* The growth in volume or margin from year to year on a monthly basis, excluding the focus group
- *Difference.* The difference in growth or margins between the focus group and the region.

Lee noted the importance of including both volume growth and margins in the objectives. "If I'm a rep and you tell me to improve my margins, well I can do that, but I may have to sacrifice growth. If you tell me to improve my growth, I can do that, but I may have to sacrifice margin. We wanted to make sure that, if we improved one measure, we weren't hurting the other, so actually we ran a growth project and a margin project concurrently." Here's how Lee explained the project:

We separated our data into the different regions, because we didn't want to compare a sales rep in New Mexico with one in New York. So we basically ran a project in each of our regions. This made it manageable and helped us determine what the market was doing in those specific regions.

The next thing was to see where we were getting the most or least gain, using simple tools. For each region, we determined which reps were declining in growth. We needed at least two years of data for a rep to be on the list, and they had to be declining while the rest of the region was growing. For example, in the northeast region, we might have 3 reps with declining growth while everybody else was growing. Those 3 were the group we wanted to improve. (Each regional vice president, or RVP, manages 10 to 12 reps.)

We found that precise operational definitions were vital in this project, because there's constant change in the sales field. For example, what do we do if a low performer in one region transfers to a different region? Do we want to keep that region as focus group or re-evaluate the performer in the new region? Our data was pulled based on their territory number, not by the rep's name. Therefore, if a rep relocated or was displaced, the data was still based on that geographic territory. Also, our regional growth numbers track growth in volume and margins from year to year, and our original growth targets had excluded the focus group. If we had included the reps who were reducing our growth, we would have reduced our targets for the region. We wanted to focus on the focus group, because that's where we were losing market share and margins.

Now, how can you gauge reps' improvement? We wanted to be able to compare them to the rest of the region. It's like buying stock. If you purchase a stock, the natural thing to do is to track it, maybe more closely than your other stocks. At the end of the year, if it's up 10 percent, that may be great. But what if the market's up 20 percent? That's kind of the methodology we used. The rest of the region—not counting the focus group—represented what the market was doing. So each month we would run data and ask, "What is the growth and what are the margins for the focus group and for the rest of the region?" And we measured that difference, that delta.

We realize that we could show improvement in that delta in several ways, but only one way would measure true improvement. For instance, we might show improvement if the rest of the region came down and the focus group stayed the same, and obviously we didn't want to call that improvement. The only way we showed improvement was if three measures that we put in place improved. The first was that the change in delta had to represent a statistically significant shift between the baseline and their performance. The second was that improvement had to be sustained for at least six months; when you're working with monthly data, you've got to look at it over time. And the third was that the improvement had to come from the focus group improving, not from the rest of the region coming down.

Each month, we would plot the average growth of the focus group, which might be two or three reps, in a region against the average growth for the rest of the reps in that region. So if we had ten reps in the region and we identified two of them as focus group, we would average the two and average the rest of the eight and compare the two to the eight. Each month, we plotted the growth of the focus group and that of the rest of the region and calculated that delta. Our key measure was the gap, the delta, the difference between the two groups within a region. Our goal was for the process to improve so that gap became zero.

It's not so much what we're measuring—in this case it's growth, and we also did this with margin—as *how* we're measuring. We're focusing very clearly on what we want to change. Our intent was to give the regional vice presidents information so they would know where to focus their attention.

Figure 7-2 plots a sample of the data that Lee is describing. Each point on the graph represents the delta—the difference—between the

FIGURE 7-2

Difference between Growth in the Focus Group and the Rest of the Region

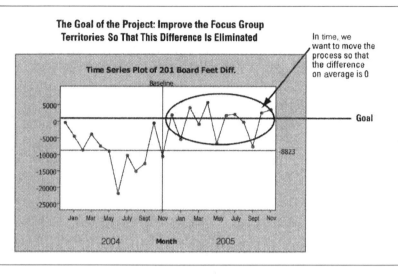

focus group's average growth and the rest of the region's average growth. As the figure shows, delta (measured on the vertical axis as the difference in board feet of lumber sold between the two groups' averages in a region) varies much more widely in the baseline year of 2004 than in 2005, after the project began. (The months are on the horizontal axis.) In other words, the difference varies much more closely around zero after the project begins. In fact, in seven months of 2005—those for which delta is above zero—the growth of the focus group exceeds that of the rest of the region. That's all well and good, but the goal of the project is to minimize the difference between the focus group and the rest of the region. The logic is that when you're done, you have removed a good amount of variability from the process in a region. Only then can you move on to improving the process so that all the reps in the region can generate more growth.

I'll discuss how this differs from the usual approaches to sales management in a few minutes. For now, back to Lee Anderson:

> We started off with this project just like any other Six Sigma project we'd been doing at LPI. We were going to map the process, identify the key input variables, associate those key

input variables with the output, things of that nature. That's where we started off. However, something happened along the way, because salespeople are very competitive. The initial list that we put out for focus group kick-started the whole project. The RVPs focused on their focus groups, coaching them and such, when before they may or may have not have been focusing on those reps. They may have been trying to manage the whole region. But they shifted focus from the region to this smaller group, which was more manageable for them to teach.

Actually, we kind of went around the main Six Sigma process. Instead of define, measure, improve, analyze, we kind of took it backwards, because that's what happened. As soon as we started pushing the numbers to the RVPs, we started seeing improvement without doing more analysis. Normally, you want to do your analysis, figure out what's causing the needle to move, implement changes, then watch the needle move. In this case, we saw the needle move but we—the Six Sigma team—hadn't changed anything. That tells me that I may have been on the wrong path by going through the process map and looking for key input variables. Because some things that were uncovered— I won't say we never would have found them with normal Six Sigma tools—but some things in sales are extremely subtle. For example, it's how the RVP conducts his or her business and the RVP's relationship with the reps. Some things involved the soft skills of the sales force, and I'm not sure we'd have found them if we had taken the traditional approach.

I feel this hits home as to why a lot of sales reps are kind of timid when it comes to Six Sigma. There are a lot of these soft skills that, if I were a sales rep, I wouldn't want to be told how to do. I don't want to be told how to do this and when to do that. Let me sell. Those are some of the things we found.

We also found opportunities for partnering among the reps, which we wouldn't have considered before. Some RVPs found that if you put a rep that's struggling near a rep that's doing well, the sales rep that's doing well will mentor that low performer.

So we now have two sources of improvement. One is that many focus groups have improved; the other is that we can better use the reps in the region who are performing at a good level or high level. We say, take the best and teach the rest. We're finding the skills and behaviors of those high performers, then teaching, mentoring, and coaching the rest of the region. Everybody improves that way.

In fact, in the first six months of this project, growth improved in 42 percent of the regions, and margins improved in 39 percent of the regions. Across the board among the focus group, we saw an 88 percent margin improvement and 55 percent increase in board feet sold.

The driving factors were really salespeople's competitive urge and the relationship between the RVP and the reps. But I might say that one key factor we improved was the reporting system itself, which may have had a gap that we filled by providing the data on the delta. For example, on the basis of that information, the RVPs required the focus group to report back to them weekly on every lead they generated. So that data improved the coaching that the RVPs gave the focus group. And then there was the tactic of partnering a low-performing rep with a high performer. Those things all brought about the results, but they all began with the data we provided.

I find two things about this very successful sales management case particularly interesting. First, no radical adjustments were made to the sales process itself, nor were process changes the aim of the project. Second, while this was not, as Lee points out, a strict DMAIC project, it did employ Six Sigma principles to good effect. I'll comment briefly on each of these points.

The project did not set out the make major process changes, but it did change one key aspect of the sales process: the information made available to the regional vice presidents, which in turn changed their behavior. The information on the performance differential pinpointed a part of the process that wasn't working up to par—the low performing reps—and directed management attention and efforts toward those reps. Thus prompted, the RVPs asked those reps to provide weekly information on the disposition of their leads and had high-performing reps partner with them.

How did the management method used here differ from the way salespeople are usually managed? In several ways, the key ones being these:

- Most sales improvement efforts lack the operational definitions, even of "low performer," and the rigor of the data used here. Managers usually look at sales trends and at who is making or not making their sales quotas, and they try to get everyone to make quota. But where do quotas come from? The data used here compares the average growth and margin numbers of the focus group with those of the rest of the reps in the region. The logic was not that everyone should be "selling more," which is the aim of quotas and so-called stretch goals, but that everyone should perform at around the regional average. When you've achieved that, then you can start "aiming higher."

- Sales managers—all managers—often try to do too many poorly defined things at once. Lee mentions focus, and this project focused management attention on what most needed fixing—the growth and margins of the low-performing reps in each region. That's where you could realize the greatest improvement in the shortest time, so that's where you focus.

- The project defined a very clear objective and in doing so defined the way to reach that objective. The objective was to close the gap between the low-performing reps and the rest of the region by raising the performance of those reps. The question each RVP had to answer was, how do I get my focus group to achieve the results that my other reps achieve? In a short time, this led them to partner low-performing reps with high performers. Often, managers try to increase sales by getting more sales from all reps, especially those already performing well, on the grounds that the high performers are best equipped to bring in even more business. This project took a different tack.

- Management avoided comparisons, as Lee put it, between New Mexico and New York. Of course, various data collection and analysis options exist for avoiding this pitfall. But by having each region competing against itself, management leveled the playing field. The team, however, could compare regions to one another based on how quickly they closed the gap between the focus group and the rest of the region and by other measures.

- Management respected the capacity of the sales process. It set goals that could be achieved within the existing sales process, as evidenced by the fact that the average sales rep had achieved that goal. That's another positive result of using the regional average as the objective.

While Lee mentions that this effort was not a by-the-book Six Sigma project, it did rely on data and measurement, it did change the way the RVPs managed the focus group, and it did define a result in terms of closing an identified gap as opposed to hitting some perhaps reasonable, perhaps unreasonable, sales quota or margin target. However, she's very right to point out that doctrinaire approaches often aren't necessary and that salespeople will often resist them. In fact, a good part of Chapter 8 covers ways to deal with organizational resistance.

SEEING INITIATIVES IN A NEW LIGHT

Clearly, a process approach will significantly impact the way management chooses and implements standard marketing initiatives and impact them for the better. Marketing and salespeople generally tend to be intuitive rather than analytical, and may at the outset resist the level of rigor employed in some of the examples in this chapter. Of course, statistical analysis has become firmly established in marketing in areas such as market segmentation, price sensitivity, and database marketing. But process approaches are more than statistics and require a shift in thinking.

This is as true, or even truer, of sales as of marketing. It's also true of entire organizations and senior management teams. So in the next and final chapter, we look at the managerial and cultural changes that com-

Special Resource

If you would like to learn about other examples like the ones in this chapter, subscribe to the Sales Performance Improvement Forum (SPIF). SPIF is free, and it is the only newsletter devoted to sales process improvement. Each month, you'll read case examples from companies like yours, new articles by me, and the latest events in the industry. To subscribe, visit *www.salesperformance.com/spif.aspx.*

panies have made both as a result of process approaches and to adopt those approaches. We also look at some cutting-edge uses of Six Sigma in marketing and sales, which several companies have used to improve their customers' processes.

KEY POINTS

- The use of a process approach to measure activities and results (causes and effects) is a prerequisite for objectively evaluating the effects of typical sales improvement initiatives, such as sales training, CRM systems, and advertising.
- Often, the biggest challenge that vendors and consultants to sales and marketing organizations face isn't in delivering what they promise but in getting clients to measure their business activities appropriately.
- While the focus in sales organizations tends to be on salespeople's activities and skills, these salespeople are often (though not always) ensnared in bottlenecks and dysfunctional processes that limit their ability to improve. If these process problems are not solved, investments in improving sales skills will produce suboptimal results.
- CRM systems hold great promise for providing instantaneous information and improving salespeople's performance. However, if the processes and operational terms are not defined properly and if measurements of activities and results are not validated, calculating an ROI on these systems will continue to be difficult.
- Good product design has a lot in common with good sales process design: both focus on identifying and solving customers' problems.
- Testing initiatives in all promotions and advertising is key to gaining the data needed to reduce risk and increase ROI.
- Establishing simple measurements where there were none can, in and of itself, produce improvements in salespeople's performance.

8

MOVING TO HIGH-PERFORMANCE MARKETING AND SALES MANAGEMENT

A variety of companies has clearly improved the performance of their sales processes with Six Sigma and Lean. Some of these companies have applied selected tools or used a process approach to make relatively minor changes, while others have implemented Six Sigma companywide. In this chapter, we examine ways of implementing process improvement in marketing and sales by briefly revisiting some earlier examples and looking at some companywide deployments. We also look at some advanced applications of Six Sigma in marketing and sales.

If this book is your first real exposure to process improvement or to Six Sigma in sales, the whole issue of implementation may seem a bit overwhelming. If, for instance, you are a sales manager looking to apply some process improvement practices in your shop, you may be wondering where to begin. The same may be the case if you are a quality professional interested in applying what you know to your marketing and sales function. In either case, you will find useful guidance in this chapter.

However, one caveat is in order before we begin on this topic: my goal is not to have you adopt Six Sigma in marketing and sales; rather, it is to show you ways to permanently improve your marketing and sales performance. That requires process improvement but not necessarily Six Sigma, which is only the most rigorous application of process improvement.

JUMP-STARTING SALES PROCESS IMPROVEMENT

To "sell" process improvement in marketing and sales, you have to make the business case and demystify the methods. I've found that marketing and sales people respond positively when I've taken the following approaches.

Start with Existing Business Goals

Given today's pressures, most managers won't even consider an initiative that doesn't support their business goals (which is good). In marketing and sales, the main goal is almost always to increase sales, usually while increasing profits. The four basic strategies for increasing sales are to:

1. Sell more existing products to existing customers
2. Sell more new products to existing customers
3. Sell more existing products to new customers
4. Sell more new products to new customers

The six major strategies for increasing profitability are to

1. Reduce the cost of bringing on new customers
2. Reduce the cost of servicing existing customers
3. Increase customer retention (customer loyalty)
4. Drop unprofitable customers or increase their profitability
5. Increase prices while maintaining or reducing product costs
6. Sell more of the most profitable products, fewer of the less profitable ones

Several cases in earlier chapters show how process improvement supports these strategies. HSBC dropped terminally unprofitable trading customers and increased the profitability of many accounts that they kept. WaterFurnace found ways to sell more to new customers by improving its dealer network. ServiceMaster increased prices by reducing discounting in two businesses. Motorola sold more products to new customers by testing promotion and merchandising tactics. Clients of

TARP discovered how to retain customers by attacking the problems most likely to result in lost customers. Lumber Products, Inc. sold more products to new and existing customers by improving the results of low performing salespeople.

While process improvement will support the above-noted strategies, it's best to avoid preconceived solutions about ways of implementing the strategies. Calling an initiative process improvement does not make it process improvement; the principles and practices make it so. If you think that you have too many unprofitable customers, that your distributors are a problem, or a lot of discounting is going on, and the data shows that that's not the case, then you have a different problem to solve. It may or may not be worth solving, but a process approach calls for locating and solving actual problems rather than assumed problems.

Anyone looking to bring process improvement to a marketing and sales function has to understand the business's goals. As John Crossmock, Six Sigma deployment champion at ServiceMaster, said, "We use our Six Sigma resources to work on projects that everybody in the field, all the branch managers, care about. If it's in their strategic objectives to improve X, whatever it is, and they're being judged on it, then we're seen as helpers rather than as working on stuff not tied to the business."

Finally, look to see that improvements flow through to the financial statements. Recall that Jon Theuerkauf mentioned that HSBC follows formal financial policies for Six Sigma. Define your measures in dollars whenever possible. Then you can measure the changes in revenue, costs, or profitability and capture them in the accounting system so people see real results. For instance, if you want to reduce the sales cycle, a common goal, you must define not only the sales cycle and measure it in days but also—perhaps with a sales operating audit—define the dollar impact of shaving each day off the sales cycle. Such calculations take time, but they support the goal of achieving measurable, meaningful process improvement. They also usually support the Six Sigma effort itself, because the ROI on projects can be quite impressive.

Take the Customer's Point of View

When someone suggests considering the customer's viewpoint, very few marketing or sales professionals can say, "Forget that!" with a straight face. It would be bad form. It would also be foolish, given the number of companies that have succeeded by focusing on customer needs.

Consider Whole Foods Markets. This grocery chain knows that affluent customers both worry about food additives and want superior service. So the stores carry only additive-free foods, and they market them cleverly ("The food, the whole food, and nothing but the food"). These are not the hippy-dippy organic food stores of the 1960s. Displays are achingly attractive, and service is paramount. When you ask for help, employees assist you in finding the item rather than waving a hand and saying, "I think that's in aisle five." This does not happen by accident. It happens when managers take the customers' point of view and build the value proposition around it. Although Whole Foods is not a Six Sigma company, they "measure the heck out of everything" and promulgate those measures all the way down to the hourly employees.

Tools that enable you to look at your products, services, and sales process from the customer's point of view include customer value mapping, sales process mapping, and Voice of the Customer. Get marketing and sales staff to focus on the value that customers derive from products and services and on the buyer's journey. If they do, they will inevitably gain new insights and probably an appreciation of the potential of sales process improvement.

By the way, customer focus is not an exercise in altruism. Recall that HSBC found two-thirds of their futures-trading customers to be unprofitable because these customers were receiving *too much value*. So the company had to help them to become profitable, move to online trading, or move out of the bank.

Examine (and Map) Your Sales Process

Whether you're in process improvement or marketing and sales, you can view sales as a process and help your colleagues to do the same. People may or may not accept the analogies between prospects and raw materials, between sales opportunities and work-in-process, and between customers and finished goods. Yet sales is clearly a process—a set of related activities designed to produce a certain result.

Keep the direct response model in mind. As you examine a marketing or sales activity, ask: "What actions are we trying to prompt the customer to take?" and "What specific results are we trying to achieve?" If you cannot identify the action or result you are trying to create, ask what result the activity actually is creating. For instance, recall the telecom salespeople who asked prospects to dig up their old phone bills. The *desired* response was for the prospect to provide the bills so the salespeople could propose a more competitive price. The actual result was a delay in the sales process. Eliminating that request proved quite beneficial.

Ask yourself what customer response you're aiming for with activities such as advertising, trade shows, cold calling, promotions, price changes, and travel and entertainment. Are you getting the desired response? Are those responses worth the resources devoted to the activity?

Develop Relevant Data and Facts

To develop useful answers to the questions in the preceding paragraph, you need measures of the activities and responses. But first you must define what you are measuring. For instance, say you want to measure the sales you are generating from attending trade shows. You first have to define what you will count as attending a trade show and what you will count as a resulting sale.

Do you define attending a trade show only as sponsoring a booth? Or do you count any form of attendance? Should you have a cost threshold? If so, do you count salaries? Do you count having one salesperson at a show as attendance? What do you count as a sale generated from a trade show? Any sale resulting from a lead generated—or qualified—at a trade show? What if the sale was already in the pipeline, but seeing the prospect at the show helped to close the deal?

These are serious questions if you're serious about allocating marketing and sales resources to activities that produce sales. Questions like these can be applied to any activity, and there are many ways to answer them. For instance, you can say, "We count any show that costs us at least $5,000 to attend in total expenses (including travel, meals, lodging, and salaries) as trade show attendance," and, "We count any prospect whom we meet or qualify at a show and who enters our sales cycle within three months as a sale, if the deal closes within the next nine months."

Of course, the questions and answers depend on the activity, result, and company. But the resulting data can be invaluable. Many people quoted in this book said, "We didn't know about the problem until we developed the data," or "We knew we had a problem, but we didn't have the data to make the case." Sometimes data reveals counterintuitive conclusions. For example, Motorola found that using more than one promotional tool did not always increase sales. There's no substitute for solid data.

Bear in mind that data need not be statistically significant to be useful. Simple counts of leads, prospects, and sales opportunities will reveal where in the process you are losing potential sales. That information can be quite enlightening. Recall the high-net-worth banking unit that lost customers at the account opening stage. They thought they needed more salespeople, when they actually needed a better method of opening accounts.

The point is that you don't measure for measurement's sake but for a purpose—to get a result. Moreover, until you know how your process works and understand cause and effect within it, you don't really know what to measure. You have to be precise. Mapping your process, defining your terms, and brainstorming the Xs and Ys are at one level simple language exercises, but they help you count things, the basis of measurement. People who dismiss this kind of measurement fail to see that the purpose is to identify the real issue, the underlying cause, the things that need to be changed to improve results.

Apply a Tool or Two

The Six Sigma approach includes many valuable tools for defining and analyzing your process and your data. You'll find a valuable list of resources for more details about these tools in the Resources section in the back of this book. Some of the tools require technical knowledge, which you can hire. Others, such as fishbone diagrams, SIPOC, data tables, and process control charts, require minimal technical background.

The tools I've developed specifically for sales process improvement—customer value mapping, qualification criteria, sales process mapping, and the sales operating audit—require no technical knowledge. For example, consider the simple table that would result from gathering the trade show data described in the previous section. Just seeing the costs and returns arrayed in tabular form could be an eye opener. Even basic analytical tools will enrich your knowledge of cause and effect in your processes.

Examine Cause and Effect

Understanding cause and effect, of course, leads to effective problem solving. For instance, an analysis of trade show attendance would examine cause and effect. If a lot of sales result from trade shows or from certain types of shows, you'll want to know why. Then you can seek other situations with similar characteristics, such as the themes, conference attendees, ways your company was represented, and so on. If low sales resulted from trade show attendance, you would want to know the same things.

When you know what caused a result, you can replicate desirable results and eliminate undesirable ones. It's not enough to conclude that trade shows are great or that they're wasteful. You want to know why, especially if trade shows used to generate good results or poor results and things have changed.

Make Common Sense Common Practice

If what I've presented in this section strikes you as common sense, I couldn't be happier. That's a typical response but, as you know, nothing is so uncommon as common sense. Much of process improvement is just codified common sense. Define something before you measure it. Measure it before you analyze it. Analyze it before you decide how to improve it. Improve it, and then control it to the new level of performance. Some people see that and still say, "What's the Six Sigma of it?" The Six Sigma of it is the dogged dedication to the principles explained in Chapters 2 and 3. Most of us use common sense now and then, with brilliant results. Six Sigma aims to make common sense common management practice.

Managing with Six Sigma may not be as exciting for some people as traditional management practices. Managing on data, facts, measurement, analysis, and experiments minimizes the politics, power struggles, personality clashes, and drama of organizational life. It works better, but mere improved performance doesn't appeal to some people. Others fear the transparency that data and facts bring to the table. Submitting to the rule of data demands maturity of mind, respect for reality, and dedication to standards. In other words, common sense. You look at what your customers are trying to accomplish. You look at what you're trying to accomplish. Do the best you can to match what you're trying to do with what they're trying to do. And then deliver, deliver, deliver.

Boring? I don't think anything is boring about high performance. Yes, it may take getting used to, but most people manage after they see the results.

MORE POWER TO YOU, AND TO YOUR CUSTOMERS

The real power of using a process approach in marketing and selling is that it genuinely aims to improve life for customers. It does this by finding real problems to solve, real opportunities to add value, and ultimately, real ways of improving customers' business results. Again, we don't use a process approach for altruistic reasons. You use a process approach to make your company worth more to the customer, to increase the value that you add for customers, and to earn more market share and share-of-wallet than your competitors. Six Sigma does this by taking value for the customer as its guiding star, then applying proven methods to improve your ability to add value.

Broadly, process approaches achieve results in the following three ways:

1. By improving the marketing and selling "production system" so that it truly assists customers on their buyer's journey. Improvement occurs when you design a sales process that adds value for customers in and of itself.
2. By moving from solution selling to what I call Six Sigma selling. This extends the arc that sales professionals have been following as they have moved from selling product features to selling prod-

uct benefits to selling solutions. Six Sigma selling focuses on helping customers achieve the business results they seek when they buy a product or service.

3. By providing on-site Six Sigma teams to customers to partner with them in achieving the business results they seek. This is truly the cutting edge of Six Sigma selling, and a number of companies are already there.

Let's examine each of these routes to results in turn.

Assist Customers with Their Buyer's Journey

The first level of bringing Six Sigma to customers would be assisting them—genuinely assisting them—on their buyer's journey. At times, this might mean directing the customer toward one of your lower-priced or lower-profit solutions, toward a solution that you don't sell, or even toward a competitor who can solve the problem better than you can. However, if you truly understand your customers and the problems they encounter on their buyer's journey, and you have solutions to the problem they want solved, you will be able to sell to most potential customers. I've covered designing a sales process that will help the customer on the buyer's journey in some depth, so I'll just reprise an example of this.

Quadrant Homes grew to become the largest homebuilder in the state of Washington by helping buyers on their journey. They realized that a couple, perhaps with a pregnancy in progress, perhaps empty nesters, has things to do other than shop for flooring materials and bathroom fixtures. But they also knew that people want a wide selection and expert guidance and that they like to know when they can move into their new home. Finally, they knew that new homebuyers mainly want high square footage at a reasonable cost. So Quadrant devised a sales process and a business model (described in Chapter 6) that achieves these things.

When you bring Six Sigma to customers in this way, they're not even aware of it. They're only aware that they are working with people who have their act together. To emulate Quadrant Homes, you must

- define the steps that your customers take, from being unaware of the problem to deciding to make the purchase, and really understand this journey from their point of view;
- design a Lean sales process that assists them at each of those steps;
- link your marketing and sales process to your production process, which will be relatively straightforward if you have already applied Lean Six Sigma to your production process; and
- elevate your performance by continually applying process improvement to prioritize changes to each activity in the production and the sales process.

Following the above steps changes your position in the market, because your interactions with customers are based on different premises than those of your competition. Generally, most companies that have taken this approach have found that they keep their most valuable customers and do a better job of meeting their needs. They've also generally found that the savings and efficiencies of relatively steady demand creation and fulfillment outweigh the cost and inefficiency associated with chasing peak demand. These companies establish a firm, profitable customer base and market position, then build from there.

Apply Process Improvement to the Customer

The next level of bringing Six Sigma to customers calls for applying it to the parts of your customers' operation that your product or service touches. For instance, consider the SIPOC (the diagram that depicts suppliers-inputs-process-outputs-customers, described in the Appendix). From your customers' point of view, your company is the supplier of inputs to a process of theirs that must produce outputs for their internal and external customers. Remember that television show *The Weakest Link*? That's what you don't want to be in this situation.

Might you know more about your customers if you understand *their* process? Which inputs do you contribute to or provide? Within the charter of your business, how can you make your customers' process more effective or efficient? Customer value maps, which I introduced in Chapter 5, can also be used in this way. In fact, that's what the company that sold ingredients for medications did. As it turned out, while the key product feature met the medical efficacy requirements, it added little value in the formulation process. However, the compound's stability across a range of temperatures was invaluable for scaling up to production quantities, reducing costs and time to market.

For another example, consider two companies selling ready-mix concrete to contractors who haul it to their job sites. Basically, they have to get the right number of loads of the right grade of cement delivered to the right job site at the right time. Now one of these companies has an automated terminal where drivers can dial their mix without getting out of the truck and be on their way in a few minutes. The other requires drivers to wait in long lines and fill out paperwork. Which company better fits the customer's process?

In this market, the number of customers is pretty much known, and relationships among suppliers are established. So the salespeople focus on customer service. The best ones gain insight into the customers' processes. Then they work with the customers to fit their product to those processes in ways that would be difficult for competitors to match. They also might help customers with technical issues or alert them to challenges that might arise from changes in the weather or supply shortages. In this way, even in a commodity market like concrete, they add more value than do competitors and reduce costs and waste for customers, all by looking at the customers' business through the lens of a process approach.

Provide On-Site Six Sigma Teams to Customers

The most innovative method of Six Sigma Selling is to have some of your best salespeople and Black Belts actually bring the methodology into the customer organization. Now I recognize that this is a highly advanced application of Six Sigma selling. However, it is already a reality at some companies. For example, this approach is taken by Ortho-Clinical Diagnostics, a Johnson & Johnson company that manufactures equipment for hospital laboratories. As Jim Ellis, director of Sales Process Excellence explains:

> Hospital labs face real cost pressures, which often involve workflow problems that Lean can solve. We saw a potential opportunity to add value beyond our line of chemistry instruments

and blood bank products, if we could help our customers solve their workflow problems and reduce some of their costs.

Most of the workflow problems in hospital labs are caused by high peak demand. Lean teaches that a consistent workflow timed to customer needs will generally work better than batch processing. So we worked with a southwestern hospital chain on an alpha test basis to see if we could apply what we'd learned about Lean in manufacturing to laboratory operations.

This was part of a two-year effort to increase demand for our products and differentiate them at the same time. I had always been a fan of Mack Hanan, who said, "You shouldn't sell the features of your products but instead sell the financial benefits that those products and services produce for your customers." That's what we wanted to do—create and sell more financial benefits—by helping labs redesign their workflows to be more efficient and effective.

Our sales force wanted us to use this project to win a prospect they had been soliciting, but we wanted a neutral hospital for the project. Our goal was to see if our idea would work. We didn't want a customer that was a fan of ours, nor did we want one that was presenting difficulties. We just wanted a lab that would be open to this experiment.

Well, we picked one out and approached it more or less cold and presented our proposition. Both we and the hospital would own the rights to any published material that came out of the project. This all happened in the early 2000s, a few years after the entire company had become involved with Six Sigma.

To make a long story short, it worked. We basically applied Lean principles to the lab. For example, instead of having all blood samples arrive at the same time, we have them come down in a steady flow by staggering the schedule for blood draws from patients. Most labs, like most established operations, just put new equipment wherever it will fit. So we analyze the walk patterns—the footsteps that an operator must take in the lab—and arrange the workflow and the equipment to enhance efficiency. You can reduce inventories by showing people there's no need to hoard supplies. Those sorts of things.

This project and others like it resulted in a consulting arm of our division. We now charge for these services, and it has been a good business. We've worked with numerous laboratories to improve workflow and productivity and reduce inventories and space usage.

I've got some numbers for you. On average, we see productivity improvement of 70 percent, inventory reduction of 50 percent, and space reduction of 30 percent. About 80 percent of our clients recover the cost of our services in less than 12 months, and 100 percent do at 24 months. After that, the savings go to the bottom line.

We try to effect a knowledge transfer, and we're comfortable with that. This is not the kind of consulting where you write recommendations and leave the customer to implement them. We work alongside customers and set them up to do what they need to do in the best ways. That's the approach we've taken all along to bring this to our customers. In the beginning, we didn't even know if it would work, let alone whether we would get anything out of it. It did work, and we've created a high value-added consulting unit that brings these principles to our customers, really enhancing the relationship between them and our company.

Jim brought a deep technical background as a research scientist to this work, along with excellent sales skills. He pointed out that a pure technician would not be the person to sell this sort of project to senior management. The salesperson has to see the big picture and convey it to the senior decision makers.

Jim emphasizes that the whole initiative had strong support from senior management. "It involved about a $2 million investment and took about two years to get off the ground. Once we had our alpha test site, we wanted to get the project done in three to six months, which was quick. But it takes a long-term management commitment to bring process improvement to customers. And, of course, you have to be using it in-house before you can take it to another organization."

Finally, Jim noted that even after they begin working with a client, they might encounter resistance to new methods. For instance, when the lab people see the blood samples arriving in a smooth flow because the people drawing the blood have changed their schedule, they are happy. But they're less happy when they have to change certain parts of the way they work, for instance to maintain smaller inventories. You have to see resistance to change as part of the situation and work through it by employing people skills as well as data, facts, measurement, and case studies.

SIX SIGMA SELLING

Six Sigma selling as described above represents the next logical step in the evolution of selling as a profession. Indeed, I believe it will transform selling into a true profession. Over the past hundred years or so, professional salespeople have evolved from pushing product to selling features to selling benefits to selling solutions to true consultative selling. That trajectory traces an arc from a focus on the product and the seller's needs to a focus on customers and their problems. The end point of that arc is not selling the benefits of the product or even selling solutions, which in practice is often just a way of positioning a configuration that basically fits the product to the customer's needs. The end point is enhancing the customers' business results as your product or service relates to them.

Fitting the product to the customers' needs is good, especially when the fit represents a genuine solution rather than mere positioning. Better yet is learning what customers are trying to accomplish with products and services of the type you sell, then working with them to accomplish that. This demands a process approach, because processes are the means by which things get done in business. Process thinking provides a template for understanding what customers are trying to do, the steps and the people involved in doing it, the inputs and outputs, the things that are known and not known about the steps and the problems (the data and the measures that are missing), the causes of problems and potential solutions. When you have salespeople who understand process, they can look at the customer and talk with the customer and question the customer in ways that simply aren't possible without a process approach.

Again, I recognize that consulting with the customer is an advanced application of Six Sigma in marketing and sales. Yet I believe that it's worth at least thinking about, even if you're new to Six Sigma.

After you have some experience, how can you adopt Six Sigma selling and use a process approach to bring more value to your customers and capture more value, loyalty, revenue, and profits for your company? Here are three steps.

1. Do It Yourself

All companies that have actually applied Six Sigma to their customers have first applied it to their own internal processes. This is true not only of Standard Register and J&J's Ortho-Clinical Diagnostics but also of GE, Sun Microsystems, Motorola, Allied Signal, and other companies that have taken this approach. As noted earlier, you learn process improvement by using process improvement. It's similar to surfing, shooting, or riding a bicycle. You have to paddle out on the surfboard or point the shotgun at some clays or get on the bicycle. You can read books or sit in classrooms for weeks, but you will never be able to surf or shoot or ride a bike unless you do it, make your mistakes (intrinsic to the learning process), and get better.

Hiring an experienced Six Sigma czar and some Black Belts and training your people with the help of an experienced vendor will help you learn faster. But you have to apply it to your own processes. That way, you really learn. Also, from the ethical standpoint you are your own guinea pig. Then, when you've made your mistakes and run successful projects, you can help others. This is not an exercise in positioning but a genuine service to customers. I can imagine nothing worse than telling a customer that you understand Six Sigma when you haven't used it yourself.

2. Take an Eclectic Approach

Though they call themselves Six Sigma companies, or at least accept the label, no outfit that I've come across takes a doctrinaire approach to using process improvement with customers. They use Six Sigma and Lean as well as balanced scorecard, best practices, and their own hybrid approaches. They match the tools to the situation. They might do the define and measure steps, see a solution they can implement without much analysis, and omit the analyze step. They gather enough data to understand causes and effects, enough to make the case for a cost-effective solution.

The idea is to work *with* customers, not to impose process improvement on them. Indeed, as recommended earlier as an internal strategy, it's possible that you could take a process approach to helping a customer without ever mentioning that's what you are doing. On the other hand, you will also find customers who actively want you to understand Six Sigma. In fact, I've heard that one major U.S. bank told an information technology vendor, "Don't even think of calling on us unless you can send some Black Belts along." When things are moving in that direction, there's little need to be defensive about broaching a process improvement to customers. As always, your approach depends on the customer.

3. Create a Dedicated Sales or Consulting Team

Creating a dedicated sales team or consulting team enables you to develop real expertise as well as a unit that can be assigned specific goals and aimed in potentially fruitful directions. Such a team evidences management's commitment to Six Sigma selling and provides internal and external visibility. It makes customers feel special and, more important, assures them that they are dealing with experts.

Such a team should include salespeople with knowledge of process improvement and process improvement people with superb people skills. Technical Six Sigma skills do not qualify a person to deal with customers, and you cannot place people who lack the requisite skills in front of customers. On the other hand, salespeople who know nothing of process improvement will quickly find themselves out of their depth in any discussion of processes. This whole issue of Six Sigma skills versus people skills surfaced several times in the interviews conducted for this book. The consensus, as one fellow put it, is that, "it's easier to teach someone Six Sigma than it is to restructure their personality." If, particularly in an early discussion with a customer, a Black Belt "geeks out" on sample selection or statistical analysis, the customers may find process improvement irrelevant or overly complex. This turnoff often occurs within companies, never mind with customers. The focus must be on the things that your customers are trying to accomplish and the ways in which they're trying to accomplish them.

Creating a sales team or a consulting team dedicated to bringing Six Sigma to customers presupposes that you have customers with the type and scale of operations that would make a process approach worthwhile. The issue of scale is perhaps more important than the product or service, which might range from the most sophisticated to the simplest. If you sell cleaning supplies, lubricants, or packing materials, you might think of these bread-and-butter products as having little to do with process improvement. But if you examine the processes around these products—delivery and maintenance schedules, all costs (including transportation and inventory), ease of use, upstream and downstream effects, safety procedures, and so on—and you initiate a serious conversation with your customer about these matters and your product, you'll see the process that surrounds the products and, in all probability, new opportunities to add value.

GETTING IT RIGHT: ELEMENTS OF A SOUND DEPLOYMENT

I've written this book for a range of readers, including marketing and sales professionals who have never (or who have only) heard of process improvement as well as people in Six Sigma companies who may be currently or soon participating in process improvement projects. This range of readers also includes process improvement professionals who are or will be applying their knowledge to their marketing and sales functions. And it includes senior managers, consultants, and vendors of services to marketing and sales—all with different levels of knowledge of process improvement. So although some readers will be familiar with Six Sigma deployments, this book would be incomplete if it failed to cover the subject.

Here then are six characteristics of successful deployments culled from Six Sigma literature and the experience of companies that have been there:

1. Senior management support
2. Training in Six Sigma
3. Establishment of a dedicated project office
4. Savvy project selection
5. Replication of successful projects
6. Control of processes to the new standards

Senior Management Support

No need to belabor this point. Anyone with any knowledge of organizational life knows that most people in the organization will adopt the goals, initiatives, beliefs, and behaviors demonstrated by management. While the CEO must spearhead a companywide effort, process improvement methods can be applied in the marketing and sales function on a small, targeted scale. The key is that the manager overseeing the function in which these methods are applied must support the effort. In a companywide effort, the CEO clearly must support it, because the CEO's span of control is companywide. An effort limited to marketing or sales, or both, can be initiated with the support of the management of the relevant function(s). Of course, senior management support of even limited efforts would be more than welcome, but senior executives often must see proof of efficacy before supporting an initiative.

Note, however, that the senior managers in companies that have really succeeded with companywide Six Sigma programs did not simply support it. They made it a way of life. They integrated the language and concepts into the company culture, used Six Sigma to set priorities and pursue goals, and ensured that managers at all levels were engaged. They also trained a good number of employees in process improvement.

Training in Six Sigma

Almost every company that has deployed Six Sigma companywide has used formal training in process improvement methods. The exceptions may be originators such as Motorola and Allied Signal. But they were firmly grounded in quality control and improvement disciplines such as Total Quality Management. Most companies that decide to use Six Sigma hire at least one person, and often more, with deep experience in leading entire initiatives or multiple projects (or both) in other companies. Standard Register hired Bob Crescenzi, who worked at Compaq Computer and received Six Sigma training through Motorola; HSBC's Jon Theuerkauf worked in GE Capital Corporation; J&J hired people from Motorola and Allied Signal.

With outside expertise on board, the company then hires a firm to train selected people to become Black Belts and Green Belts. Some of these people will report to the head of the Six Sigma effort but have experience in one or more functional areas of the company. The number of people who receive training varies from company to company. Some companies work with a relatively small team of Black Belts who run projects, while other outfits want greater "density."

But a word of caution is in order. As with sales training, it's useless for people to learn a new method and then return to their former modes of operation. They must apply the method on actual projects. That's the purpose of the Black Belt and Green Belt certifications. Be sure that any training you use includes a strong dose of relevant, practical application. That means classroom training followed by work on an actual project, then more classroom time followed by more work on the project over a period of weeks or months. Bear in mind that training is only one characteristic of a successful deployment. It is necessary but not sufficient.

Establish a Dedicated Project Office

The only things that get done in an organization are things that someone is responsible—and accountable—for doing. That's why organizations that have successfully deployed Six Sigma companywide have placed a high-level executive with senior management support in charge of the initiative. As you've seen, that person typically has experience spearheading process improvement deployments or projects. That person also is tasked, not only with bringing process improvement to the functional areas of the company, but with producing gains. Gains are usually defined in terms of the ROI on the cost of the initiative but sometimes in terms of cost savings or revenue or profit increases expressed in dollars or percentages.

Now responsibility and accountability are key management principles but what about authority? What authority does the vice president of process improvement have over the areas intended to adopt these methods?

Usually the head of quality has to "sell" the initiative to the operating units and functional areas. Selling is inevitably easier with strong senior management sponsorship. Recall HSBC's Jon Theuerkauf who came from GE, an environment in which mandates drove a lot of change. At Service-Master, Chief Executive Officer Jonathan Ward decided that the company would use Six Sigma to pursue its growth and profitability goals. Similarly,

Standard Register CEO Dennis Rediker decided that this business forms company would use Six Sigma not only to remain relevant to customers but to transform itself as well. With that kind of "air cover," the prospect of promulgating Six Sigma becomes far more realistic. Yet it still must be promulgated rather than shoved down people's throats for a very simple reason: The managers and employees in functional areas need to do their jobs and meet their objectives, whether or not the company is using Six Sigma. So their focus tends to be on that rather than on Six Sigma. (We'll look at ways to address that source of resistance later in this chapter.)

The process improvement czar usually has the authority to hire Black Belts, choose a vendor for training, and chart the course of the deployment. But the czar rarely, if ever, can order the manager of a department to undertake a project. Of course, if the manager's area is performing poorly, the manager's motivation will be higher and resistance lower. Yet even in those circumstances, you need cooperation rather than rote compliance. The promise of increased top- or bottom-line performance makes the business case, but helping people to do their jobs makes the human relations case.

Savvy Project Selection: Pick Your Shots

Mention project selection to a group of Six Sigma practitioners, and you have their attention. The importance of the issue stems from three factors. First, as in most endeavors, the way in which you define a task partly dictates the chances of success. Second, pursuing the wrong project—one that wastes resources, takes too long, or doesn't pay off—can squander the goodwill established with an operating manager and his or her people. Third, choosing the wrong project creates an opportunity cost—in the form of the project not undertaken—that can be high, especially if you don't get another chance in an area for a while.

Proper project selection means carefully defining and scoping the project, setting realistic expectations, and gathering data that enables proper measurement of potential costs and benefits of various projects. In the early stages, selecting the right projects produces quick wins while demonstrating the application and benefits of the methodology. Consider the marketing and sales projects presented in this book and how they came about:

- Lumber Products, Inc. built a project around the seemingly straightforward task of improving the performance of the lower-performing salespeople in each region. Recall the scope of the project: in each region, the goal was to get the low performers to the level of the region's average. That goal was reasonable, measurable, and doable for the regional managers.
- When it examined its whole sales process, the private banking division of an international financial institution found that it was losing new customers at the account-opening stage. Improving that part of the process generated gains without adding any new salespeople, the original solution.
- TruGreen ChemLawn management suspected that discounting was a problem but never had the data to make the case. That data, plus research into prevailing prices in each market, revealed that controlling discounts would be a feasible and potentially profitable project.
- HSBC built a project around customer profitability and holding salespeople responsible—on the basis of sound data, account analysis, and "expectation pacts"—for bringing customers to acceptable levels of profitability or moving them to online trading or out of the trading business.
- At American Residential Services, a business of ServiceMaster, Steve Burnett looked at a Six Sigma project that speeded up the contract cancellation process and asked: why are customers canceling and what can we do about it? His question led to research revealing that cancellations were due mostly to customer service problems that could be resolved. This insight led to a project that established a very successful Save Desk.

It may be useful to use one or more of the following steps to help your team select sound marketing and sales project:

- Conduct Voice of the Customer surveys and ask managers and employees in the area about their biggest problems, frustrations, and bottlenecks.
- Develop one or two simple tools, such as a preliminary sales process map, so you can better visualize, understand, and discuss the process.

- Count leads, prospects (qualified leads), and opportunities at various stages of the sales process to see where they are lost; calculate yields for activities such as lead generation, sales calls, proposal submissions, and price negotiations and look for opportunities to increase these yields.
- Calculate the costs of, and returns on, various marketing and sales activities, particularly those that appear to require significant resources; consider conducting a sales operating audit.
- Look for areas where your company may be delivering significant value but not getting paid for it.
- Identify areas where basic information—accurate definitions and useful data—seem to be missing; develop at least summary data on repetitive customer service problems, customers who leave or don't repurchase, and on basic costs such as those of developing a lead, making a sales call, and preparing a proposal.

Experimentation is intrinsic to the scientific method and to process improvement. The initial iteration of virtually any project may be considered an experiment insofar that, if it succeeds, it will be replicated across all areas and locations in which it would apply. Implicit in the notion of an experiment is the possibility that it might not work. The pilot project might show that the supposed cause was not the cause, or the improvement might be miniscule. In that case, you must identify the true cause of the problem and launch a project to fix it. In practice, however, given that quality and process improvement have been in use in one form or another for decades, a large base of experienced Black Belts and successful projects mean that these days, the number of failed projects is remarkably low.

Replicate Successful Projects, Site by Site

In a companywide deployment, successful projects are replicated at every location that can benefit. As you might imagine, there are better and worse ways of going about that. ServiceMaster provides an excellent example of effective replications. The company had conducted DMAIC projects, which found opportunities to increase revenue by reducing discounting at TruGreen ChemLawn and American Residential Services

(ARS). In Chapter 7, I mentioned that these businesses standardized their price books and established procedures for pricing and discounts. I also mentioned that compliance doesn't happen automatically.

Replicating projects in manufacturing is usually easier than in sales. Production workers tend to follow procedures, the materials they work on are inanimate, and locations tend to be fewer and more tightly managed. So process improvement professionals may have to work harder to gain cooperation in marketing and sales.

For instance, the ServiceMaster Six Sigma team started with extremely solid data, based on their own primary research on pricing, discounting, and customer perceptions of value in plumbing and heating repairs. The team also conducted a successful pilot program at an ARS location. With that data and experience, the team set out to replicate the project across other branches. Here's how John Biedry, senior vice president of continuous improvement and Six Sigma, describes that replication initiative:

> We took our data and ran smack into a big cultural wall. Service technicians in that business really believe they know how to price projects, and the experience of other locations just doesn't matter to many of them. So the real battle is in the trenches of getting folks to change the way they work. We found early on that sending memos out didn't do the trick. Nor did using our Black Belts traditionally, as others have, by coming up with a solution and then handing it off to the units.
>
> So we got our Black Belts heavily involved in implementation and compliance. We weren't a manufacturer with three locations in North America, or five, or ten. We had hundreds of service locations with 40 to 50, maybe 60 people involved. So as we got better at this, we found that sending process improvement people out to many of the locations, doing hands-on training, following up on a location with metrics, using compliance charts—simple green-yellow-red charts to track the metrics for them—keeping it on the president's weekly conference calls, having our Black Belts at region meetings—all that helped us become effective. We had high-level support, and the changes and discounting were tied right into the profit expectations for the year so that people were measured on it. We've had our struggles, but we've had some real success along the way.

John emphasizes that although the company wanted compliance with the new pricing policies, its efforts to tailor things to the branch locations were genuine.

> At the branches, our Black Belts sat down not only with company data, which some branches could care less about, but with their own branch data. This data said, "Here's what you gave away through discounting. Here's your breakeven analysis. Here's what you will have to sell this year to make up for that discounting. And, by the way, here's what your customers said about pricing and about their willingness to take price increases."
>
> Then, the branch people would ask what they could do to change things. We, of course, had company recommendations, but we also gave the branches the ability to fine-tune them and come up with their own recommendations. So we didn't have one way to do pricing in all of ARS from day one. We went from no way to do pricing, where every branch did its own, to gravitating first to regional price lists and now to national price lists.
>
> We're not perfect. We've got a long way to go. But we made real progress and brought in $5 million or $6 million of incremental profit. Also, this isn't so much a Six Sigma success story as it is a business success story. The Six Sigma teams are there to provide support and add some rigor and to use the methodology. But this succeeded because the business got behind it. The Six Sigma team did great work, but the credit goes to the leaders of the business that continue to push this.

John's final comments may put some readers in mind of Harry Truman's saying, "It is amazing what you can accomplish if you do not care who gets the credit." Yet it's true that the actual work must be done by people not on the Six Sigma team. Six Sigma pros help to discover, justify, and recommend process changes, but the people working in the process make the changes. That's key to remember in replication efforts. Also, the fact is that conditions and challenges do vary across locations. So even when you're replicating a very successful project, a process improvement team must resist the urge to try to force adoption. They'll be tempted to, given a successful project and a clear way to secure gains. However, considering the local situation and those who must live with the changes will work better and faster than trying to force people to change.

Control Processes to the New Standards

Replication—and then controlling the process to the new level of performance—are necessities for success with Six Sigma. Indeed, the control step in DMAIC tends to receive the least attention in most discussions of Six Sigma. The detective work, the experimentation, and the eureka moments occur in the first four steps. However, failure at the control phase has often been cited as a key problem with the methodology. That failure occurs most often when managers lack the data required to manage the process to the new standards.

Evan Miller, president of the enterprise software firm Hertzler Systems, says, "One of the ugly secrets of Six Sigma—especially in transaction environments [such as sales and marketing]—is that most business systems weren't built to produce the kind of data necessary to implement Six Sigma projects." As a result, Black Belts must often spend a lot of time picking through data files to collect and prepare the right data for analysis. Then, once the project is finished, the process owners are left to manage at the higher level of performance but without the systems needed to keep the process in control.

Because companies often don't recognize this problem, getting the right systems in place can become a political football. In sales and marketing, the issue centers on CRM systems, which depend on the sales force to generate the right data. The challenge is to design a sales process that helps salespeople succeed, build systems that help them do their jobs easier and faster, and then pull the right data out of those systems.

Successful Six Sigma deployments have other characteristics, yet the ones I've discussed above will enable a company to avoid the most serious mistakes. This, of course, presupposes that senior management understands Six Sigma as a way of managing and not as a fad, an investor relations tool, or a cost-cutting program.

BLACK BELT, HEAL THYSELF?

Here is a tale of a Six Sigma initiative gone horribly wrong, told by a Black Belt in his own words. He would like to remain anonymous, and he extends that courtesy to his former employer.

I was a Black Belt in consumer financial services, at what I'll call The Company, reporting to the original quality leader, whom I'll call Larry. After missing its financial goals for several quarters, The Company bought some loan portfolios to boost earnings, and that worked for a while. But then it all hit the fan. The Company was found guilty of multiple violations under Sarbanes-Oxley [post-Enron legislation regarding senior managers' and directors' responsibilities], and we wound up paying a few hundred million in fines and penalties.

Six Sigma had been launched a few months earlier, and I think management saw it as a way to avoid future sins. Five of the first ten Six Sigma projects focused directly on the problems that had led to our violations, and we fixed them.

But shortly after that, management learned of problems in our insurance group. They had been hearing that the group head, whom I'll call Ron, was incompetent and the place was falling apart. So the president asked my boss, Larry, to take over the insurance group and fix it, and Larry agreed. But—and this is the killer—because Ron had been around forever and was well connected, they put *him* in charge of the Six Sigma project office.

The guy hated Six Sigma. He had been on one of the first project teams and spent all his time mocking the methodology. Not only that, as the Six Sigma head, he now reported to the vice president of strategic projects instead of to the president. That sort of demoted the whole initiative.

But for me, the death knell was this: I'd always heard that 15 percent of our customers came into a branch in person to make their monthly loan or mortgage payment. That means that across our huge branch system, salespeople who were tasked with generating $300,000 a month in new business had to take a check, create a receipt, prepare the remittance, and all the rest of it to process each of these payments.

I told Ron about this and for reasons he never explained, he told me not to pursue it. I found an IT guy who had been on one of my project teams, and he and I secretly collected two months of data on the entire branch network. We found that payments of over $300 million *a month* were going into over 500 different banks—none of them ours, so our banking division wasn't getting the use of those funds. Collectively, our salespeople were spending 25 full-time equivalents dealing with these checks. Plus, we weren't even trying to sell anything to all these customers who visit us every month.

Long story short, I compiled the data and presented the analysis and potential solutions to management. The solutions employed check scanners that printed instant receipts and deposited the funds directly to our affiliate bank and so on. The payback period would have been a few months. Well, some of it was implemented, but a lot of it wasn't, because most of the benefits went to the banking division, not to our division.

What can you do? I've since moved on.

Ironic, isn't it? Companies can build waste, errors, and defects into their own Six Sigma programs. This case is somewhat extreme, fortunately, but it illustrates the sheer wrongheadedness of some executives' views of Six Sigma. Yet even without someone actually trying to undermine their efforts, many companies have had problems implementing Six Sigma. Those problems, however, usually stem not from Six Sigma per se but from the ways management views it or implements it. Like any tool, Six Sigma can be used in the wrong ways, for the wrong purposes, and even in a dangerous manner. Such failures are clearly not a shortcoming of the methodology.

Most companies that take it seriously get it right. For a superb example of a Six Sigma deployment and a case of the methodology being used to transform a company and its culture, let's turn to Standard Register.

A COMPANY REINVENTS ITSELF WITH SIX SIGMA

Standard Register was founded in 1912 and, with about $1 billion in revenues, is a leading provider of business forms. In 2001, CEO Dennis Rediker brought on Bob Crescenzi, who had been through Motorola University in the early 1990s, to head up the Six Sigma initiative—and to achieve a one-year payback. More challenging still, however, was the underlying purpose of the initiative: transformation of the company.

The business forms industry has experienced an upheaval over the past decade. The personal computer's desktop printing and electronic forms capabilities were one thing. Add print-on-demand technologies, plus networking and the Internet, and you have a business in total flux. Standard Register's customers include some of the largest outfits in their industries, which have adopted these new methods. Business forms are a commodity product, and when you're selling a commodity in a changing market, the challenge is first to remain relevant, then set the bar higher.

To do this, Standard Register had to reinvent itself, and it chose process improvement as the vehicle. Bob Crescenzi, vice president of Six Sigma, explained:

> Our customers have three options: desktop printing, on-site print center, or contracted printing firm. But they don't have the expertise in workflow, paper flow, and cost management to make those decisions in the best way. They need someone with that expertise, a "concierge" who can route each job to the lowest cost print option. We had to transform ourselves from selling forms to selling workflow analysis and management, and from a service approach to an enterprise approach.

Bob, who helped the company integrate Six Sigma into the workflow analysis, describes Standard Register's Six Sigma deployment as "textbook." As with Six Sigma in every company, early projects focused on internal processes and hard-dollar cost savings in areas such as order processing, printing, delivery, and billing. In 2003, about a year-and-a-half into the deployment, the company moved the focus from cost reduction to revenue generation, that is, into the customer-touching functions, including sales and marketing. Here's how Bob explains that shift and its results:

To create a customer focus, we launched a comprehensive Voice of the Customer initiative. We needed to identify current and future customer needs, learn about customers' business problems and how we could help solve them, and find out how we were meeting their expectations. We wanted our customers to see and feel the effects of Six Sigma. So this VOC included metrics such as loyalty assessments, transaction and satisfaction surveys, win-loss analyses, and customer scorecards. We used telephone and Web-based surveys to measure loyalty on an annual basis, satisfaction on a quarterly basis, and transaction execution on an event basis.

Several useful things came out of this. We identified gaps between customers' expectations and our performance. We gathered metrics for improvement and control in areas such as order turnaround, quality, convenience, cost, and reliability and used customer scorecards to track that data. We used the Burke Secure Customer Index to gauge customer loyalty and the factors that go into it, and we looked at our customers across industries to learn where we did well and where we could improve.

We took the Baldridge categories [leadership, strategic planning, customer focus, measurement and analysis, human resources, process management, and business results] and used a balanced scorecard to drive performance in four areas: learning and growth, internal process, customer benefits, and financial results. Our logic is that *learning and growth* will give our people the expertise they need to build the needed capabilities into our *internal processes.* That, in turn, will enable us to deliver the *benefits* customers require, which will generate *financial results.*

While our initial efforts helped us internally, for instance by reducing costs and waste, our customers rarely felt those changes. For that to happen, we first did the VOC surveys and then, based on the findings, launched an effort to help customers achieve business results with our services. Everyone wants to do whatever they're doing better, faster, and cheaper. In our area of expertise, we showed them how to do all three.

We went all out on measurement. You have to understand what's important to the customer today and in the future, but you also have to develop very sensible ways of measuring those things. We prepared a comprehensive set of customer loyalty measures, transaction customer surveys, and win-loss analyses and took them seriously. For example, the loss analysis is done by our senior executives. I do some. Our chief marketing officer does some. The vice president of investor relations does some. We want to see firsthand why our company loses business from customers and why we win business.

We worked hard to find what's important to customers and how they rated us on those things. If they rate something at 5 [on 1-to-5 scale] in importance and rate our performance at 3, there's a gap there—a missed opportunity. You need to understand the correlation between what the customer views as important and what you're doing. You can't do that without measures. You've got to get beyond the customer saying, "I don't like what you're doing," and have factual discussions that result in measurable concepts.

We do an annual review with every major account, using a comprehensive set of metrics that they grade us on. They have actually used our approach to change how they deal with their other suppliers. I believe that any supplier that's not measuring things in this way doesn't really have a clue about how they're doing.

So it all ties together, metrics on your customers' requirements, on your processes, and on your performance in the eyes of customers.

Standard Register's results came from of an all-out adoption of Six Sigma. By 2005, more than 50 percent of Standard Register's employees had been through some level of Six Sigma training, including Black Belts, Green Belts, and Yellow Belts. (The latter receive two to four hours of training in basic Six Sigma.) Bob Crescenzi says, "At that density, Six Sigma starts to change the culture and the language of the business." In fact, as of 2005, *the majority of Standard Register salespeople* had received at least two hours of Six Sigma training, so, in Bob's words, "They at least know that the Black Belts are not the enemy."

That's good, because the company found that major customers were asking about Six Sigma. Given their size and industry positions, many Standard Register customers have used process improvement and constantly seek ways to remain competitive. Many of them want to squeeze out wasted cycle time, excess inventories, and non-value-adding steps in processes. Printing and routing forms represent a logical place to look for such savings.

Standard Register has developed a consulting group composed of Black Belts and Green Belts. This group works with customers to redesign their processes with an on-site Standard Register consultant, who helps people route their printing to the lowest cost option: desktop, on-site print center, or off-site printer. These consultants use a personal computer-based tool as a print procurement gateway, which enables customers to control their documents and costs. However, as Bob points out, with any new effort come challenges:

> Our biggest challenge is the customer, not our salespeople. Customers often have no data and often don't understand our approach. So there's a lot of discovery and a lot of knowledge sharing that goes on. But we are definitely getting to the C-level managers in many organizations [chief information officer, chief procurement officer, and so on]. And we are definitely in the process of reinventing ourselves as a company.

Many companies follow the path of deploying Six Sigma first in operational areas and then in marketing and sales. Indeed, it's almost necessary for several reasons. First, you have the greatest control over processes that don't directly touch customers. Yes, you look at what customers need from those processes, but the customer interface with them is limited. Second, it's best to master process improvement in-house before you apply it to customer-facing functions just for the experience. Third, it's a matter of priorities: why pursue ways to add high value for customers if you can't even process their orders correctly and send them accurate invoices? Do those things first, then start thinking big. Finally, it's again an issue of priorities: Because most internal systems function at low levels of efficiency and effectiveness before process improvement, that's where you'll find the biggest bang for the Six Sigma buck at the outset, especially in marketing and sales. As one fellow put it: "The fruit's not low hanging. It's on the ground!"

THERE'S NO TIME TO WASTE

This book is not meant to be the last word on applying process improvement to marketing and sales. On the contrary, it's actually the first word, in book form that is. My publisher and I could not wait until we had a perfect or exhaustively comprehensive book on the subject. In that same vein, I suggest that you do not wait for the perfect time to apply Six Sigma to your sales process.

Depending on your organizational role, you can apply it in ways ranging from one-off projects to boost the performance of an activity, such as lead generation, to—if you are a senior marketing officer—a redesign of your entire sales process or—if you are a CEO—a companywide deployment. You can use formal Six Sigma by hiring consultants or Black Belts and getting training. Or you can informally map your sales process, gather some data, and identify points that clearly demand a process approach. Even applying process *thinking* to marketing and sales can produce positive results.

Similarly, after you have adopted process approaches internally, don't wait until you think you have a perfect method before bringing Six Sigma to your customers. You will probably never reach that point. Yet you should be able to add greater value for customers in a matter of months after you have employed process improvement in your marketing and sales function. Remember: Designing your sales process around the buyer's journey will assist your customers in very real ways while reducing your costs and increasing your revenue. With such a process in place, you can consider ways of bringing higher levels of Six Sigma selling to your customers by helping them improve their processes, perhaps with special sales or consulting teams and value-added services.

It's interesting that for some companies, and perhaps for many more in the future, Six Sigma selling ultimately dovetails with consulting. Consulting itself is moving toward a much more client-focused mode of operation. David Maister, author of *The Trusted Advisor* and *True Professionalism*, is one of the chief proponents of this model, in which a company adds value by truly understanding customers. "Having the solution is not really enough," David says. "If you want customers to trust you, you actually have to add a layer of consulting behaviors that enable them to understand that you understand them. You're not doing this and taking people and their goals into account just because it's the right thing to do. You're also doing it because people won't listen to your advice or purchase your solution—even if it's totally correct—unless you take a truly consultative approach. You have to have the solution, but you have to have the relationship, too." In addition, David notes that you will discover more opportunities to help the customer in the context of that kind of relationship.

Finally, be aware that a competitor of yours may bring Six Sigma selling to your customer before you do, thus gaining first-mover advantage. To be the second mover on something this innovative may permanently relegate your company to also-ran status.

If you are a process improvement professional and you have read this far, you probably realize that marketing and sales represent areas of tremendous opportunity. You may even have seen the redirection of Six Sigma from cost reduction to revenue enhancement in your own company. You probably now have a better understanding of the ways in which applying process improvement to marketing and sales differs from applying it to production functions—and of ways to deal with those differences.

If you are a marketing or sales manager or a general manager and you have read this far, you may have as many questions as you had when you picked up this book. However, I trust that they are different questions and that you have gained an understanding—and an appreciation—of the differences between managing marketing and sales with Six Sigma and managing without it. I also trust that the examples of the companies that have used this approach will inspire you to do the same in the ways that make sense for you and your customers.

Indeed, regardless of your professional position, I would like to leave you with a bit of data and something to consider. In his book *Diffusion of Innovations,* first published in 1962, Everett Rogers classified adopters of new technologies into five categories depending on their willingness to adopt an innovation. At that time he also introduced the bell-shaped technology adoption curve and organized his categories under that curve. Rogers stated that with respect to a given technology, only about 3 percent of a given population will be Innovators, and another 13 percent will be Early Adopters. The remaining *84 percent* consists of the Early Majority (34 percent), Late Majority (34 percent), and Laggards (16 percent). That translates to a fairly large percentage taking a cautious, wait-and-see approach to new technologies, products, and ideas. It also translates to a small percentage reaping major gains and establishing prominent positions in the early stages of an innovation's diffusion.

When it comes to Six Sigma in marketing and sales, the companies covered in this book are Innovators and Early Adopters. I hereby invite you to join them by investigating and, yes, experimenting with process improvement in your marketing and sales function. After all, if it doesn't work, that itself is valuable information that enables you to move on with enthusiasm to your next initiative. However, if it does work, you may very well revolutionize your company's sales process and boost its performance to otherwise unobtainable levels while genuinely helping your customers.

My hypothesis is that process improvement will improve your sales process. In the spirit of scientific inquiry, I am ready to be proven right or wrong. However, on the basis of the evidence I've gathered so far, I must admit a bias toward being proven right.

KEY POINTS

- Process improvement techniques should be implemented to help businesspeople achieve their goals and objectives. Doing this requires organizations to begin at a high level and take the following steps:
  1. Start with existing business goals.
  2. Take the customer's point of view.
  3. Examine (and map) your sales process.
  4. Develop relevant data and facts.
- Far from some people's perceptions that Six Sigma is primarily about arcane and complicated statistical techniques, it is really about sound reasoning regarding the fundamentals of managing sales and marketing activities.
- Six Sigma process improvement can apply in sales and marketing organizations in three basic ways:
  1. Improving your ability to assist customers on their buyer's journey
  2. Applying process improvement to customers in the way you sell to them
  3. Providing on-site Six Sigma teams to customers

- Successfully deploying Six Sigma within a company requires the following:
  - Senior management sponsorship
  - Training in Six Sigma
  - Establishing a dedicated project office
  - Savvy project selection
- Organizations must respect the human nature of their employees. This means doing things in a way that allows those employees to exercise their own judgment and generates their buy-in rather than their compliance.
- Process improvement and Six Sigma represent a deep well of opportunities for companies to reinvent themselves as more profitable, more resilient enterprises.

SUPPLEMENT TO CHAPTER 4

The first section of this Appendix contains the examples of tools and more detailed data that were omitted from Chapter 4 for simplicity. In this section, the bolded items are the ones not covered in Chapter 4. The second section asnwers technical questions concerning the data.

PART 1—DEFINE PHASE: WHAT'S THE PROBLEM?

The define phase must define the goals and benefits of the project. It must ensure that you have a valid problem, that the team understands the problem, that the problem is solvable, and that the stakeholders want it solved. It must ascertain that you've got the resources and that applying them to the project will produce benefits. In some early versions of Six Sigma, the define phase was assumed rather than explicit, causing problems in later phases. Thus the define phase states the problem clearly enough to keep everyone on track as the project winds its way to completion.

Tools of the Define Phase

The define phase of this project employed the following tools:

- **Project Charter**
- Brainstorming
- Fishbone diagram
- XY matrix
- Measures of the process
- High-level process map
- **SIPOC diagram**
- **FMEA**
- Screen shots of TRG Web pages

Project charter. The charter lays out the scope, background, team members, and other basic information about the project in a standard format. Figure A-1 shows the charter for this project.

Note the key questions being asked and answered in the third column:

- What is the importance of the process?
- What is the problem?
- What is the cost of the problem?
- How do we know these things? What measurements are available?
- Who are the stakeholders?
- What are the boundaries of the process (beginning, ending)?

As you can see, these templates are more structured and thorough than is typical of the methods for most marketing and selling decisions. The purpose, of course, is to elevate the quality of your thinking at the outset of the project so that the quality of your results will be more assured. Studies have shown that when projects do not turn out well in business, failure is usually due to not answering these kinds of questions carefully enough, or early enough.

SIPOC (suppliers, inputs, process, outputs, customers). A SIPOC (*sy'pock*) diagram lays out the five key elements of any process: suppliers, inputs, value-adding process, outputs, and customers. A SIPOC, which can apply to internal or external customers, is extremely useful for showing who performs which tasks on what materials for whom. A properly prepared SIPOC requires very little explanation, as evidenced by Figure A-2.

FMEA (failure modes and effects analysis). Failure modes and effects analysis (FMEA) is exactly what it sounds like—if you stop and think about it. Yes, it's a mouthful, but the tool provides a structured way to identify all possible modes of failure in a process. That is, it first identifies all the ways in which the process can fail to do what it's supposed to do. Then the effects analysis determines the ramifications of each failure on other activities and results.

FMEA also ranks and prioritizes the causes and effects causes of failures, and it can be applied to a product or service as well as to a process. The Severity, Occurrence, and Detectability columns are simply ranked

FIGURE A-1
Project Charter

Project	TRG Revenue Improvement	
Project Leader	Michael Webb	**Process Importance** This process is fundamental to the success of TRG and to the constituents of TRG (potential employers and employees)
Master Black Belt	Rob Tripp	**Cost of Poor Quality** Low revenue to TRG, lost opportunity for employers and potential Black Belt employees
Project Start	October	
Project End	September	
Team Members		**Process Problem** Too few people are aware of the potential or convinced of the value of TRG. Too few employers are signing up with TRG so they can find employees. Too few people know how to use TRG
Sponsor	John Smith	
Black Belt	Michael Webb	
Master Black Belt	Rob Tripp	
Subject Matter Experts		**Process Goals** To express the value of TRG in the customer's terms. Devise a more effective way of finding, gaining, and keeping customers. Leverage Internet tools without hiring employees
John Webb	Marketing, sales, and Web site marketing	
John Smith	TRG business needs	
Process Start/Stop		**Process Measurements** Gross TRG visitor statistics, conversions to relationships, conversions to (employer) customers
Start Point	Employers visit the TRG Web site seeking potential employees.	
Stop Point	Employers continue using TRG to find potential employees and provide testimonials.	

Project Time Frame

Milestone	Project Kickoff	Completion
Define	October • Michael Webb • Rob Tripp	September
Measure	April	May
Analyze	May	June
Improve	June	
Control	September	

FIGURE A-2
SIPOC (TRG)

SIPOC Diagram: Technical Resume Group

Note: This diagram represents only the employer side of the TRG selling process. Job candidates are not considered for purposes of this project.

Suppliers	Inputs	Process	Outputs	Customers	Requirements
Press	Publicity		Awareness of potential value	Employers with general needs for job candidates	
Market partner	Referrals Inquiries (visitors)		Provide information about services and candidates		
Potential clients (employers)	Job opportunities Functional design and information Functional Web site		Provide information about services and candidates Easy, simple purchase process	Employers with specific needs for job candidates	Credibility of supplier Positive testimonials Reason to buy Reasonable fee schedule
Web site owner			Positive testimonials	Web site owner	Selling done by Web site, not salespeople; agreement to provide services
Web site builder and ISP			Process yield information Revenue		No- or low-cost advertising only Accurate, on-demand reporting

Attract potential clients	Establish trust and credibility	Establish specific need or value	Service transaction	Satisfaction/ value assessment

---

from 1 to 10. The Risk Priority Number (RPN) is simply the product of all three. It is amazing how following simple logic like this allows the team to discover or articulate things that may have been suspected but not confirmed.

Although at first glance, an FMEA may seem too technical to apply with sales teams, my experience shows otherwise. Once salespeople and marketers get the idea of what an FMEA is, filling in the blanks can generate a lively debate. People learn a great deal about their work and about each other when they apply what they already know to the structured way of thinking inherent in these quality tools.

Although a process FMEA is often done later in a project, we used the one in Figure A-3 in the define phase to give us an idea of what might be going wrong.

PART 2—MEASURE PHASE: WHAT WILL WE MEASURE AND HOW?

Six Sigma projects often move back and forth between the measure and analyze phases, as my project did. The team can formulate and test hypotheses in an iterative way and validate variables as they're identified. This section presents the tools of the measure phase in the sequence.

Tools of the Measure Phase

Part A of the measure phase of this project employed the following tools:

- Defect, opportunity, unit, and metrics
- **Detailed process map**
- Data collection plan
- Data table
- Process measurement charts
- Situation assessment
- **Process capability**

Detailed process map. The detailed process map in Figure A-4 enabled us to define precisely the metrics we would gather. As the map indicates, each page plays a role in finding and gaining customers. (The function of keeping customers was beyond the scope of the project.) For each page (home.asp, pricing.asp, and signup.asp), the map delineates the activities conducted by each page and, at the bottom of the column for that page, the intended output, effect, or result.

Process capability. Process capability is a statistical test to determine the extent to which a process is capable of producing what is required of it. The chart in Figure A-5 is presented by way of illustration.

FIGURE A-3

FMEA (Failure Modes and Effects Analysis)

Failure Effects	Severity	Failure Causes	Occurrence	Detectability
What happens if such a failure occurs?	I to 10	What could cause a failure?	I to 10	I to 10
Low traffic, and resulting low business level	7	Lack of publicity, promotion, or awareness in the market	4	3
Prospect leaves for another site	6	Cluttered unattractive or confusing layout/design	3	3
Prospect leaves for another site	9	Lack of useful information/content	8	2
Prospect doesn't come back	9	No promise of future value, not enough depth	8	2
Prospect doesn't come back	9	Lack of permission marketing (e.g., newsletter)	9	2
Prospect doesn't sign up.	8	Failure to communicate value in specific terms prospect can relate to. Or page may seem difficult to use.	8	4
Transaction fails, customer leaves before completing it, or errors (billing, information) are produced.	10	Design or programming error. Lack of feedback from customers.	5	3
Customer decides not to transact any more.	7	Quality of quantity of job candidates is lower than employer's expectations. Information about candidates might be incorrect or incomplete	5	3

FIGURE A-3 *(continued)*

Current Controls	RPN	Recommended Actions	Responsible Person
What are the current methods to prevent failure?	*Risk priority number*	*Outline improvements for items with high RPNs*	*Who is responsible?*
Visibility in TRG Web site	84	Improve visibility and number of external links to the site. Get market partners to provide links.	John Smith
Site appearance seems acceptable; however, there isn't much for visitors to do	54		
Minimal: information value seems weak	144	Provide resources employers might use: how to interview candidates, how to maximize culture fit, evaluating technical vs. leadership skills, new hire orientation programs, organization and individual assessments, etc.	John Smith
Product offer is only reason for someone to come back.	144	Demonstrating that the site is on a trajectory that increases the value to customers. Enhancing functions/services step by step.	John Smith
No permission marketing in effect	162	Provide stay-in-touch services for nonclients. Perhaps giving them stats on available candidates in their area of interest, without providing specific names, etc. Adding helpful content continually over time via the newsletter.	John Smith
None	256	Provide employers with indication of quantity and quality of candidates available. Make sign up simple and attractive. Provide risk reversal (guarantees, etc.)	John Smith
Error logs	150	Gather feedback from visitors (a survey of some kind, perhaps).	John Smith
None	105	Develop and incorporate feedback mechanism for customers to ensure reporting of this information.	John Smith

FIGURE A-4

Detailed Process Map (of the Process "As Is")

Detailed Process Map (as is): Technical Resource Group

Finding	Winning	Keeping

Web Page Process Detail

External TRG Home Page	Employer's Home Page	TRG Pricing, more information	TRG Signup	
Jobs link on TRG site (for employees)	Top: TRG logo Other customers	Same as default page	Same as default page	Servicing Elements are not within the scope of this project
External links to TRG employer site	Menu: My Open Jobs Resume Search Job Stats Help Employee Link			
John Smith conversations with people				
Other external promotion?	Left: Log in Quick fact BBB Membership			
	Right: Featured Jobs	Employer pricing copy	Sign up instructions	
	Center: Image Sales Copy Link to pricing Testimonial	Subscription menu: 1 year 6 months 3 months Month to month	Company/admin details	

Attract potential clients	Establish trust and credibility	Establish specific need or value	Service transaction	Satisfaction/ value assessment

The histogram is compiled by adding up the numbers of weeks where various numbers of orders were achieved. The specification limits and mean were set to illustrate the desired capability of the process.

PART 3—ANALYZE PHASE PART A: WHAT'S CAUSING THE PROBLEM?

Again, we did the analyze phase in two parts, applying the tools of part A of the analyze phase after part A of the measure phase, then doing

FIGURE A-5
Process Capability of Orders

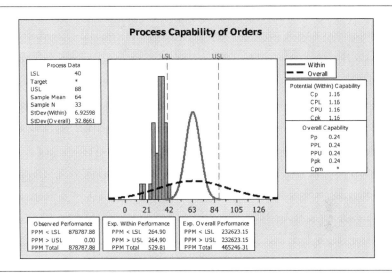

part B of the measure phase—Voice of the Customer—and then doing part B of the analyze phase.

Tools of the Analyze Phase: Part A

- Performance objectives $Y = F(x)$
- **Root cause diagram**
- Key input variables

Root cause diagram. Root cause diagrams are another form of structured brainstorming. Like the fishbone diagram, which helps organize potential causes of a problem into categories, root cause diagrams help to identify chains of causes in an attempt to simplify understanding a problem. An example of a root cause diagram for our project is shown in Figure A-6.

To-be process map. The to-be process map in Figure A-7 illustrates the functions of the pages in the new design.

FIGURE A-6

Root Cause Diagram

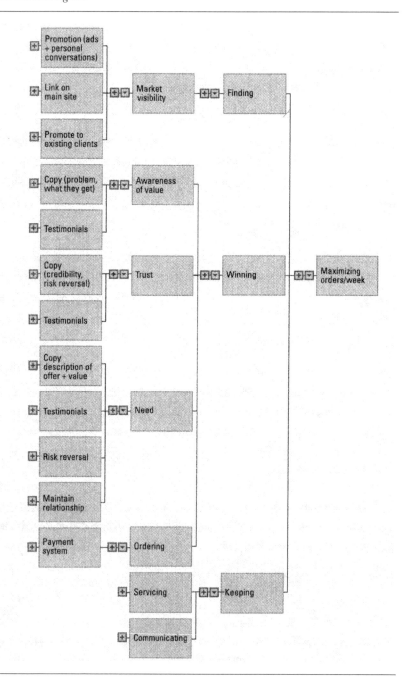

FIGURE A-7

To-Be Process Map

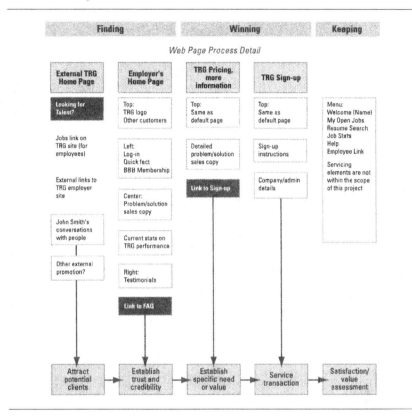

Web Page Process Detail

| Finding | Winning | Keeping |

Tools of the Control Phase. TheThe control phase is one of the most important phases of a project. This material was left out of the chapter, because on this particular project, once the Web site was changed, the change would remain in place and the issues around the control phase were less critical. However, you should have an idea of what a control phase involves, because in other kinds of projects, special steps and procedures will be required to ensure that all your hard-earned improvements actually stick.

Tools of the control phase include:

- **Control plan**
- **Documentation**
- **Monitoring plan**

- **Response plan**
- **Training plan**

Control plan. In the three preceding steps, we measured the Web site's performance, conducted a survey to identify potential changes to improve the results, then made those changes and realized the improvement. As in many Six Sigma projects, gathering and analyzing the data was time consuming, because the information systems had not been designed to supply the data the project required. (This is usually the case with software systems that generate Web site traffic statistics.) Fortunately, the information needed to manage a Web site like this isn't complicated and can be obtained easily and analyzed once a system for capturing it is in place.

- *Control plan part one: foundation.* The first requirement for the control plan was a system that captured and logged the following information by day and date:
  - Page views for each page on the Web site
  - Number of orders received
  - Dollar value of each order received
  - Source of each order (new or existing customer)

  This essential information must be collected, logged, totaled on a weekly basis, and analyzed with process control charts and the rolled throughput yield (as discussed earlier).

  By monitoring this information, the process owners can ensure that the process remains in control—and know when it isn't. They will also see future changes in performance as they continue to experiment with sales copy, site features, and promotional campaigns. In addition, when this kind of monitoring is automated, you have the entire universe of sales data, which minimizes the problem of small sample size.

- *Control plan part two: ongoing VOC for satisfaction and value.* Because the TRG Web site basically provides information to its customers, it can incorporate an automated follow-up system to check that customers received what they requested and to assess the perceived value of the information.

  In lieu of occasional major surveys, the control plan recommended that the TRG interact with prospects and customers in a way that "surveys" them continually. This can be done with autoresponders that ask visitors a few questions at a time about themselves and their experiences. These "minisurveys" would probably foster more participation than occasional major surveys and generate statistically significant amounts of information in a shorter time.

The plan recommended starting with questions on the topics identified as key in the VOC survey. Then over time, the site could add questions that would reveal increasingly more about prospects and customers.

- *Control plan part three: split testing.* The project pointed to other changes that might enhance the Web site, and split testing would quickly reveal which ones work and which do not. While split testing goes beyond a control plan per se, it would establish a rapid means of gathering the data needed to identify and validate useful changes to the process.

   Split tests would direct visitor traffic to two different versions of a specific page, such as the FAQ page. One page—usually the current one—serves as the control, while the test page has different sales copy, service configurations, or pricing, depending on what is being tested. The server would be programmed to support the different versions of the pages, distribute them across the visitors, and place a cookie on their systems to ensure that they see the same page on each visit. The alternative version of a page would have corresponding downstream pages, such as pricing pages and thank-you pages. This enables the page-view counting system to determine which version of the page being tested is causing more people to take the desired actions.

Documentation. Few of TRG's systems had been thoroughly documented, partly because the people involved knew how the systems worked. However, as TRG grows and its systems become more complex, documentation will become essential. In addition, if all elements of the control plan are implemented, TRG will be able to develop, test, and move on to iterations of Web pages much more quickly, heightening the need for documentation. Someone within TRG must be responsible for managing the business and continuing to improve its performance and for maintaining process and control plan documentation.

FIGURE A-8
FMEA for the Control Plan (TRG)

Failure Effects	Severity	Failure Causes	Occurrence	Detectability	Current Controls	RPN	Recommended Actions	Responsible Person
What happens if such a failure occurs?	*1 to 10*	*What could cause a failure?*	*1 to 10*	*1 to 10*	*What are the current methods to prevent failure?*	*Risk priority number*	*Outline improvements for items with high RPN's*	*Who is responsible?*
Low traffic and resulting low business level.	7	Lack of publicity, promotion, or awareness in the market.	4	3	Visibility in TRG website	84	Improve visibility and number of external links to the site. Get market partners to provide links.	John Smith
Ratio of visitors moving from one page to the next falls out of control	8	Copy has been inadvertently changed, technical problem	2	4	View the site regularly	64	Return the site to previous state	John Smith
Order conversion rate falls out of control	9	Copy has been inadvertently changed, technical problem, competitive threat	2	8	View the site regularly, interact with visitors by responding to their e-mails	144	If changes have occurred, return site to previous state. If environment has changed, conduct VOC and adjust offers accordingly.	John Smith

The necessary documentation includes process documents such as

- process maps and flowcharts;
- standard operating procedures; and
- FMEA (failure modes effects analysis).

The documentation must also include the control plan documentation such as

- training manuals;
- monitoring plan-process management charts and reports;
- response plan (FMEA); and
- job descriptions and performance objectives.

Below, I'll explain the monitoring plan and response plan documentation in more detail.

Monitoring plan. The control plan above sets forth the essential data needed to monitor the performance of this business. The only other requirement would be the attention of a manager with the knowledge and authority to control the process. This manager would monitor visitor and customer traffic on the basis of monthly, or perhaps weekly, reviews of the automated control charts and respond accordingly.

Response plan. If the trends in the data reveal that the process is moving out of control, the data from the iterative customer surveys should indicate where to look for the problem and solution. Also, the FMEA for the control plan in Figure A-8, which differs from the FMEA in Figure A-3, can be used to guide managers in responding to potential problems. In addition, split tests and experiments with site changes should be the responsibility of the site manager and must be included in that position's performance objectives.

Training plan. Finally, once the documentation has been assembled, the process owner should conduct training with the process manager to explain and review the systems and set management objectives for moving forward with improvements.

FIGURE A-9

Comparing Daily Page View Data with Weekly Totals

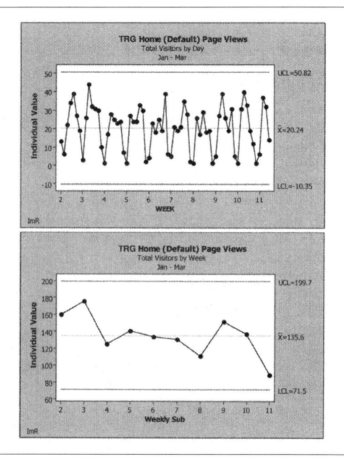

TECHNICAL QUESTIONS CONCERNING THE DATA

Why Is Data Presented in Weekly Totals, and Is That Summation Valid?

The data was actually gathered on a daily basis. However, the daily data produced a cyclical pattern every week (high in the middle of the week, low on weekends). This cycle introduced unnecessary variation and complexity to the numbers and made it harder to see what was happening to the underlying process. Because a week is always seven days while months vary in length, it made sense to work with weekly totals of page views, as shown in Figure A-9. (For technical reasons, we did not use averages.) This approach enabled us to examine the changes and the stability of the underlying process much more clearly. That is the purpose of the run charts.

Here is a vivid example of this idea. Suppose you were to try to measure the height of waves in the ocean. An examination of the surface of the water reveals that although waves come in the 1- to 2-foot range, within each of those are also smaller variations—waves on the order of a fraction of an inch within the 1- to 2-foot waves. Likewise, waves also occur on the order of 10 to 20 feet in height (or higher), and each of these larger waves includes the smaller ones as well. Which order of magnitude is most suitable for the purpose of your study?

Why Was a MultiVary Chart Used in Figure 4-14 Instead of a MultiVary versus Mood-Median Test on VOC Data?

Sharp-eyed readers who are familiar with MiniTab may have noticed that the illustration Figure 4-14 in Chapter 4 was taken from a MultiVary chart. However, because the data is not normal data, it is more suitable for a Mood-median test. I selected the MultiVary only because it made a better illustration of the data. The actual Mood-median test is in Figure A-10.

FIGURE A-10
Moods Median Test

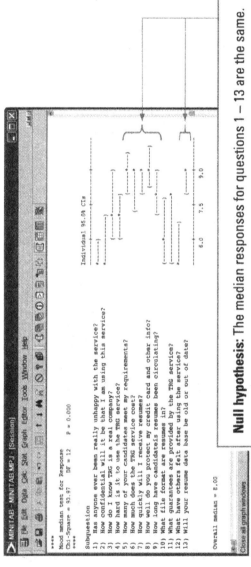

Null hypothesis: The median responses for questions 1 – 13 are the same.

Alternate hypothesis: At least one of the medians for questions 1–13 is different from the others.

Conclusion: The probability of being wrong in assuming that at least one is different from the others is very low (p=0). Therefore, at least one median is different from the others. In fact it appears from the graph that the medians for questions 5–9 and 13 are similar to each other but significantly different from the rest.

Excellent resources for more information about Six Sigma can be found at *www.isixsigma.com*, the leading Internet site for the Six Sigma community.

BOOKS

Abramowich, Edward. *Six Sigma for Growth.* Singapore: John Wiley & Sons (Asia) Pte Ltd., 2005.

Bosworth, Michael. *Solution Selling.* New York: McGraw Hill, 1994.

Caples, John. *Tested Advertising Methods.* Paramus, NJ: Prentice Hall, 1997.

Davidow, William. *Marketing High Technology.* New York: Free Press, 1986.

Friedman, Lawrence G. and Timothy R. Furey. *The Channel Advantage.* Worburn, MA: Butterworth-Heinemann, 1999.

Goldratt, Eliyahu. *The Goal.* Great Barrington, MA: North River Press, 1986.

Hanan, Mack and Peter Karp. *Competing on Value,* New York: Amazon, 1991.

Holden, Jim. *Power Base Selling.* New York: John Wiley & Sons, 1990.

Hopkins, Claude. *My Life in Advertising & Scientific Advertising,* Lincolnwood, IL: NTC Business Books, 1998.

Juran, Dr. Joseph M. *Managerial Breakthrough.* New York: McGraw Hill, Revised Edition, 1994.

Juran, Dr. Joseph M. *Quality Control Handbook.* New York: McGraw Hill, Third Edition, 1974.

Konrath, Jill. *Selling to Big Companies.* Chicago: Dearborn Trade Publishing, 2005.

Macfarlane, Hugh. *The Leaky Funnel*. Toorak, Australia: Bookman Media Pty Ltd, 2003.

Maister, David, Charles Green, and Robert Galford. *The Trusted Advisor*. New York: Free Press, 2000

Maister, David. *True Professionalism*. New York: Free Press, 1997.

Mello, Sheila. *Customer-Centric Product Definition*. Boston: PDC Professional Publishing, 2003.

Miller, Robert and Stephen Heiman. *Strategic Selling*. New York: Warner Books, Reissue Edition, 1988.

Moore, Geoffrey. *Inside the Tornado*. New York: HarperBusiness, 1995.

Nick, Michael and Kurt Koenig. *ROI Selling: Increasing Revenue, Profit and Customer Loyalty through the 360 Sales Cycle*, Chicago: Dearborn Trade, 2004.

Pande, Peter S. et al. *The Six Sigma Way*. New York: McGraw-Hill, 2000.

Rackham, Neil and Howard Ruff. *Managing Major Sales*. New York: Harper Business, 1991.

Rackham, Neil and John DeVincentis. *Rethinking the Sales Force*. New York: McGraw-Hill, 1999.

Rackham, Neil. *SPIN Selling*. New York: McGraw Hill, 1988.

Roff-Marsh, Justin. *Re-engineering the Sales Process*. Brisbane: Ballistix, 2004

Rogers, Everett. *Diffusion of Innovations*. New York: Free Press, Fifth Edition, 2003.

Schaffer, Robert H. *High-Impact Consulting*. San Francisco: Jossey-Bass, 2002.

Schmonsees, Robert J. *Escaping the Black Hole: Minimizing the Damage from the Marketing-Sales Disconnect*, Mason, OH: Thompson/South-Western, 2005.

Selden, Paul. *Sales Process Engineering: A Personal Workshop*. Milwaukee, WI: ASQ Press, 1997.

Shonka, Mark and Dan Kosch. *Beyond Selling Value*. Chicago: Dearborn Trade, 2002.

Wallace, Thomas and Robert Stahl. *Sales Forecasting: A New Approach*. Cincinnati, OH: T. F. Wallace & Company, 2002.

Wallace, Thomas F. *Sales and Operations Planning: The How-To Handbook.* Cincinnati, OH: T. F. Wallace & Company, 1999.

Wheeler, Donald. *Making Sense of Data.* Knoxville, TN: SPC Press, 2003

Wheeler, Donald. *Understanding Variation: The Key to Managing Chaos.* Knoxville, TN: SPC Press, Second Edition, 2000.

Womack, James P. and Daniel T. Jones. *The Machine That Changed the World: The Story of Lean Production.* New York: Scribner, 1990.

WEB SITES

The following Web sites provide valuable information and resources for sales and marketing and process improvement:

www.csoinsights.com

www.isixsigma.com

www.marketingexperiments.com

www.marketingsherpa.com

www.mathmarketing.com

www.pdcinc.com [Product Development Consultants, Inc.]

www.perrymarshall.com

www.salesperformance.com [Sales Performance Consultants, Inc.]

www.tarp.com [TARP Worldwide]

Michael J. Webb founded Sales Performance Consultants, Inc. to help business executives make their sales funnels flow faster, and he is the foremost expert on sales process improvement. He gave the keynote presentation at the first two conferences ever held on applying Six Sigma to sales and marketing. He has worked with clients such as American Express, DuPont, Marriott, and many smaller companies to improve their sales processes and results. He also works with sales training and CRM firms to help integrate the best selling practices into their client's sales operations. Mr. Webb achieved certification with the ASQ as a Quality Manager in 1998, is a Six Sigma Black Belt, and has completed a Lean Masters training course. Prior to becoming a sales trainer and consultant in 1996, he held a variety of increasingly responsible positions as Account Manager, Field Marketing Manager, and Director of Sales and Marketing in several industries.

Sales Performance Consultants, Inc. offers resources to help marketing and sales executives make their sales funnels flow faster through process improvement.

- *www.salesperformance.com:* offers articles from the fields of sales management, quality management, marketing, sales, CRM, and sales training.
- **SPIF!** – *Sales Performance Improvement Forum:* A free e-zine devoted to ongoing insights from work with clients and research around sales process improvement
- **White papers:** Leading-edge resources *(workbooks, white papers, and conference calls)* you can use to help your organization with sales process improvement.
- **Guidebooks:** Sales Performance Consultants, Inc. publishes popular guide books to help consultants and business managers lead teams to apply powerful and logical approaches.

- **Consulting:** Mr. Webb's client engagements produce faster flowing sales funnels, improve margins, and better measurement of marketing, selling, and servicing activity through process-improvement techniques such as:
- improving the performance of working sales processes through *Sales Kaizen Events*
- *supporting Lean and Six Sigma deployments* in customer facing groups such as sales, marketing, service, and program/project management.
- assessing the financial profile of marketing, selling, and servicing operations through *sales operating audits.*
- implementing *Sales Process Improvement* (using techniques such as customer value mapping and qualification criteria development), often in combination with sales training, CRM, or other initiatives.

For more information please visit www.salesperformance.com, e-mail mwebb@salesperformance.com, or call (877) 784-6507.

About the Coauthor

Tom Gorman has written or collaborated on more than a dozen business books, including three very successful Complete Idiot's Guides and *Writing the Breakthrough Business Book.* Tom is based in Newton, Massachusetts and at *www.contentbizbooks.com.*